BOULDER AND ELDORA

Time Table No. 10 — June 29, 1913

EAST BOUND

THIRD CLASS 10 Freight (Arrive D'ly Ex. Sunday) PM	SECOND CLASS 8 Mixed (Arrive D'ly) AM	FIRST CLASS 36 Mail and Exp (Arrive D'ly) PM	Coal, Water and Turning Station	Station Number	Distance from Eldora	STATIONS	Distance from Boulder	Length of Siding in Feet Between Head Blocks	ALTITUDE
	9 20	6 00			33 4	DENVER U.D. (AR) LV			
	8 25	4 45				BOULDER U.D. (AR) LV			
	8 25	4 40		0	33 4	BOULDER U.D. B-DS-BR (DRT ‡)	0		
	s	s		0	33 3	C. & S. AND D. & I. CROSSING	1		5351
4 55	8 20	4 37	CWYs	0	32 6	5TH ST. SHOPS (R § ‡)	8	355	5800
4 43	f 8 13	f 4 28		3	30 5	†ORODELL	2 9	200	
				4	29 9	*OLD ORODELL	3 5	184	
				A 6	27 5	† TWO BROTHERS (T §)	5 9	569	
4 23	s 7 58	s 4 11	W	6	27 2	CRISMAN	6 2	300	6300
4 17	7 52	4 06		A 8	26 2	*BLACK SWAN	7 2	1254	
4 16	s 7 51	s 4 05		8	25 9	SALINA (D ‡) SN	7 5	400	6571
4 08	7 45	4 00		A 9	24 9	†TAMBOURINE	8 5	545	
4 06	s 7 43	f 3 58		9	24 4	WALL STREET	9 0	585	6825
3 55	f 7 29	f 3 49		12	21 8	COPPER ROCK	11 6	440	7375
3 48			WY	12½	20 9	SHALE	12 5	1065	7750
	s 7 21	s 3 43		13	20 1	SUNSET (DRT) SU	13 3	368	8475
	f 7 01	f 3 23		E 17	16 1	SUGAR LOAF	17 3	342	
	f 6 58	f 3 21		E 18	15 5	TUNGSTEN	17 9	1928	
	s 6 35	f 3 02	WY	E 22	11 0	GLACIER LAKE (T § ‡)	22 4	639	9050
	f 6 30	f 2 58		E 23	10 1	†HILL	23 3	584	
	f 6 13	f 2 42		E 26	6 7	BLUE BIRD. No Siding	26 7		
	f 6 11	f 2 40	W	E 27	6 1	ANSON	27 3	639	8595
	f 6 05	f 2 35		E 28	4 9	†LAKEWOOD	28 5	375	
	f 6 00	f 2 32		E 29	4 0	*WOLFRAM	29 4		
	s 5 57	s 2 30		E 30	3 4	*CARDINAL (D ‡) CA	30 0	842	8710
	f 5 47	f 2 21		E 32	1 3	SULPHIDE	32 1	953	8530
	f 5 44	f 2 17	WY	A 33	7	*LAKE ELDORA	32 7	258	
	5 40	2 15		E 33	0	*ELDORA (DR) DO	33 4	608	8730
	(Leave D'ly) AM	(Leave D'ly) PM							

WEST BOUND

STATIONS	FIRST CLASS 35 Mail and Exp (Arrive D'ly) AM	SECOND CLASS 7 Mixed (Leave D'ly Ex. Sunday) PM	SECOND CLASS 11 Mixed (Leave Sunday Only) PM	THIRD CLASS 9 Freight (Leave D'ly Ex. Sunday) AM
DENVER U.D.	8 05			
BOULDER U.D.	9 15	12 25		
BOULDER U.D. B-DS-BR	9 30		5 30	
C. & S. AND D. & I. CROSSING	s	s	s	
5TH ST. SHOPS	9 33	12 28	5 33	8 30
†ORODELL	f 9 45	f 12 43	f 5 45	8 48
*OLD ORODELL				
† TWO BROTHERS				
CRISMAN	s 10 01	s 1 07	s 6 01	9 13
*BLACK SWAN	10 08	1 14	6 08	9 23
SALINA	s 10 11	s 1 16	s 6 11	9 25
†TAMBOURINE	10 19	1 24	6 19	9 34
WALL STREET	s 10 21	s 1 26	s 6 21	9 40
COPPER ROCK	f 10 35	f 1 43	f 6 35	10 00
SHALE	s 10 45 / 10 50	s 1 55	s 6 50	10 10
SUNSET	s 11 01	f 2 20	f 7 10	
SUGAR LOAF	f 11 12	f 2 23	f 7 12	
TUNGSTEN		s 3 02	f 7 33	
GLACIER LAKE	f 11 33	f 3 06	f 7 37	
†HILL	f 11 37	f 3 26	f 7 57	
BLUE BIRD	f 11 57	f 3 28	f 7 59	
ANSON	f 11 59	f 3 34	f 8 05	
†LAKEWOOD	f 12 05	f 3 39	f 8 10	
*WOLFRAM	f 12 10	s 3 43	s 8 13	
*CARDINAL	s 12 13	f 3 53	f 8 24	
SULPHIDE	f 12 24	f 3 56	f 8 27	
*LAKE ELDORA	f 12 27	4 00	8 30	
*ELDORA	12 30			

Opposite Page

Original painting by Howard Fogg

The high canon walls bordering rushing Four Mile Creek reverberate the full-throttle exhausts of a double-header Denver, Boulder & Western freight hauling cement for the construction of the Barker Dam in the spring of 1910. The hard even blasts of No. 33 and the rapid sharp beat of No. 25 make a new sound in the hills.

THE Switzerland Trail

of AMERICA

WITH AN ADDED CHAPTER

An Illustrated History of the Romantic Narrow Gauge Lines Running West from Boulder, Colorado: The Greeley, Salt Lake & Pacific and The Colorado & Northwestern, later The Denver, Boulder & Western.

By Forest Crossen

Hardcover Edition
Published by Pruett Press, Inc.
Boulder, Colorado

Second Printing Published By
Robinson Press, Inc.
Fort Collins, Colorado

Softcover Edition
Published by
Robinson Press, Inc.
Fort Collins, Colorado
1-800-747-5395

SOFTCOVER EDITION

OF

THE SWITZERLAND TRAIL OF AMERICA

With an Added Chapter

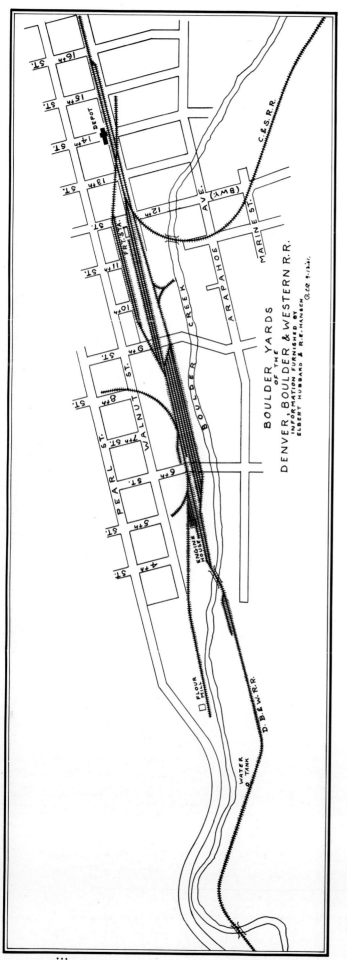

BOULDER YARDS
of the
DENVER, BOULDER & WESTERN R.R.
INFORMATION FURNISHED BY
ELBERT HUBBARD & R.E. HANSEN

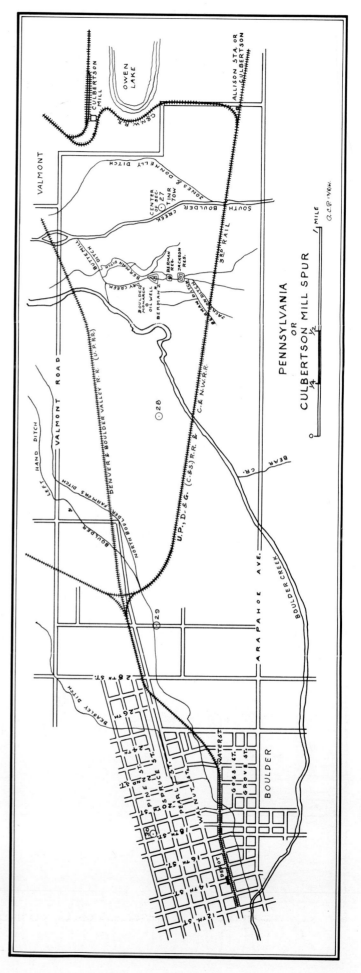

PENNSYLVANIA
OR
CULBERTSON MILL SPUR

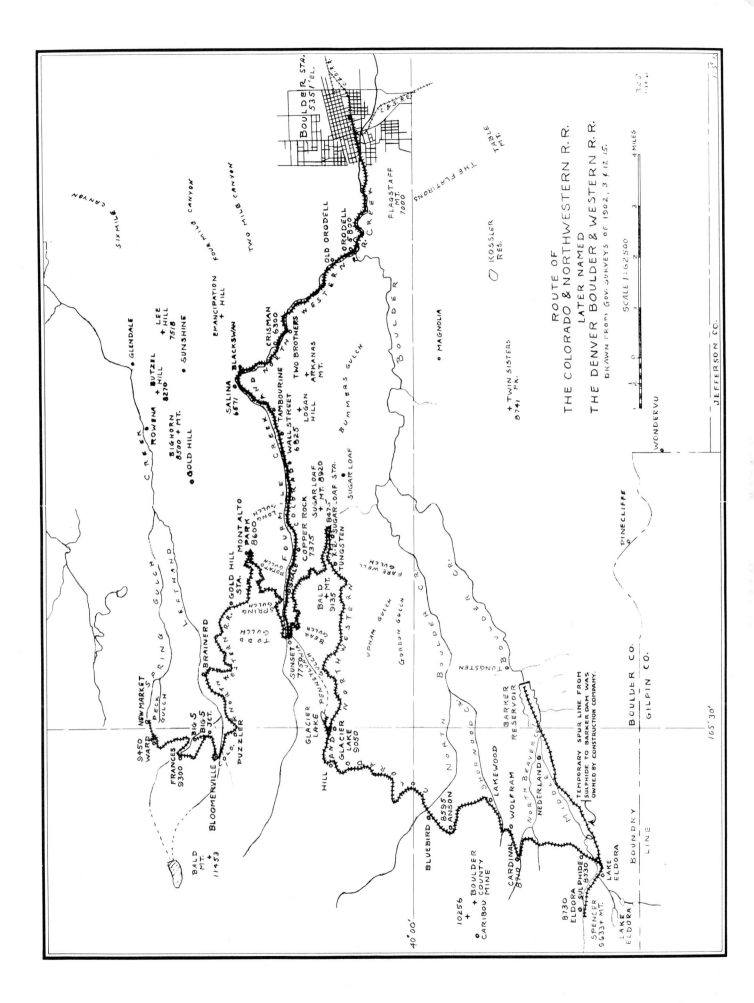

ROUTE OF
THE COLORADO & NORTHWESTERN R.R.
LATER NAMED
THE DENVER BOULDER & WESTERN R.R.
DRAWN FROM GOV. SURVEYS OF 1902, 3 & 12. 15.

SCALE 1:62,500

ix

TABLE OF CONTENTS

LIST OF FULL-COLOR PAINTINGS

MAPS

PREFACE AND ACKNOWLEDGMENTS

(First Printing—1962)

The Switzerland Trail of America! The flowing beauty of the name fascinated me when first I heard it long ago. When I saw the abandoned grade curving along a mountainside, my imagination conjured up pictures of ghost trains so real I could almost hear the whistles. The stories of old railroaders and people who rode the trains brought to me the excitement and color of the little lines running west from Boulder into the Rockies. Even as I read old books and papers, the dry bones of history came alive. All those things pushed me, unconsciously, toward the day when I began this book.

Now telling the story of even a little railroad like the Switzerland Trail of America is a big undertaking. I could never have completed it had there not been the help of many wonderful, unselfish people. They put their hearts into it. Whatever I have put down I owe largely to them.

I pay tribute first to A. A. "Gov" Paddock, publisher of the *Boulder Daily Camera,* whose love of local history has led to the collection and preservation of a treasure of material that only the future will properly evaluate. He encouraged me to interview old-time people and write their stories of true adventures on the Switzerland Trail for the *Boulder Daily Camera.* He gave free run of files of the *Daily Camera* and the *Boulder Tribune.* He opened his big photo files, his collection of pamphlets and papers. He has been behind me every step of the way.

I'm glad that I was urged to the writing of this book by E. J. Haley, R. H. Kindig, and Bryant McFadden, old-time members of the Rocky Mountain Railroad

Club, who had a big hand in publishing *Denver, South Park & Pacific, Rails Around Gold Hill,* and *Pictorial Supplement to Denver, South Park & Pacific.*

To their voices were added those of Morris Cafky, author of *Rails Around Gold Hill,* and M. C. Poor, author of *Denver, South Park & Pacific* and co-author with Kindig and Haley of *Pictorial Supplement to Denver, South Park & Pacific.*

For research I'm indebted to Miss Ellen Jackson, head of the Department of Government Documents and Microfilm Records of the Norlin Library of the University of Colorado, and her able assistant, Miss Martha Campbell.

I remember kindly the encouragement and help of Dr. Robert C. Athearn, History Department, University of Colorado, author of *Westward the Briton, High Country Empire,* and other valuable books on the West.

I thank Dr. John B. Schoolland, University of Colorado faculty member and narrow gauge specialist, who read the manuscript. He kindly gave me use of his considerable file of photographs and material on the Colorado & Northwestern and its predecessor, the Greeley, Salt Lake & Pacific.

For reading the manuscript I likewise thank E. J. Haley, R. H. Kindig, Bryant and Shirley McFadden, and W. C. Gordon.

My thanks go also to Ralph Peters, retired electrical engineer and employee during his University of Colorado student days of Morse Brothers when they were wrecking the Denver, Boulder & Western, for reading the manuscript and drawing maps of the DB&W.

For valuable assistance in preparing this

manuscript I wish to thank Dr. Charles H. Nilon of the English Department of the University of Colorado.

For the long and arduous task of proof reading, I thank Claire Rokala, Ralph Peters, Robin Arnett, Dwight Rokala, and Charles Gibbs.

Additional photographs and illustration material to that already mentioned came through the courtesy of R. H. Kindig, M. C. Poor, Otto C. Perry, Elbert Hubbard, Clint O. Dumm, Mrs. Jack Gilman, Mrs. Mary E. Wirtz, Martin Parsons, Reva Hickox Larson, staff of the Denver Public Library Western Collection, Librarian Gladys R. Gary of the University of Colorado Museum, Library staff of the State Historical Society of Colorado, Mrs. Erna Viele, Frank and Jewell Black, Waldo Bliss, H. B. Rosenkrans, M. C. Trent, Bob Richardson, Richard Lind, Jim Ehrenberger, Neal Miller, Stuart Anderson, Herbert O'Hanlon, John Strong, Jo and Newell Fogelberg, R. E. "Mickey" Hansen, John W. Maxwell, Glenn Sisson, W. N. Hofer, Mrs. John G. Oldaker, A. Joe Bell, David S. Digerness, and R. A. Curtis.

My warmest thanks go to Michael Koch, who volunteered to let me use the painting he had commissioned Richard Ward to do on the Colorado & Northwestern. This winter train scene rounded out our paintings for each of the four seasons.

For technical information and help in writing captions I am indebted to Elbert Hubbard of Wall Street, one of the last living employees of the Switzerland Trail.

I extend my deepest appreciation to Howard Fogg, celebrated railroad artist who lives in Boulder, for his enthusiastic cooperation. His three paintings bring back the glory that was the Switzerland Trail's.

Above all, I wish to thank my publisher, Fred Pruett of Pruett Press, Boulder, whose deep appreciation of the colorful adventure of the Switzerland Trail and its mountain land led him into this work.

In preparing the manuscript and illustration captions we have striven long and hard to avoid errors. That there may be some, even many, we have no doubt. If there are, they are honest errors. We hope you readers will treat them with tolerance and will help us to make corrections.

The writing of this book has been a labor of love. Now I give it to you, wishing you good reading and good looking.

SOFTCOVER EDITION - 1992

Seventeen months after its publication in July of 1963, the first printing of "The Switzerland Trail of America" was sold out. That printing was 4,000 copies, and when available, sold for as much as $200.00 per copy.

In 1978, a second limited printing was issued. It was an exact copy of the original book, with an added chapter on the career of Bill Tipps, the Switzerland Trail's senior engineer. The material for this chapter came from his son, Carl Tipps. Some previously unpublished photographs were added to the final chapter, and the spirited color picture of No. 32 on the Eldora line was reproduced to create a beautiful front cover. Special screens were purchased to capture the detail of some of the original photographs, as several negatives were no longer available at that time.

Since 1978, Crossen's autographed, numbered, limited edition hardcover book has enjoyed tremendous success among railfans the world over. Collectors in Germany, Japan, Australia and other countries have treasured the 1978 edition. In fact, it has been so popular that demand has risen for a softcover edition easily affordable for the general public: thus, this edition. It is a complete reproduction of the hardcover, and we trust that you will enjoy your copy of "The Switzerland Trail of America" for many years.

Forest Crossen

The Switzerland Trail of America

WITH AN ADDED CHAPTER

DEDICATION

To the men with bold hearts who built and operated the narrow gauge railroads west from Boulder, Colorado, into the Rocky Mountains, and the miners who blasted from the hard rock its treasure of gold, silver, and tungsten, this book is affectionately dedicated.

Part I

Chapter I

THE GOLD AND SILVER HILLS

There are old-timers in Boulder, Colorado, who swear that the hills have never been the same since the narrow gauge was ripped out. By "the hills" they mean the Rocky Mountains that rise suddenly out of the plains to nearly nine thousand feet at Boulder's edge, by "the narrow gauge," the never-to-be-forgotten Switzerland Trail of America.

It was only a tiny railroad and it did not last very long, but for sheer grandeur of scenery, stirring train operations, and colorful life along its curving track it can lift its head proudly.

It was built to serve the gold and silver mines and the adventurers who went down in them to bring out the stuff of dreams—and well it served them. The tragedy that came upon it was in no way deserved.

To understand its reason for being we must go back to an ancient day when the first Indians, having crossed the Bering Straits from the Asian homeland, came south from Alaska. They made a trail that men used from then on, parts of it even today. Adventurers came over this trail to mine gold in the wild canons of the Rocky Mountains and build railroads in to them.

(The Old North Trail the ancient Indians called it.[1] Then it became the Cherokee Trail, named for a party of Cherokees who came north along the eastern foothills of the Rockies over it in 1850 headed for the California gold fields.) The Cherokees had mined gold in north Georgia before the invading whites drove them west. They prospected as

they traveled and on Ralston Creek, northwest of present-day Denver, found gold.[2] In the mining camps along the Sacramento with other miners they swapped yarns of their adventures along the trail to California. The Cherokees told of the gold they had discovered near Pike's Peak.

Among their listeners was a hardy Georgian by the name of William Green Russell. Green Russell went east with pokefuls of gold dust and nuggets and settled down to the good life in Georgia. But he could not stay quiet, not after he had made the California gold rush and breathed the exciting air of Downieville, Hangtown, and the American River camps. He kept remembering the story of the Pike's Peak Country gold. In February, 1858, he took the trail west.

With Russell went his two brothers, Oliver and Levi, along with several other Georgians. On the way out a party of Cherokees joined them, then another group from Missouri and Kansas. Well armed and numbering one hundred and four they rolled up the old Cherokee Trail past the foot of Pike's Peak. On June 23, 1858, they camped on Cherry Creek, which runs through present-day Denver.

They prospected the creeks flowing into the South Fork of the Platte River. They found gold but it was so fine they could not recover it. Some became discouraged and frightened, for they had seen signs of Indians about. They were completely alone, a tiny dot of men in an immense savage land.

The Cherokees pulled out and so did

[1]*The Whoop-up Trail* by Gerald L. Berry, Applied Arts Products, Ltd., Edmonton, 1953.

[2]"Cherokee Goldseekers in Colorado" by Dr. Leroy Hafen in *Colorado Magazine*, May, 1938.

1

most of the others, until only twelve men remained with Russell. He told them bluntly that they had come far and that he intended to prospect the Pike's Peak Country — if only one man would stay with him. They would settle, once and for all, the question of whether there was gold here. The twelve decided to stay.

They started up the Platte and soon found flake gold worth four or five hundred dollars on Dry Creek, near present-day Englewood. Gold in the Pike's Peak Country was a reality.[3]

The news reached the Missouri River settlements via a Government wagon-train. At once parties of adventurers headed west, their slogan, "Pike's Peak or Bust." Each saw himself riding in a shining coach and drinking champagne with gay, lovely ladies.

Most of them had nothing to lose. In 1857 a panic had begun, bringing to an end a wild inflation and speculative era caused by the influx of California gold, railroad building, and unstable state banks. Railroads, banks, and businesses failed. Factories closed down. Farmers had no markets for their crops, though hungry people begged in the streets. The men of wealth, whose greedy, unwise policies had brought on the panic, told the people that it was an "Act of God"— but that put no food in empty stomachs. So the men who had lost farms and jobs set their faces west.

In mid-October, with the leaves of the cottonwoods turning golden, a loose collection of parties headed up the South Fork of the Platte toward the Pike's Peak Diggings. They stopped for the night at Fort St. Vrain, built on the right bank across from the mouth of the St. Vrain River, named for Colonel Ceran St. Vrain, a power in the fur trade.

The next morning a couple of men of one small dissatisfied party climbed the adobe walls of the abandoned fort. Off to the

west lay a lovely valley leading up to the great foothills of the Rockies. They eased down and told their partners about it.[4] They were tired of traveling with so large a company, which was scaring the game out of the country. They would have to winter largely on game.

The little party let the others pull out. Then they yoked their oxen and hitched their teams, forded the shallow Platte, and started up the St. Vrain. When they reached the mouth of Boulder Creek they went up it, their pleasure growing with each mile they traveled.

Finally they came to the beautiful but awesome mountain wall and camped in a grove of cottonwoods where the Boulder (Creek) flows out of its narrow canon.

On the 15th of January, 1859, six of them went prospecting. They discovered rich placer gold on Gold Run, near the present town of Gold Hill, twelve miles northwest of Boulder.[5]

The experienced miners knew that the source of the gold was upstream, in the rock. Not far away one found the Horsfall Lode, which he and his partners developed into a mine with streaks of high-grade that glittered in the light of their candles and set their blood dancing.

Meanwhile, over to the south about fifty miles, a frontier Missourian named George Jackson found rich placer gold January 7, 1859, on Chicago Creek near present-day Idaho Springs. And at a lesser distance John H. Gregory, a wandering Georgian miner, struck gold May 6th in the gulch that today bears his name. It was destined shortly to hold the lively mining camps of Black Hawk, Mountain City, and Central City.

In the spring more stampeders from the Missouri River arrived and swarmed to the hills. Thousands came to Boulder City and

[3]*History of Colorado*, Volume 1, by Wilbur Fisk Stone, S. J. Clark Publishing Co., 1918.

[4]*History of Boulder & Clear Creek Counties* by Amos Bixby, 1880.
[5]*Colorado, The Centennial State* by Dr. Percy Fritz.

Crossen photo

Modern Boulder at the foot of the Rocky Mountains, "the hills" to the old-timers. The big buildings in the background are on the campus of the University of Colorado.

3

struck out into the Rockies with pick and shovel and gold pan.

It was not long until a prospector discovered the Niwot gold mine, named for a friendly Arapahoe chief, 25 miles northwest of Boulder. The camp of Ward grew up around it and later discoveries on the great Columbia Lode.[6]

Gold mining near Boulder went along quietly for ten years. Then a hunter who had come down from the north walked into a Central City saloon and showed some pieces of float (surface ore). He did not know what it was but a sharp-eyed woodchopper who had worked in the great Comstock Lode of Nevada at once spotted it as high-grade silver. This man was Billy Martin.

He whispered the news to his partners, bought the hunter a few drinks, and listened carefully to his story of where he had found the float. They made a deal with the stranger, who was obviously Sam Conger.

The next morning Billy Martin and George Lytle, who had mined in British Columbia and over most of the West, struck out to the north with a little cart pulled by a yoke of oxen. The others had staked them with their last cent.

At the Valley of the Middle Boulder they struck northwest. After a hard five miles through thick virgin timber, they reached the base of the long hill Conger had described. They started up it and soon found the float.

Martin began digging. Before long he let out a yell. He had come upon the vein. It was so rich in silver it made them gasp.

They named it the Caribou, because George Lytle said that the place looked like the Caribou Range of British Columbia. It was the last day of August, 1869.

A short time later George found and staked the Poor Man. He laughingly said that he could not have been poorer at the moment but that he would not be poor any more.

They returned for their woodchopping partners, who staked claims before the stampede started. The camp of Caribou sprang up and for years was a flourishing place.

For years a heavy mineral had showed up in the Gold Hill mines that had to be thrown out on the dumps. No one knew what it was but it was as heavy as gold. No one could break it down. Finally in 1872 a metallurgist identified it and a new and valuable gold ore started a boom west of Boulder.[7] It was tellurium, and camps with romantic names: Sunshine, Magnolia, Salina, Wall Street, Crisman, Gold Hill, Glendale, Rowena, Summerville, Jamestown, and Balarat sprang up.

For a long time prospectors going through a belt of mountain country some eighteen miles west of Boulder had been coming across a heavy mineral that they called black iron. In 1900 a metallurgist found it to be tungsten, which, alloyed with steel, produced tool steel that would continue to cut at high speeds after it became hot.[8] It was also in increasing demand for making filaments for electric light bulbs. The big boom camps of Nederland, Tungsten, and Lakewood were destined to come on during World War I. Their production to the present totals nearly $32,000,000.[9]

In a beautiful setting at the foot of the Rockies, men formed the Boulder City Town Company in February, 1859. Boulder was destined to become an important educational center with its University of Colorado, health resort, and tourist mecca. And of its fame nothing has been more romantic than its narrow gauge railroad, the Switzerland Trail of America.

---

[6]*Mining in Boulder County, Colorado,* Silver Jubilee Edition of the Boulder County Metal Mining Association, Boulder, Colorado, 1919.

[7]*Mining in Boulder County,* Boulder County Metal Mining Association, 1910.
[8]*Mining in Boulder County, Colorado.*
[9]Compiled from Colorado Mining Yearbooks.

Sturtevant photo. M. R. Parsons Collection

In April, 1888, Rocky Mountain Joe Sturtevant made this photo of Boulder from Lover's Hill east of 15th Street. The building in the center is the new Boulder County Courthouse, built on the old town square. Taxes to build it came largely from the silver mines at Caribou, 22 miles west, which were still rolling out a flood of wealth. The two-story brick house in foreground in line with courthouse was the home of County Treasurer A. E. Lea, father of Homer Lea, little hunchback who would become famous as a General of the Chinese Revolutionary Armies and author of the prophetic "The Valor of Ignorance."

5

Crossen photo

Modern Gold Hill, Colorado. Once a lively mining camp, it is now a summer resort and year 'round residence town. The big log building in the left foreground is the old Gold Hill Hotel, for years the summer camp of the Holiday House Association of Chicago. One-half mile to the left, on Gold Run, the six intrepid Fifty-niners discovered gold.

Part I

Chapter II

ROADS TO THE MINES

Roads had to be built to the mines to transport people and supplies and bring out the ore. Miners produce nothing but raw treasure; their needs must be supplied by others, usually from a distance.

The first primitive road to Gold Run followed the route of the six prospectors. It had steep grades, sharp turns, and tight squeezes between big trees.[1]

Practical men among the stampeders resolved to build a better road. They formed the St. Vrain, Altona, Gold Hill and Gregory Road Company and built up open Left Hand Canon to Aikens, now Lickskillet, Gulch. They ran up this steep gulch to the top of the hogback where Gold Hill stands today and down to Gold Run.[2]

The first road from Boulder City to Central City was up Gregory Canon. It was one of the most difficult and dangerous roads in the mountains.

Boulder Canon was a challenge. Cliffs jutted up from the edge of the creek, boulders formed the stream bed, and the brush along the banks was enough to tear the hide off a mountain lion. However, the canon was the natural gateway to the Central City mines— rich market for the hay, grain, vegetables, beef, and butter that the farmers of Boulder Valley were producing.

On March 11, 1864, the Territorial Legislature granted a charter for the Boulder Valley and Central City Wagon Road. It was capitalized at $50,000. Work began in March, 1865.

"My grandfather, James N. Maxwell, was in charge," explained Marc N. Maxwell, son of a famous Boulder pioneer. "When they came to a bad place — they couldn't blast out rocks like they do now — they put in a bridge and went across to the other side of the creek where it was easier going. That's what made so many bridges in the early days.

"All they had to work with were teams of horses and mules pulling scrapers and plows—oxen when they needed more power. The rest of it was pick and shovel."

In three months they reached the mouth of Four Mile Creek, four miles up Boulder Canon. The cost was $9,000.

"Below the mouth of the present Silver Lake Ditch the road went around the point of a hill, then sharply down. That was the only way they could build it, for there wasn't any bank there, only a sheer cliff. This made a very steep grade or pitch. It was always called the Maxwell Pitch."[3]

The Maxwell Pitch is one of the landmarks of Boulder Canon, located a short distance above its mouth. Directly below it is the Silver Lake irrigation ditch. Below that is the grade of the Greeley, Salt Lake & Pacific narrow gauge railroad and the masonry piers of its bridge crossing Boulder Creek, later used by the Colorado & Northwestern.

Toll charges ran $1.00 for wagon and team (two animals), 25 cents for each additional animal, 75 cents for a one-animal vehicle, loose animals 10 cents a head.[4]

Later the road was extended up Boulder

---

[1]Interview with Martin Parsons, January 12, 1955, at Boulder.

[2]Martin Parsons' articles on toll roads, *Boulder Daily Camera*, February 7, 8, 1952.

[3]*Boulder Daily Camera*, February 22, 1956, by Forest Crossen.

[4]*Boulder Daily Camera*, February 7, 1952, articles on toll roads by Martin Parsons.

McClure photo. A. A. Paddock Collection

Maxwell Pitch in Boulder Canon of the original wagon-stagecoach road, built in 1865. It is the high rock-walled road above the wooden flume of the Silver Lake Ditch and the trestle of the Colorado & Northwestern. Trestle piers were originally built by the Greeley, Salt Lake & Pacific in 1882. The two trestles shown here carry a pipeline with water from high Silver Lake, at the foot of the Arapahoe Glacier, for Boulder. Railroaders called the Maxwell Pitch Windy Point.

8

Sturtevant photo
University of Colorado Museum Collection

Six-horse team on freight wagon at toll gate house at the mouth of Boulder Canon. The steep grade often required six horses.

Sturtevant photo. M. R. Parsons Collection

The Boulder-Nederland stage in Boulder Canon. The driver-owner is Johnny Carmack, veteran stage operator out of Boulder. The coach is a big Concord, built by the Abbot-Downing Company of Concord, New Hampshire. It was built on special order for Col. J. L. Sanderson, at that time active head of the famous Barlow and Sanderson stage lines, and was beautifully finished.

10

Sturtevant photo
University of Colorado Museum Collection

Big Marine boiler enroute from Boulder to the Star Mine, located in a side canon running into Left Hand Canon a short distance below Rowena. The nearest station of the Colorado & Northwestern was far from this spot. Boulder Mayor Lou Johnson standing beside wagon. Driver at left is Elmer Cobb, with

Lew Thomas, owner of the outfit, to the right. Driver of push cart is Jack McGee. Such trips over the narrow mountain roads of steep grades and sharp curves were long, arduous, and dangerous.

11

Canon to the foot of steep Magnolia Hill and up it and over to Black Hawk.[5]

Lured on by a promise of Wells-Fargo & Co. to put stagecoaches on from Cheyenne to Boulder and on to Black Hawk if Boulder would build a suitable road into the mountains, the road builders began work again. In February, 1869, they started extending the road up Boulder Canon.

Then Fortune leaned down and kissed them. While their men were slowly working upstream in the late summer of 1869, the great silver discovery at Caribou broke. They at once ordered a speed-up, reaching Brown's Ranch, later Nederland, in the summer of 1871.[6]

Wells-Fargo & Co. forgot its promise to Boulder, so Lee and Walter Smith opened a stage line. They ran daily from Boulder to Nederland and Black Hawk, with a profitable branch line to Caribou.[7] For a while they operated from the end of steel of the Denver & Boulder Valley Railroad at Erie.

These were the great days of beautifully matched four and six-horse teams stepping along smartly with rocking Concord stagecoaches, their drivers expertly keeping them right-side up on the sharp curves and narrow shelf roads. Of less glamour were the freight

[5]Ibid.
[6]Ibid.
[7]Ibid.

wagons, pulled by fours and sixes, their "skinners" hardened to weather and long trails.

The road builders fanned out up the principal canons. Some of their roads failed to pay, but all in some way served people in the new country. The toll roads ran their allotted charter terms and became free public roads.

These pioneer roads, built at low cost, were one-way, with turn-outs at intervals for passing. When two outfits met, the upgrade driver had the right-of-way, the one coming down getting into a turnout. The down driver was usually in the clear before they met; they fastened bells on the hames of their leaders and the musical sound warned approaching drivers.

Freighters and stagecoach operators provided the first transportation to the mines. They gave faithful service in all kinds of weather. In winter their lot was truly hard, for, coming down grade, they had to stay on the rigs to work the brakes, nearly freezing. To be out twelve hours was nothing unusual.

They paved the way for building the first railroad from Boulder into the mountains. After it began operating, they provided valuable feeder service, hauling supplies to the mines and lumber camps and bringing ore and lumber back to the little stations. They helped make possible the Greeley, Salt Lake & Pacific.

Part I

Chapter III

A RAILROAD TO THE MOUNTAINS

After the first placer gold and the shallow free gold surface ores were worked out in the early 1860's, hard times fell upon Boulder. In the early 1870's prosperity returned as new business came in from the silver mining at Caribou. When a method of extracting the gold in tellurium ore was discovered, more money flowed into Boulder. The two standard gauge railroads that reached the town in 1873 — the Colorado Central and the Denver & Boulder Valley—raised hopes again.

Then came a mighty stirring as 1881 broke over Colorado, made a state only five years before. From scores of mining camps over her vast Rockies poured a river of gold and silver. In 1880 it had made Colorado the leading gold and silver producing state.[1] Men looked to the mountains and dreamed the lavish, bold "the sky's the limit" dreams of the frontier West. Many of these dreams were of railroads.

Few people today can understand the magic that the word railroad carried when the United States was new. Every crossroads settlement felt that with a railroad it might grow into a city. A railroad would unlock Nature's lavish treasures. A railroad meant sure-fire prosperity, growth, exciting living.

The railroad fever gripped Boulder as the spring of 1881 came to this town of 3,000 at the foot of the Rockies.[2] With their inner eyes men saw railroads threading the wild canons and gulches, nosing into the camps: Caribou with its hill of silver, Jamestown with

its fabulously rich Golden Age Mine, Ward with its Niwot producing ore worth up to $2,500 a ton, Salina with the Melvina's tellurium running $500 a ton, Magnolia with its Sac and Fox hoisting tellurium worth $300 a ton. These were only about half of the camps.[3]

The biggest items were the undiscovered leads, which prospectors were bound to strike once they had railroads up there. Railroads would reduce freight rates on ore down and supplies back—the slow wagon freight outfits could never develop a country. Only the Iron Horse and Steam could do that.

Exciting talk beat the air. Two great railroad systems were squaring off to see who would control business in this part of Colorado—the Union Pacific or the Burlington.[4] They were going to build right up through the mountains, tap the mining camps, cross the Continental Divide, and go on to the Pacific Ocean. As for Boulder, it was right in their path, destined to become a great railroad terminal—probably for both lines—with humming machine shops, noisy locomotive shops, car shops, and foundries.

Mining? It really had only started. There would be smelters here. The *Boulder News & Courier*, an excellent weekly, said editorially in the April 29, 1881, issue: "Attention is called to this town as being a favored locality in which to erect large smelting works, providing the projected railroads up Left Hand, Boulder and South Boulder canons are built. . . . Abundant coal fields

[1]*Boulder News & Courier,* July 29, 1881.
[2]*Boulder News & Courier,* July 30, 1881.

[3]*Colorado Directory of Mines,* 1879.
[4]*Boulder News & Courier,* April 29, 1881.

13

This house at 7th and Pearl streets in Boulder with its wooden gingerbread trim and tower with a widow's walk was built at the height of the silver and tellurium booms, in 1877. It was built by Williamette Arnett, Boulder pioneer, who died in the Klondike in 1900. The exterior of this house is almost unchanged from the original finish.

are at our doors with roads already constructed thereto. What better opportunity offers
for the investment of capital in smelting?"

The coal fields lay at Marshall, six miles
south, tapped by the Colorado Central Railroad. Thirteen miles east lay the Erie field,
on the line of the Denver & Boulder Valley.
Both lines were standard gauge. The mountain lines would probably be narrow gauge,
but third rails could be easily laid. Then coal
could be shipped directly to the gold and silver camps, replacing the more expensive
wood as boiler fuel.

Suddenly the rosy hopes and high-flown
talk assumed reality. Building north from
Denver to Longmont was the Denver, Western & Pacific standard gauge. Many of Boulder's leading citizens had urged its officials to
run the line through Boulder. At the end of
June came the announcement that the DW&P
would build a branch to Boulder from Buffa-
lo Hill, three miles south of Louisville.[5] This
would place Boulder on an airline route to
Denver, 29 miles against the 49 via the Boulder Valley and Denver Pacific Railroads.

Nor was that all. The DW&P announced that it was a trunk line, going through
Boulder north to the mouth of St. Vrain
Canon, thence up it and across the Continental Divide to the Pacific. The *Boulder News
& Courier* in reporting the company's request
for sixteen acres of land for depot buildings
and announcement that they would be compelled to purchase more "indicates that Boulder is to become to this Company what Lara-
mie City is to the Union Pacific, the com-
mencement of the mountain division where
all the big machine shops are to be located
. . . . We have reason to believe that this
DW&P is but a link in a great transcontinental line which is to extend from the Atlantic
to the Pacific. . . ."

At the same time came news that a narrow gauge line, the Denver, Utah & Pacific,

had already started northwest from Denver.
It would run up rugged South Boulder
Canon, four airline miles to the south, up
through Rollinsville, that saloon-less and
dancehall-less town founded by old John
Quincy Adams Rollins. It would cross the
Continental Divide and run on to the Pacific. From Rollinsville a branch line would
extend south to Central City and Georgetown, etc., while to the north a branch would
run to Caribou. Boulder, that natural railroad town, might also be touched with a
branch.[6]

On July 8, 1881, Boulder buzzed with
the announcement that the Union Pacific
would build a narrow gauge line up Boulder
Canon and through the county to the west.
Thomas L. Kimball, General Western Manager of the U. P. lines, arrived in his special
car and met with Boulder's head men. He
asked for a subsidy, spoke of the great advantages that would accrue to Boulder. The
company would "should the citizens comply
with his request, put up an elegant brick passenger depot in the center of town, between
Twelfth and Eleventh (Streets), also put up a
freight depot in the same locality.

"The company asks that the citizens donate the right-of-way through town and six
half-blocks for depot purposes. . . ."[7]

The Greeley, Salt Lake & Pacific Rail-
way Company was incorporated under the
general laws of Colorado January 17, 1881.
The incorporators were Colorado men: John
J. Bush, Junius Berkley, A. A. Egbert, C. W.
Fisher, and Willard Teller. Egbert was
Superintendent of the Colorado Division of
the U. P.

The capital stock was placed at $500,-
000. The railroad was to run from Greeley
to Fort Collins, thence up the Cache la
Poudre Canon to the Utah line and on to Salt
Lake City.

Amendments provided for building rail-

[5]*Boulder News & Courier*, June 24, 1881.

[6]*Boulder News & Courier*, July 22, 1881.
[7]*Ibid.*, July 8, 1881.

Photo by John Strong

The grade of the Boulder, Left Hand & Middle Park clings to the foothills of the Rockies two miles north of Boulder (along Colorado No. 7) as it bravely heads for Buchanan Pass. No track was ever laid on this grade.

A. A. Paddock Collection

Location engineers of the Boulder, Left Hand & Middle Park Railroad and Telegraph Company on the west side of the Continental Divide. This projected narrow gauge railroad, running north from Boulder along the foothills of the Rockies, turning west at the mouth of Left Hand Canon, was to extend over Buchanan Pass. The grade, which may be seen today, was finished to Left Hand Canon and for some distance up it. No rail was ever laid and it remains a ghost railroad, a tribute to brave pioneers of great enterprise.

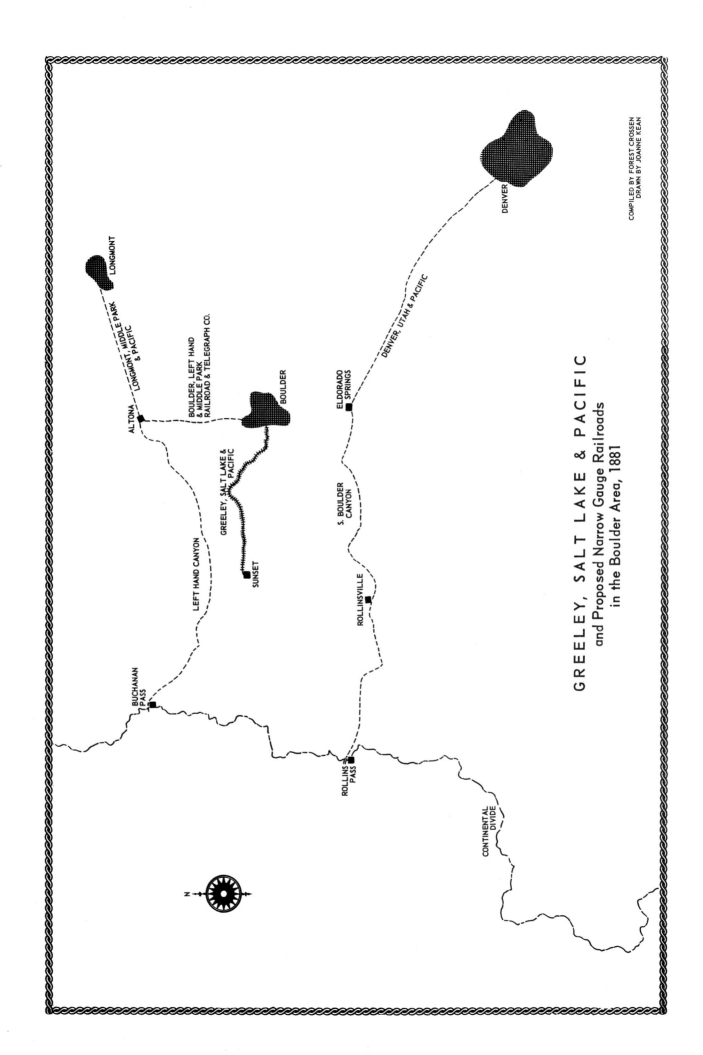

GREELEY, SALT LAKE & PACIFIC
and Proposed Narrow Gauge Railroads
in the Boulder Area, 1881

COMPILED BY FOREST CROSSEN
DRAWN BY JOANNE KEAN

LONGMONT

DENVER

ALTONA

LONGMONT, MIDDLE PARK & PACIFIC

BOULDER, LEFT HAND
& MIDDLE PARK
RAILROAD & TELEGRAPH CO.

BOULDER

GREELEY, SALT LAKE &
PACIFIC

SUNSET

LEFT HAND CANYON

ELDORADO
SPRINGS

DENVER, UTAH & PACIFIC

S. BOULDER CANYON

ROLLINSVILLE

BUCHANAN
PASS

ROLLINS
PASS

CONTINENTAL
DIVIDE

N

roads up nearly every canon on the eastern slope of the Continental Divide in Colorado and many on the western side. Among these was "From the main line of the road of said Company at Boulder up Boulder Creek to the mouth of Four Mile Creek, thence up Four Mile Creek to the mouth of Penn Gulch."[8]

Building north from Boulder was another narrow gauge railroad, the Boulder, Left Hand and Middle Park Railroad & Telegraph Company.[9] It was a home corporation, C. G. Buckingham, a leading banker, its President. Great hopes were held for this road, for it would tap the growing gold camps of Left Hand Canon, Jamestown, and Ward. When the rails reached Middle Park, they would bring out untold riches of coal, timber, oil, ranch and farm products.[10]

'Tis little wonder that people lost their heads and began to see themselves rich. Boulder growing by the thousands, big shops and factories and smelters darkening the sky with smoke. Every man to be in on the take, becoming a capitalist and living a high and mighty life. The real estate promoters rubbed their hands unctuously. The saloonkeepers, gamblers, and lissom girls in the sporting houses smiled and prepared to make life merrier for the footloose men who always follow booms.

Big events are seldom born without violence. Immediately after the U. P. announcement Boulder awoke to find a railroad war on its hands. During the night of July 7, 1881, a large force of men and horse-drawn equipment of the Denver, Western & Pacific built a grade through town, going north on Eleventh Street, cutting the proposed line of the narrow gauge Greeley, Salt Lake & Pacific.

The town authorities ordered the men to stop. They pulled out and shortly afterward along came Union Pacific men, who be-

gan shoveling away the grade, so that they could put in their own line. Again the authorities ordered a halt, arresting three men who were slow to obey.

The next day and the next, both railroads' crews were at work. They eyed each other suspiciously, although they had agreed not to jump grades.

Both sides called a truce on Sunday, but on Monday the tension heightened. The arrival of Senator Henry Teller and Superintendent A. A. Egbert of the Colorado Division of the U. P. in a special train brought out the curious, itching to see excitement. The town board met in special session, failed to agree, to the glee of the onlookers. That afternoon they met again, and this time were successful, establishing grade locations satisfactory to both railroads.

The Greeley, Salt Lake & Pacific would be pushed through, so would the airline Denver, Western & Pacific road. The U. P., however, lost on one point: it would have to build its depot farther west. "It is thought that the depot grounds will be on Ninth Street or just above, a beautiful place, and near the heart of the town."—reported the *Boulder News & Courier*. Then it added gleefully, "Boulder's boom is fairly inaugurated."[11]

The Union Pacific quickly made a grade west through Boulder, starting from its standard gauge Boulder Valley line at the eastern edge of town. The grade swarmed with men, lured by wages of $3.50 a day for common labor. Again the idlers gathered.

Following the graders came the tie layers, planking down hand-hewed standard gauge ties in the soft dirt and gravel. Later they would tamp them into ballast. A double line of men came forward with a length of rail, lowered it carefully onto the ties. The spikers moved up, and the air resounded to the rhythmical clang of steel on steel. Rail

[8]Copied from original incorporation papers in Secretary of State's office, Denver.
[9]Bill head, Martin Parsons' collection.
[10]*Boulder News & Courier*, April 1, 1881.

[11]*Boulder News & Courier*, July 15, 1881.

by rail the track went forward, a little old U. P. engine pushing the work train.

The rails reached the western limits of the frontier town. They went on approximately a half-mile, tapping the Boyd Smelter, Mrs. Yount's flour mill, and the Golden Smelting Company's agency.

"In response to an interrogation concerning the evident haste of the (U. P.) company, Captain Reed, the herculean wheelhorse, informed us it was to get material in for the narrow gauge through the (Boulder) Canon upon which work would begin as soon as contracts could be let. He avowed that Caribou would be reached before winter," the *Boulder News & Courier* (July 15, 1881) informed its readers.

Bold words. Caribou was at least 30 miles west by a rail line survey from Boulder and 4,600 feet higher.

The Greeley, Salt Lake & Pacific had bold plans. It was to run up Boulder Canon to Four Mile Creek, up this creek to Pennsylvania Gulch, thence to Williamsburg, Nederland, Caribou, and over the Range through Middle Park via Hot Sulphur Springs to Salt Lake and the Pacific. A branch line was to be run from near Nederland to Central City. "This road across the range will be the grandest tourist route in the world," stated the *Boulder News & Courier*.[12]

The first twenty miles of grading contract fell to W. H. Cox. He at once advertised in the Denver newspapers for sub-contractors and a large force of men.

Evidently the wages that Cox offered did not tempt the men hanging around Denver's busy Larimer and alluring Holliday Streets. The Leadville boom was on; they could always go up to the Cloud City and go to work. So Cox turned to the Negro. A rumor ran through Boulder's saloons that he had employed one thousand Negroes.

Soon Cox arrived, accompanied by a man named Stone. He put out the word that

500 Negroes were now engaged for his work, with one thousand sent for.[13]

Presently Cox & Stone began work in Boulder Canon—with 200 Negroes. It was not long before the people of Boulder heard of Mr. Cox again.

Six of Cox's men walked off the job. They were arrested in Boulder for breach of contract and thrown into the local jail. The next day the rest of the gang came in.

Their story was all too typical of the so-called good old days. They had been lured from Kansas by promises of $1.75 a day, without board. They had no written contract, except that the contractors did not have to return them to Kansas should they quit before their time expired. They became apprehensive about their wages once they found flour $6.00 a sack and sugar 14 cents a pound at the camp commissary, so they asked Cox. He flatly told them it was none of their business how much they were getting and to get back on the job.

Cox denied the charges, and the men had to return to work or lay out jail sentences. Law and order broke the strike.[14]

Less than two weeks later Cox had another run-in with his men. He ordered them out with leveled shotgun, told them to get to work. This time the workers had him arrested for assault and he was tried before a justice of the peace and fined.

The *Boulder News & Courier* was published by Western men and what they had to say is to their credit. "Again the contractor W. H. Cox comes into unenviable notoriety in the role of bulldozer. Coming from the South, evidently Mr. Cox is of the opinion that the crack of the slave-whip has the same ring as of old. In this he will find himself mightily mistaken. The shackles have fallen and the negro arises from his serfdom a man, equal in rights of citizenship to Mr. Cox or any of us."[15]

[12]July 22, 1881.

[13]*Boulder News & Courier*, July 29, 1881.
[14]*Boulder News & Courier*, August 19, 1881.
[15]*Ibid.*, September 2, 1881.

19

Sturtevant photo
J. B. Schoolland Collection

Boulder's industrial section west of the city limits during narrow gauge days. The Boyd Smelter, erected in 1871, stands at left on the bank of Boulder Creek. The Delano Mill is at the right, with the Yount Flour Mill in the distance straight ahead.

20

This blast must have tamed Cox down, for no more mention of ramming his Negro laborers around appears.

The grading went steadily ahead, but its progress would seem slow indeed to us today. No great machines clanked and roared; the builders had nothing but the muscles of men and patient horses and mules. The men worked with pick and shovel; the horses and mules pulled little dump carts.

Boulder Canon was almost entirely rock work — and hard rock at that. The wagon road builders in 1865 had naturally taken the easiest route. The railroad graders had to literally blast out a shelf at the bases of the beetling cliffs. They drilled holes by hand, one man holding the drill, the other hammering it with a long-handled eight-pound hammer called a doublejack. After each blow the man holding turned his drill a quarter turn, so that the sharpened chisel end chipped away the rock. They worked steadily, changing off on the hammering. Two men could put down a 36-inch hole in one to two hours if all went well.

Black powder was their only explosive. The powder men filled the holes with coarse blasting powder, set their fuses. When they had everything ready, they lighted the fuses and hot-footed it to safety. The blasts tore away the rock, but feebly compared to sawdust soaked with nitroglycerine, the later invention (dynamite) of a Norwegian named Alfred Nobel.

When the last high-flung rock thudded to the ground, the laborers loaded the carts pulled by a horse or mule. The cart man led his animal away to the spot that the dump boss indicated. A quick throw of a lever, and the cart dumped its load, raising the grade.

Along Boulder Creek and gentler Four Mile lay the tent camps of the sub-contractors, who were building short stretches of the grade. Their men and the Negroes of Cox and Stone walked out to the job, back for dinner, out to the job again and back at quitting time. Men thought nothing in those days of walking three and four miles to work. And all for $1.50 to $2.00 a day, board not included. The days were 10 hours long.

Not every man collected his pay. Some of the sub-contractors, unable to pay their bills, offered ten cents on the dollar. One man skipped the country. The late John Borgstrand, retired Colorado and Southern section foreman of Boulder, remembered this incident well.

"I worked hard on this job, but like the rest of the men of my gang I got beaten out of my last two months' pay. We were working for the sub-contractor who had taken a stretch of grade under Cox.

"This sub-contractor told us to stay in camp while he went to Denver to collect the money for his work. That was the last we ever saw of him. . . . Instead of paying us, he bought a good farm near Windsor."

John and his buddies had to tramp wearily into Boulder, find an empty boxcar, ride to Denver with the sympathetic train crew looking the other way, and start hunting another job. Many had not a cent. No unemployment compensation then. Only a few people had heard of such a thing, and then only from Socialist speakers in obscure halls closely watched by the police.[16]

Not until the end of June, 1882, did carloads of bridge material and railroad iron begin arriving. Stone for the bridge piers came in, 150 carloads of it, and the masons went to work. Some of their fine craftsmanship may be seen today in the remaining bridge piers in lower Boulder Canon.[17]

One morning in early November things began to stir again. A Colorado Central train crew switched several flatcars with unusual loads onto a sidetrack at the west end of the new U. P. yards. As a gaping crowd looked on, they unloaded a narrow gauge en-

[16]*Boulder Daily Camera*, July 31, 1939.
[17]*Boulder News & Courier*, June 30, 1882.

LOOKING EAST FROM MOUTH OF BOULDER CANON

Louis Meile photo. A. A. Paddock Collection

Looking east from the mouth of Boulder Canon along the new line of the Greeley, Salt Lake & Pacific, probably in 1882. Note handsome masonry bridge piers of trestle at right. In the distance, to left of center, is the tiny University of Colorado.

Colorado Central No. 6, an 0-6-0, helped build the Greeley, Salt Lake & Pacific and was its first locomotive. She is **shown here about 1880 running along Clear Creek toward Idaho Springs.**

Sturtevant photo. M. R. Parsons Collection

The Union Pacific station in Boulder in the 1880's. The locomotive of the waiting standard gauge train is No. 111 with fancy cap stack, oil headlight, and link and pin coupler. Behind it is another locomotive with a diamond stack. Note third rail for narrow gauge Greeley, Salt Lake & Pacific, which ran west up Boulder Canon, in background. At the left is Preston ore mill with the high smokestack. Also at left is the 9th Street bridge over Boulder Creek, fated to be washed out by the flood of 1894. This red frame U. P. station stood at about 10th Street.

gine, the first ever seen in the frontier town, and several flatcars.[18]

Soon the narrow gauge locomotive crew had steam up and made up their work train. A big work gang loaded the flatcars with rails, spikes, fish plates, etc. The conductor gave the highball, and the first narrow gauge train headed toward Boulder Canon, laying rail as it went.

The *Boulder News & Courier* said in the November 10th issue: "Track laying up the canon is progressing as rapidly as could be expected, considering that there is scarcely a straight rail to be put down. . . ."

On November 24th the newspaper said: "Accepting the invitation of Conductor Reid Tuesday afternoon, we mounted the cow-catcher of No. 6 and were soon on our way up the canon. . . . We came upon the track layers a short distance this side of Orodel-phan. . . . Four Mile will probably be reached tomorrow. The rails used weigh 41¼ pounds to the yard and are 30 feet long. The roadbed is a splendid one, although the grade averages 195 feet to the mile."

Number 6, Colorado Central narrow gauge locomotive, was an 0-6-0, built by Porter-Bell, probably in the early 1870's. She had a big balloon stack, 13 by 16-inch cylinders, 34-inch drivers, weighed 32,450 pounds on drivers. She was in first-class shape, black paint and brass fittings shining, for she had been rebuilt in September, 1882.[19]

The crews laid track all that winter of 1882-83. By January 19, 1883, they reached Woods Mill—above Crisman.[20]

A Boulder pioneer, Mrs. Mary E. Taylor, a fine handsome woman with silver hair and the warm courtesy of the Old West, remembered this time well.

"My father, Gardner P. Wood, was very much in favor of the Greeley, Salt Lake & Pacific being built up Four Mile," she said.

"He had begun developing the Wood Mountain Mine at Wall Street — it was called Sugar Loaf at first — in 1867."

"Do you remember the Greeley, Salt Lake & Pacific?" We scarcely expected an affirmative answer, so long ago it had been.

She nodded. "My first recollection of the railroad was when they were blasting out the roadbed on the south side of the creek, right across from our house. Father had been ill and he was sitting there in an easy chair near the bay window.

"All at once a big blast went off and a rock same sailing through the window. It shattered glass over the room but fortunately Father wasn't touched. We were all glad, though, when they were finished over there.

"The railroad meant a great deal to Father, for he could now bring up supplies easier. We were pleased with the idea of having a railroad running right in front of our house. We could now go back and forth to Boulder quicker and easier than with horses."

She laughed. "The man who owned property west of us was angry at the railroad coming up the canon. Evidently he didn't get his price for the right-of-way. The railroad went through anyway.

"Seymour Johnson was his name. He was an old bachelor and an old-timer in the country. He had several mining claims in Four Mile.

"So one day he went down and flagged the train. 'I've just blowed up the bridge,' he told the engineer.

"They backed the train down, all the way to Boulder. He went to Boulder and gave himself up.

"The next day the railroad sent out a work train and crew. They rebuilt the bridge, and traffic continued as before."[21]

A grand jury later indicted Seymour Johnson for blowing up the bridge.

Suddenly spring quickened the steps of

[18]*Ibid.,* November 3, 1882.
[19]*Denver, South Park & Pacific* by M. C. Poor, Rocky Mountain Railroad Club, 1949.
[20]*Boulder News & Courier,* January 19, 1883.

[21]*Boulder Daily Camera,* March 1, 1957.

people in Boulder, and with this spring came a great event. On April 6, 1883, the *Boulder News & Courier* announced:

The first passenger train run over the Greeley, Salt Lake & Pacific road up the Canon was run last Sunday. The train leaves Twelfth street at 11 o'clock, and arrives at Pennsylvania Gulch (Sunset), the terminus of the road, at 12:40. Returning it leaves Penn Gulch at 1:10 and arrives at Boulder at 2:50.

In the next issue we find that a large force of men had begun work on the new depot, located between 9th and 10th Streets, with the intention of completing it in three weeks. The depot would be 24 by 80 feet, including a platform 48 by 106 feet.[22] It would be used for both passengers and freight. Before the end of May a paint car arrived, and the crew painted the new depot a "bloody red."[23]

Boulder did not get an elegant new brick depot and a separate freight station — but at least it had an uptown depot.

More significant, perhaps, was the newspaper comment that "From the number of side-tracks being put down between Ninth and Twelfth streets, one would suppose the U. P. company expected to do a heavy business in Boulder."[24]

The proud new mountain railroad was very much in the news. Up at Penn Gulch workmen completed a new depot, a one-story frame structure 21 by 49 feet, with a platform 7½ by 11 feet.[25] Three carloads of telegraph poles arrived at Boulder for the narrow gauge line. Workmen extended the grade from Pennsylvania Gulch nearly six miles, the line running up along the side of the mountain east to the base of Sugar Loaf Mountain, then west nearly to present Glacier Lake.

In the May 18, 1883, issue of the *Boulder News & Courier* we read that:

The excursion to Penn Gulch, given by the Congregational Society was a success in every particular. . . . The train left Twelfth street a few minutes late and the run to Penn Gulch was made without an accident. . . . Arriving at the Gulch, dinner was in order and after that the party broke up into small groups, some hunting flowers and others climbing the grade around the mountain, taking in the magnificent view from the top of Sugar Loaf. At 4 o'clock the train started back and the run was made without incident worthy of note. At Twelfth street three cheers were given for Conductor Ackroyd, Engineer Thorne and the success of the first excursion over the "narrer gouge."

[22]*Boulder News & Courier,* April 13, 1883.
[23]*Ibid.,* May 25, 1883.
[24]*Ibid.,* May 25, 1883.

[25]*Ibid.,* May 18, 1883.

Part I

Chapter IV

THE GREELEY, SALT LAKE & PACIFIC

Boulder looked upon the Greeley, Salt Lake & Pacific as its own, despite the fact that it was a part of the mighty Union Pacific. It was the first step toward making Boulder a terminal on a transcontinental railroad. It tapped the precious metal mines. It was going to bring great prosperity.

From the start the little railroad was popular. The press announced that parties visiting Penn Gulch could now secure a good lunch there; the carpenters who were building the depot had opened a refreshment stand. An enterprising outfit had put on a stage-coach between Gold Hill and Bloomfield— one of the many stops on the narrow gauge. The Masons planned an excursion to Penn Gulch, the round-trip $2.00. The Congregational Sunday School scheduled an excursion to Penn Gulch, round-trip $1.00, children 50 cents.[1]

"Squire Thorne and Jeff Hall laid themselves out when they decorated the engine that pulled the (Masonic) excursionists up to Penn Gulch on Tuesday. 'Twas a good job and the little engine looked splendid," said the *Boulder News & Courier*.

In the same issue of the *Boulder News & Courier* we read that "The offices will be removed from the old depot to the up-town depot tomorrow afternoon, and hereafter all trains coming into Boulder will come up to the 10th Street station, and all business will be transacted there. . . ."[2]

The management of the narrow gauge obligingly changed the schedule, so that people could have two hours and forty minutes between trains at Penn Gulch to enjoy the wonderful scenery. It announced the opening of an eating house and the setting up of tents for tourists and others who might wish to stop overnight.

"We understand that the Union Pacific Company will expend $1,000 on the wagon road between Penn Gulch and Ward, which should make a good road. Also, that the company will put the road from Bloomfield's to Gold Hill in good shape for heavy freight wagons to pass over," announced the *Boulder News & Courier* of Aug. 31, 1883.

Even the building of a new water tank (10,150 gallons) at Crisman was news.[3]

From the *Boulder County Herald* something is learned of the difficulties of railroading over the new line. "The average grade between Boulder and the mouth of Penn Gulch is about 190 feet to the mile. The steepest grade is between Crisman and Salina, where, for a distance of 2,700 feet, the road climbs at the rate of 237 feet to the mile. It is doubtless the worst road for curves and reverse curves in the state. . . ."[4]

Nor was that all. "A History of the Denver, Boulder & Western," published in *Bulletin No. 65, Railway and Locomotive Historical Society* by M. C. Poor, author of the invaluable *Denver, South Park & Pacific,* tells us many things: The little railroad had 66 bridges and trestles between Boulder and Sunset, as the town which grew up at the mouth of Pennsylvania Gulch was later called. The road snaked back and forth across Boulder Creek six times between

---

[1]*Boulder News & Courier,* June 22, 1883.
[2]*Ibid.*

[3]*Boulder News & Courier,* September 4, 1883.
[4]*Boulder County Herald,* March 14, 1883.

27

Colorado Central No. 10 at Sunset. Engineer Squire Thorne in cab, Fireman Sam Speas in gangway. No. 10, unloaded in Boulder January 23, 1884, replaced the original engine, C. C. No. 6. Small "U" on cab denotes Union Pacific ownership. The big oil-burning headlight is on display in the State Museum, Denver.

Colorado Central No. 10 at Sunset making up train to return to Boulder. Note pilot and link and pin coupler on tender for backward running, also oil headlight on cab. Bridge over Four Mile Creek was part of ambitious program to extend the Greeley, Salt Lake & Pacific to the Pacific Ocean. Station was or- iginally called Pennsylvania or Penn Gulch for Pennsylvania Gulch, up which wagon road at upper left runs. Sunset was a lumber shipping center then, as indicated by piles of lumber along track, flatcar which men have completed loading, and lumber wagon in left foreground. Time is 1884 or later.

Boulder and the mouth of Four Mile Creek. It crossed Four Mile 45 times between there and Sunset. The bridges and trestles varied in length from 12 to 288 feet. The most congested section lay immediately above Orodell: between mile posts 3 and 4 the track crossed 15 trestles. In this railroad, 14.43 miles long, there was over three-quarters of a mile — 3,885 feet—in trestles and bridges. Some were iron, but most were wood. The fire hazard was a constant worry.

Business on the little line picked up, the public avidly following every move. On January 23, 1884, the *Boulder County Herald* ran this story:

A large crowd, mostly boys, with a sprinkling of men, were at the C. C. depot Saturday evening to witness the unloading of the new Brooks locomotive engine (rebuilt and repainted). . . . At its side No. 6, the old engine, looked like a play thing. No. 6 weighs 17 tons, No. 10, the new engine, weighs 28 tons (M. C. Poor's roster of Colorado Central locomotives in the *Denver, South Park & Pacific* lists No. 10 as weighing 46,960 pounds on drivers). Engine and tender with water and coal together weigh 36 tons. There are some of the broad gauge freight engines which weigh more but perhaps none is more powerful because of the smallness of the drivewheels. It will be able to do most of the hauling necessary between Boulder and Penn Gulch for some months to come. . . .

The same newspaper later reported that the little railroad was a financial success. It entertained hopes that the Union Pacific would lay rail on its six or seven miles of grade west from Penn Gulch and continue on over the Snowy Range (Continental Divide) to Middle Park. It especially wanted the railroad to tap Caribou, for $20 a ton wagon freight rates were holding back its immense silver development. If the Greeley, Salt Lake & Pacific did not reach Caribou, the enterprising builders of the Denver, Utah & Pacific were going to do so. Boulder businessmen had better look out for Boulder. . . .[5]

In the spring of 1884 the railroad management obligingly changed the schedule again. "The narrow gauge road from the mountains arrives in Boulder at 9:10 a.m. and leaves at 10:30. It arrives in the afternoon at 3:50 and leaves for the mountains at 4:30. This is quite an accommodation to the men who want to come to Boulder to do their business here in one day and return home the same day. Heretofore they were obliged to stay over night," stated the *Boulder County Herald.*[6]

The same paper on July 23rd commented: "A number of Boulder people are summering at Penn Gulch. If the railroad track would run to the end of the present grade, there would be still more people who would seek its 'cool, sequested shades' for the dogday residences."

To the mountain people the Greeley, Salt Lake & Pacific was more than a moneymaking venture run by some far-off corporation. Mrs. Mary E. Taylor recalled their feeling:

"The railroad company built a platform alongside the track on the south side of the creek, almost directly across from our house (boarding house of the Wood Mountain Mine, also the postoffice, called Sugar Loaf). There were steps leading down for the passengers to cross the footbridge over Four Mile (Creek). They put up a post with a hook so that the trainmen could pick up a sack of mail without stopping."

She paused, a smile going over her face. "One thing stands out in my childhood memories — Father bringing us down to Boulder to see the Barnum and Bailey Circus. We got up at four o'clock in the morning to board the train. They ran a special up from Boulder to pick up the people. It was in July or August. The train was crowded with people.

"We got off at the station near 9th Street and spent the entire day at the circus. Then

---

[5]*Boulder County Herald*, February 13, 1884.

[6]*Boulder County Herald*, April 9, 1884.

The Greeley, Salt Lake & Pacific

R. H. Kindig Collection

Greeley, Salt Lake & Pacific train at Oredel, heading for Sunset. Locomotive may be Colorado Central No. 10. The dam was built by Tyler and Maxwell in 1865 to catch logs floated down Boulder Creek for their sawmill. They abandoned the sawmill in 1870 and the Hunt and Barber Smelter was built on the site. It is the frame building at the right. The flume carried water to operate a power wheel.

31

Denver Public Library Western Collection

Colorado Central No. 10 at Wall Street backing down to Boulder with flatcar loaded with poles. Time: 1884 or later.

Meile and Sturtevant photo. R. H. Kindig Collection

Men working on a Boulder County road in Boulder Canon have placed a barricade across the bridge to protect themselves against the snorting Moguls of the Greeley, Salt Lake & Pacific.

Sturtevant photo. R. H. Kindig Collection

Tourists enjoy walking around Sunset while Colorado Central No. 154 switches her train.

Janes and Sturtevant photo
Charles Cobb Collection

Denver, Leadville & Gunnison No. 60 stops at Gold Hill station, later Salina, on her run to Sunset. Locomotive type boiler beside track, brought up on a flatcar, will be hauled to one of the rich tellurium (gold) mines nearby by horse-drawn wagon.

we came back on the special, arriving home after dark, worn out but happy.

"People used to come up to visit, especially after the railroad was in. It was a very attractive place for people to come to in the summertime. Miss Mary Rippon of the University (of Colorado at Boulder) was one of Mother's great friends, and she used to visit us a lot.

"There were lots of picnics at Sunset—church groups, lodges, and fraternal organizations. They built a big pavilion there, where people danced and had a big time. Bands always accompanied the fraternal groups. We went up there to picnics often during the summers."

She laughed merrily. "There was the cutest little bulldog that used to come up on the train. He'd get off at a place, stay a while, then get back on and ride up to the next stop. The trainmen named him Grover Cleveland, for the President of the United States then. He used to stay with us a week at a time. We never learned who owned him, whether he had a home or not, but we were always glad to see Grover Cleveland.

"I remember Mr. (D. R.) McGaffey, the conductor of the mixed train. He was a fleshy man, always nice to us kids. He'd wave to us as the train rolled along. Squire Thorne was the engineer with him. Lots of times he'd toot the whistle when he'd see us."[7]

The railroad was fun for Boulder youngsters too and always an adventure. One day the author was talking with a tall bearded pioneer named Oscar Anderson, who was born in the homestead house of his grandfather, Jonas Anderson, in west Boulder.

"I grew up with the railroad," he said. "They used to keep the engine right across from where we lived. I knew the engineer and fireman well.

"I was going to Sunday School, to the Swedish Mission Church, and we used to

have picnics up in the mountains. The first time I remember—I'd judge I was nine or ten years old—we went to Crisman on the railroad.

"There were at least fifty, maybe seventy-five of us, children and parents. We rode on the regular train, which left Boulder in the morning about 8 or 9 o'clock. The railroad put on a special coach for us. We had lots of fun."

Oscar sat up straighter, the bright memory of those golden years vividly with him. "The next picnic we got off just above Orodell. I remember we walked around the Poorman Mine. It was wonderful to see them hoist up ore.

"Yes, that was some old railroad. Right across the street from our house they had a long coal bin where they coaled up the engine. They filled the tender tank with water here, from the City water line."[8]

Still another reminiscence of the railroad came from Mrs. John Pughe, whose black eyes twinkled as she relived the bright days of mountain childhood.

"When I was eight or nine years old my folks took me down one day to Sunset to get a load of feed. We lived on a ranch near Nederland and had to buy some feed for the stock. We went down past Washington Avenue (now a ghost mining camp near Glacier Lake), on east and down Pennsylvania Gulch.

"At Sunset I saw my first train. I thought it was the most wonderful thing I'd ever seen. I couldn't believe anything could run on a track."[9]

Her foster father, kind-hearted pioneer Stephen Sanders, waited until the train started back to Boulder, so that she might see it in action. He was intensely interested in the Iron Horse which had penetrated the mountains

[7]*Boulder Daily Camera*, March 1, 1957.

[8]*Boulder Daily Camera*, October 9, 1947.
[9]*Ibid.*, September 11, 1957.

and which might run on across the main range of the Rockies.

Fortune favored us in meeting others who knew the little railroad. In the autumn of 1941 the *Boulder Daily Camera* published the following:

Young John Kline's eyes glowed as he heard Conductor Ward's "all aboard" hurry the straggling miners onto the Greeley, Salt Lake & Pacific narrow-gauge train at the Boulder depot. He saw Engineer Squire Thorne twist in his seat and open the throttle, heard the chuff of the exhaust in the diamond stack. Proud of his standing as a trainman, John swung aboard for his first trip to Sunset. It was a summer morning, 1887.

The stout old Boulder pioneer looked torwards the blue foothills, a smile wreathing his face. In a moment the caressing hand of Memory had transformed him, in thought, to the slender youth swaying to the lurch of the narrow-gauge car. To his ears came the clik-clack-clikety-clack of wheels over rail joints as the little train picked up speed towards Boulder Canon.

"Yes sir, I worked on that first narrow-gauge railroad to Sunset," said John, nodding. "My job was to help load and unload freight at the old depot at 9th (nearer 10th) and Water streets. Then I'd go out on that morning train. We'd leave at 9:30."

He was hearing the rumble as the train crossed the long trestle over Boulder Creek, the echoing exhausts as they entered narrow Boulder Canon. He heard the whine of wheel flanges as the combination baggage-mail car and the coach rounded curves. His scalp tightened, and he knew the thrill of the men who conquer space.

"We stopped at Orodell, Crisman, Salina, Sugar Loaf station (now Wall Street), and Copper Rock. At each stop the miners got off, so that by the time we got to Sunset there were only a few aboard."

He was grinning at the good-natured "kidding" given the returning miners by their comrades on the little station platforms. He knew that many had been to visit sweethearts, stealing kisses when the eyes of watchful parents were turned. He knew that others had met the smiles and parted lips of gayer girls in Denver's dance halls.

"When we got up near Sugar Loaf station, I saw the Chinese placer miners at work. They had quite a camp there."

John was staring at the strange men from the Orient, men who turned over the gravel with a pa-

tience that no white man could equal, gathering the shining gold dust. He started as he saw the queues hanging beneath black hats, the baggy blue cotton trousers and blouses. He felt the mystery of them: buried pots of virgin gold, opium pipes in the evening, the hopes for an early return to a rich full life in old China.

"We had lots of flag stops. Whenever a miner wanted us to bring anything up to him, he'd flag us. We'd deliver it at that same place."

Young John was enjoying these frequent stops. He smiled at the hush in the leaf-shadowed floor of Four Mile Canon, the rapid requests, the smiling goodbyes of the adventurers digging in the flinty hills for gold. Then, once more, the creak and sway of the little train, the locomotive's exhausts tearing away the silence of the brooding mountains.

"We reached Sunset at 11 o'clock, left the box-car and turned on the wye there. (We believe John in error here; there was no wye or turntable at Sunset, as will be shown in a later incident.) Then we started back to Boulder and got here about one. That wasn't bad for those days; it was 13 miles to Sunset."

John paused a moment. "When we got down here, Lou Green, the brakeman, and I did the switching."

He was concentrating his every energy on helping Lou with the old link couplings, listening to the brakeman on how to handle the difficult connections without losing fingers or a hand. He caught the steps of a coal car with a flying leap, feeling himself every inch the railroader. The quick charging exhausts of the engine was powerful music to his ears.

"Yes, sir, that first narrow-gauge was some railroad." John sighed. "It seemed like something went when it was washed out during the big flood of 1894."[10]

Many people fitted into the picture of keeping the little railroad operating, and one was a frail Swedish woman, still bright of eye and spirit.

"I came to Boulder from Sweden in 1888," said Mrs. Matilda Borgstrand, widow of John Borgstrand, pioneer railroad man. "In 1891 Mr. Borgstrand and I were married and two years later we went to Crisman to live. Mr. Borgstrand was in charge of all the track of the railroad from Boulder to Sunset.

"The section house at Crisman was log

---

[10]Article by Forest Crossen in the *Boulder Daily Camera*, October 25, 1941.

Workmen finishing the flume of the Silver Lake Ditch in Boulder Canon above trestle No. 3 of the Greeley, Salt Lake & Pacific. Train is eastbound.

Construction is underway on the flume of the Silver Lake irrigation ditch, which has its headgate in Boulder Creek slightly over a mile above the mouth of Boulder Canon. The Greeley, Salt Lake & Pacific

Denver, South Park & Pacific No. 160 with east-bound train on one of the longest trestles of the Greeley, Salt Lake & Pacific in Four Mile Canon.

A. A. Paddock Collection

East-bound Colorado Central No. 59 pauses at Crisman. Station is also postoffice and grocery for the little camp.

Engineer and fireman evidently love No. 59, from the sleek look of her.

Sturtevant photo. M. R. Parsons Collection

Denver, South Park & Pacific No. 160 with east-bound train in rock cut in Four Mile Canon not far above Orodell. Behind No. 160 is a low wooden gondola and an outfit car. The uniformed trainmen indicates that it is a mixed train.

Note long link and pin coupler on the locomotive pilot and bent steel guards at the sides. They kicked many a dangerous rock away from the track.

Sturtevant photo. M. R. Parsons Collection

Sunset, looking west, June 12, 1887. Colorado Central No. 154 is about to start the return trip to Boulder with her trainload of excursionists. She will back the 14.43 miles, a dangerous practice. Beyond the station can be seen a bridge over Four Mile Creek and to the left a short trestle over Pennsylvania Gulch on the six-odd miles of grade built by the Greeley, Salt Lake & Pacific. So far as we know, no rail was laid across these bridges.

with a frame addition built onto it. I cooked for the men. Mr. Borgstrand had three or four men in the summer, when he did most of the track work. In the winter he had only one or two." She smiled. "They were all Old (Country) Swedes, like we were. Once in a while during the summer he would have a carpenter gang come up to work on the bridges."[11]

The long stretch of track with its heavy grades and sharp curves called for heavy maintenance work. But John Borgstrand was equal to the task. In 1877 he had come from Sweden directly to the Kansas Pacific Railway. In 1881 he worked on the grade of the Greeley, Salt Lake & Pacific. Then he went over to the Denver, South Park & Pacific to help build the line over Boreas Pass to Leadville. Yet this 14.43 miles of track, winding back and forth across Boulder and Four Mile Creeks taxed his patience.

Never would she forget those mornings, when she watched her husband and the men take the little handcar out of its shed, load on the tools and start up or down the track. There they would go, their bodies moving up and down as they furnished their own motive power. The motor car to lighten the labors of track men was far in the future.

Agitation continued for extension of the Greeley, Salt Lake & Pacific track. Now and then hopeful news cropped up like the following in the *Boulder County Herald* of March 19, 1884:

We are informed that the iron for the extension of the narrow gauge road from Penn Gulch to the end of the present grade on top of Bald Mountain has been secured and that tracklaying will begin about the first of May.

An observation car to be used on the narrow gauge up Boulder Canon, was unloaded from a broad gauge flat car to-day. Another passenger coach is expected in a few days.

These were Colorado Central coaches,

---

[11]*Boulder Daily Camera*, August 29, 1952.

as was most of the rolling stock. The Greeley, Salt Lake & Pacific had no rolling stock or motive power of its own. All was borrowed from the Colorado Central.

Despite this optimism no work began on the proposed extension. Then on April 1, 1885, we read:

The Herald got it pretty straight Monday that the narrow gauge road would very likely be extended ten miles further this summer. The arrangements seem all but perfected.

But, alas, for all the hopes, all the wealth of Caribou's silver hills, and the great Middle Park, the tracks stubbornly ended at Sunset.

We have preserved for us much of the warmth and color of the Greeley, Salt Lake & Pacific in photographs taken by J. B. Sturtevant, Boulder photographer and artist. Rocky Mountain Joe tramped the mountains, took pictures of everything. Through the efforts of Martin Parsons of Boulder we have many of his glass negatives today.

One shot shows Colorado Central No. 10 at Sunset. In the cab are the engineer, Squire Thorne, and his fireman, Sam Speas. Both look capable and quietly proud of their places as mountain enginemen. Both look friendly and full of fun.

Luck one summer morning brought a human contact with this photo. The exhausts of a steam locomotive drew me out to the junction of the U. P. and C&S tracks east of Boulder. Here I found C&S No. 909, a 2-10-2, standing on a leg of the wye after switching. The engineer invited me up into the cab. When we shook hands he gave his name as Sam Speas.

The name immediately rang a bell, and I referred to the photograph.

"Yes," he said, " my father, Sam Speas, ran on the Greeley, Salt Lake & Pacific. He was born in Missouri and came out here in the early '80's. He was with Squire Thorne for a few years. In 1887 he went to Como, was

Denver, South Park & Pacific No. 160 pauses on trestle over Four Mile Creek near Sunset with her daily train.

West-bound Colorado Central No. 155 switching at Gold Hill station, later Salina. Steam in left foreground is from an ore mill using both water and steam power to reduce the gold ore to powder fineness to separate the yellow metal from the rock.

The Greeley, Salt Lake & Pacific

Sturtevant photo. R. H. Kindig Collection

Sunset on the U. P. Terminus of the Greeley, Salt Lake & Pacific, Union Pacific subsidiary, it lay near the head of Four Mile Creek, 14.43 miles west of Boulder. Denver, Leadville & Gunnison No. 60 stands ready to pull out to the east. She has backed up, in contrast to the ordinary practice of heading up and backing down. Loading on the south side of the platform is a stage with four horses for Nederland or Ward, carrying passengers, mail, and express.

43

promoted to engineer, and was on the South Park run to Leadville until he retired in 1922."

We spoke of Squire Thorne, who came to Boulder from Golden to open service on the GSL&P. He returned briefly to marry his sweetheart, and they made their home in a railroad house in Boulder. Later they moved to Sunset, then back once more to Boulder.

People liked Squire, as this news story shows:

Squire Thorne was excused from service on the narrow gauge train Wednesday. A 9-pound boy who arrived Wednesday wanted his papa to stay with him. Squire feels better now. — *Boulder County Herald,* Oct. 27, 1886.

Another member of the crew well liked in Boulder was D. R. McGaffey. The late Fred White, a white-haired little Scotsman, knew him well, for Fred was manager of the Scottish-Colorado Mining and Smelting Company's mill at Salina.

"Conductor McGaffey was quite a character," he said. "Often we wouldn't have time to buy our tickets before boarding the train. McGaffey once said to me, 'I'll show you the rule of the road.' He tossed up a coin I had given him. 'Now if it sticks to the ceiling, it belongs to the company. If it falls, it's the conductor's.'" Mr. White laughed merrily, then sobered. "But I'm sure he was strictly honest."

A small dark cloud appeared on the horizon. A rumor ran about that the narrow gauge line's days were numbered. Old-timers shook their heads, recalling that the railroad had graded seven miles of line beyond Sunset to Pennsylvania (later Glacier) Lake but had never laid a foot of rail on it. The big plan of going over the Rockies to the Pacific was only a dream.

The optimists, however, would not give up. "Three cars for the narrow gauge road arrived in Boulder yesterday," s a i d the *Boulder County Herald* of Feb. 19, 1890.

"This does not look as if it was intended to take off the narrow gauge train."

The little railroad had never had an accident, a sharp testimonial to the careful operation of the crews. But it did engage in a dangerous practice which brought forth the following editorial in the *Boulder County Herald* of June 23, 1886:

Is it not against the law to have a locomotive pull a train with tender ahead? If it is not a law, it ought to be. . . . The engineers as they come down from Sunset must trust to luck and run by guess. They cannot look ahead far enough to tell where danger is lurking. If there is a law which can reach the U.P. it ought to be compelled to put in a turning table at Gold Hill station and also at Sunset, or else a wye. The present mode of backing down is very dangerous.

The practice continued and nothing happened. Then, five years later, lacking but one day after the warning:

The narrow gauge engine and tender (Denver, Leadville & Gunnison No. 60) went into Boulder Creek at the reservoir ditch head-gate Monday (June 22, 1891). The engine was on her smokestack, whistle and cab remnants. The cab is virtually a wreck. In coming down from Sunset the train backed down. The tender jumped the track near Sunset in the morning delaying the train quite a while. At the reservoir ditch head-gate the tender jumped the track again, and followed by the locomotive both went down the eight-foot embankment. Engineer Thorne and fireman Monroe barely escaped with their lives. The cars broke from the train and were left standing on the track. This is the first serious accident that ever happened on the road. — *Boulder County Herald,* June 24, 1891.

The company sent up another narrow gauge engine and a wrecking train from Denver. The crew lifted the engine out of the creek, loaded it onto a standard gauge flatcar at Boulder, and sent it to Denver to be repaired.

The spring of 1894 came late; snow lay deep on the mountainsides and filled the gulches. As May drew to an end the weather

Sturtevant photo. M. R. Parsons Collection

Colorado Central No. 154 arrives at Sunset August 1, 1886, with special observation car hooked behind regular coach. The special car has open sides, which are now protected by canvas curtains. From the fresh dark look of things a summer shower has just fallen.

turned warm and moisture-laden winds from the east struck the cold heights. It began to rain, and with fearful eyes the mountain people watched the creeks for signs of rising water. They had not long to wait.

"Sixty hours of almost continuous rain had transformed the quiet little stream (Boulder Creek) into a raging river," stated the *Daily Camera* of May 31st. "The creek had swollen into a river in Boulder canon, boulders crashed and roared, wagon roads and railroad bridges, washed from their timbers came crashing down the street.

"At Fourth street the long railroad bridge was twisted into a semicircle with the rim and rails of the track remaining, while the timbers blocked the flow of the stream and sent its waters far out upon low lying land, inundating a wide tract between the south side and Pearl street. . . .

"The Narrow Gauge railroad which operated out of Boulder to Sunset, at the head of Four Mile canon—the Greeley, Salt Lake and Pacific—was so badly damaged that it ceased operating."

C. O. Jones, a tall, slender, old-time steam engineer at the mines, told about his experiences during the flood.

"The next spring after I landed in this country I went to work for Boulder County. They were putting in a road from the mouth of Four Mile Creek to the foot of Poorman Hill. We had a tent camp up there.

"There at the end of May it began raining. It was snowing up around Sunset. That afternoon it began raining hard and we had to quit work. The tent where we slept started to leak.

"So a bunch of us—ah, there were six or eight, I guess—decided to go down to Boulder until the rain let up. So we kept a watch out for the train. It'd gone up in the

morning to Sunset and we wanted to catch it.

"Here she came, so we flagged the engineer down and got on. We rode down the canon to Boulder and got off at the old depot, never thinking any more about it.

"The next morning I started to walk back up to the camp. I got up to about where the Sanitarium is now and it began raining. So I turned around and came back to town.

"As soon as I got to Eleventh Street I saw the flood water. It was out of the creek banks and commencing to do damage. Then I walked up towards the mountains. Everybody in town was down there.

"The engine (Union Pacific, Denver & Gulf No. 155) was sitting on its sidetrack up at 6th Street. But she was in bad shape. The flood had already washed away the roadbed underneath her. She'd tipped down into the hole.

"I rode her the last trip she ever made up here."[12]

The flood hurt Boulder and the mining country badly. The newspapers faithfully reported the news but with a doleful note. Take the June 13, 1894, issue of the *Boulder County Herald*:

An engineer representing the Gulf road (Union Pacific, Denver & Gulf) started up over the narrow gauge line Monday for the purpose of estimating the damage done and reporting to the receiver and to Judge Hallett. An officer of the road also went up to Sunset to get the telegraph instruments, company books, etc., at the station.

Squire Thorne left for Denver last Monday. His wife and child left yesterday. They will make that place their future home, now that the narrow gauge is no more.

So ended a bright dream of railroad greatness in the swirl of a mountain flood.

[12]*Boulder Daily Camera,* December 31, 1952.

Sturtevant photo. M. R. Parsons Collection

View taken from the grade that the Greeley, Salt Lake & Pacific made along the south wall of Four Mile Canon. Colorado Central No. 154 has been switched around to the head end of the train for the return trip to Boulder. Time is August 1, 1886.

Sturtevant photo. M. R. Parsons Collection

Colorado Central No. 154 with trainload of gay excursionists on Colorado Day, August 1, 1886, at Horse Shoe Curve below Sunset.

Sturtevant photo
University of Colorado Museum Collection

Greeley, Salt Lake & Pacific train at Copper Rock during the flash boom of 1891 caused by the discovery of high- grade gold ore in the nearby Orphan Boy and other Mines.

ROCKY MOUNTAIN OFFICIAL RAILWAY GUIDE. 73

Union Pacific Railway.
October 1893

Denver and Morrison.

	No. 21	No. 23	Mls	STATIONS.	No. 22	No. 24	
	8 45AM	6 00PM	0	Lv......Denver....Ar	8 00AM	3 40PM	
		6 25	8	....Sheridan Junc....	7 35		
	9 45	6 30	9	......Fort Logan.....	7 30	2 45	
	10 35AM	7 05PM	17	Ar.....Morrison.....Lv	6 55AM	2 00PM	

Cheyenne to Julesburg.

8	2	Mls	STATIONS.	1	7
4 25PM	3 45AM	0	Lv...................Cheyenne....................Ar	5 35AM	11 40AM
5 20	....	32	.................................Egbert................		10 24
7 45	6 20	102	...............................Sidney	1 50AM	8 10
8 50PM	7 30AM	144	Ar ....Julesburg................	12 18AM	6 35AM

WEST			Boulder Canon Branch.		EAST		WEST		Fairplay Branch.		EAST
357 Mixed	355 Mixed	M's	STATIONS.	356 Mixed	358 Mixed		475 Mixed	M's	STATIONS.		476 Mixed
7 40AM	....	0	Lv.... Denver.....Ar	6 15PM	....		8 30AM	....	Lv.... Denver ....Ar		....
11 25	....	29	Ar.... Boulder.... Lv	1 45PM	5 45		....	....			....
2 30PM	9 00AM		Lv.... Boulder.... Ar	12 45AM	5 45		2 00PM	....	Ar ...Como.... Lv		12 55PM
2 50	9 20	....	.......Oredel........	12 30	5 28		2 10	....	Lv....Como.... Ar		12 10PM
3 18	9 48	32	......Crisman........	12 05	5 05		3 15	....	........Garo's........		11 05AM
3 30	10 00	25	.....Gold Hill......	11 55	4 55		4 05	....	......Fairplay		10 15
3 45	10 12	36	....Sugar Loaf.....	11 45	4 45		5 30	....	Ar.. London Jc ..Lv		9 40AM
4 03	10 32	38	....Copper Rock....	11 27	4 27						
4 15PM	10 45AM	42	Ar.... Sunset Lv	11 15AM	4 15PM						

—Collection of M. C. Poor.

Copied from "Rocky Mt. Official Ry. Guide"—Oct. 1893.

R. H. Kindig Collection

A wreck on the Greeley, Salt Lake & Pacific a short distance below Sunset. Denver, Leadville & Gunnison No. 60 was derailed with her train. No. 154 stands by with relief train.

49

A. A. Paddock Collection

Boulder Canon

East-bound mixed train of the Greeley, Salt Lake & Pacific in Boulder Canon, in the 1880's. Locomotive is probably No. 10, from Congdon stack and position of back-up headlight on cab. The engineer has stopped short of trestle imme-diately below the Maxwell Pitch, two miles west of Boulder, on wagon road built in 1865. Boxcar and outfit car bear the initials, C.C.R.R.; the coach, Colorado Central Railroad.

Wreck of the east-bound Greeley, Salt Lake & Pacific passenger train at Goat Rock, a short distance above the mouth of Boulder Canon, June 22, 1891. The train was backing down from Sunset. Denver, Leadville & Gunnison No. 60 landed on her cab against a big boulder. Engineer Squire Thorne and Fireman Joe Monroe jumped before she toppled over the eight-foot wall.

A. A. Paddock Collection

Denver, Leadville & Gunnison No. 60 lies on her side with train, a victim of one of the accidents that plagued mountain railroads. Location is .4 miles below Sunset. UPD&G No. 154 heads another train on the regular daily schedule.

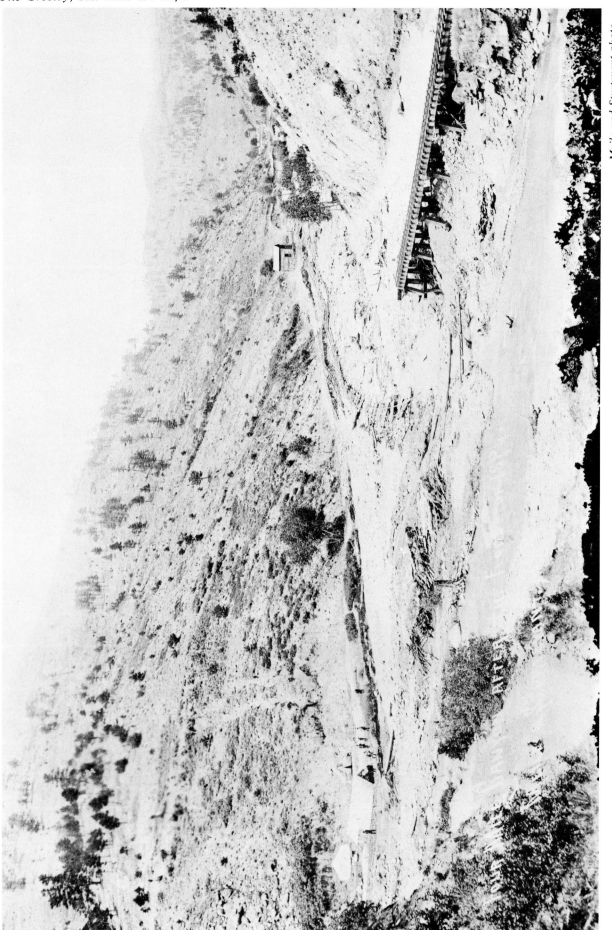

Meile and Sturtevant photo
R. H. Kindig Collection

The rails and ties of main line and siding extending up the canon show the flood's destructive power.

Mouth of Four Mile Creek after the flood of 1894. The trestle in the foreground alone remains intact with its track of the Greeley, Salt Lake & Pacific.

Meile and Sturtevant photo. J. B. Schoolland Collection

The trestle of the Greeley, Salt Lake & Pacific over Boulder Creek was a sorry sight as the stream resumed its normal flow. Note temporary footbridge.

Bass photo. J. B. Schoolland Collection

The flood of Decoration Day, 1894. This photo, looking west from the top of the Sternberg Flour Mill at 11th Street, shows the Union Pacific and Greeley, Salt Lake & Pacific station on an island. Boulder Creek, to the left, is a raging torrent. West of the station are two coaches, probably of the narrow gauge GSL&P. Beyond them is the black blot of UPD&G No. 155, nose down in the water. She will run no more to Sunset.

Looking west from 9th Street during the 1894 flood. UPD&G No. 155 in background to right is bravely facing the flood.

Bass photo. J. B. Schoolland Collection

Looking east from top of the Sternberg Flour Mill at flooded Boulder railroad yards. Note third rail track and harp switch in foreground. The crossing sign is for 12th Street, now Broadway.

Union Pacific, Denver & Gulf No. 155 after the 1894 flood waters subsided a little. She was later pulled out, loaded onto a flatcar and sent to Denver.

Meile and Sturtevant photo. J. B. Schoolland Collection

Looking east down the third rail track of the Boulder yards as the 1894 flood waters begin to recede.

Bass photo. J. B. Schoolland Collection

The fine new stone passenger station in Boulder was flooded. Note third rail track and water tank to the west.

Part II

Chapter I

THE COLORADO & NORTHWESTERN

Gloom hung heavily over Boulder long after men cleared away the debris left by the flood of 1894. The country sagged under the Panic of 1893, and in that same tragic year came the demonitization of silver. The Caribou mines shut down, and hundreds of miners and their families pulled out. The mountains lay quiet, even the gold camps were hard hit. Worst of all, Boulder lost her bright dreams of greatness as terminus of a mountain railroad; the little narrow gauge Greeley, Salt Lake & Pacific was not to be rebuilt.

In April, 1895, came an announcement of the construction of a railroad that would tap every mining camp in Boulder County and make Boulder the ore milling center. Low shipping rates were expected to bring shipments in excess of 500 tons a day.[1]

On April 6th the Inter-Mountain Railway was incorporated by Boulder citizens: Samuel C. Brown, Jacob S. Switzer, James Cowie, Eugene A. Austin, and George F. Fonda. The capital stock was $300,000, with 30,000 shares at $10 each. The company was said to have heavy eastern backing. Work would begin within a few weeks.[2]

Hope sprang up in people again. Gold mining began to pick up. On July 1, 1897, enterprising men incorporated the Ward Struggler Gold Mining Company, with capital stock of $600,000.[3] The famous Logan Mine, near Sugar Loaf, exhibited 22½ ounces of gold, the product of fourteen pounds of

ore. At Ward miners began sinking the shaft deeper on the B&M Mine. Charles W. Caryl, in the interests of a Wall Street, New York, syndicate, began driving a tunnel through the rich Melvina-Gold Hill mining district from Four Mile Creek. Four leasers on the Celestial Extension netted a little over $8 a day for 30 days—big money then.

Work, however, did not begin on the Inter-Mountain Railway in a few weeks—or ever.

A former locomotive engineer named M. F. Leach took over the inactive company.[4] He proposed to build a low-cost 22-inch tramway from Boulder to Ward primarily to haul ore down. He hired a bearded Civil War-trained railroad location engineer, J. L. Frankeberger, to run a survey for the new line. Frankeberger began work in February, 1897.[5]

Leach interested New York and Pennsylvania capital in his project. On July 22, 1897, Charles W. Mackey of New York; J. T. Blair of Greenville, Pa.; E. C. Thompson of Meadville, Pa.; T. W. Waltemeyer and M. F. Leach of Boulder incorporated the Colorado & North Western Railway Company.[6] They set the capitalization at $500,000, and two days later the State of Colorado issued them a charter.

The Colorado & Northwestern took over all rights, privileges, and franchises of the Inter-Mountain Railway Company. It

[1]*Boulder County Herald*, April 3, 1895.

[2]*Boulder County Herald*, April 6, 1895 and "History of the Denver, Boulder & Western Railroad Co." by M. C. Poor in *Bulletin No. 65, Railway and Locomotive Historical Society*, 1944.

[3]*Boulder County Herald*, July 1, 1897.

[4]Interview with Ernest Greenman of Boulder, April 10, 1954.

[5]*Frankeberger Autobiography.*

[6]*Boulder County Herald*, July 2, 1897.

would build and operate a railroad from Boulder to Ward and points west.

The *Denver Republican* picked up the story, saying that the Ward district would soon have a railroad, a facility that would more than double the output of the gold camp.[7] The heavy rates for wagon transportation—50 cents a hundred pounds going in and half that sum coming out—had kept several valuable mines from operating.

Gold Hill mining was booming. The stage was set for a boom at Eldora, with its promising veins of sulphide gold ore. H. A. W. Tabor, who had made and lost a multi-million dollar fortune in the Leadville silver mines, was developing a gold mine at Ward. Many people saw him again a millionaire.

Again Boulder people looked to the wooded hills. From them had come the wealth to start and develop their town. Again they squared their shoulders. The dream of a railroad to the west glowed brightly.

The Eastern men, who had made their money in railroads, lumbering, and steel mills, made a careful study of the complete operation. They abandoned the proposed 22-inch gauge line and settled on a 36-inch — the ordinary narrow gauge. Although more costly to construct, equip, and operate, it would widen the scope of their operations. Already they envisioned an attractive tourist business in the summer months.

The (Boulder) *Daily Camera* of August 12, 1897, reported that bids for building the railroad had been submitted by the most prominent contractors of Colorado.

The new survey placed the line on higher ground, particularly along Four Mile Creek, abandoning most of the old Greeley, Salt Lake & Pacific roadbed. The original railroad had a maximum grade of 4.39%, with curves running as high as 25 and 30 degrees. It had 66 bridges and trestles between Boulder and Sunset. The new line would have 17 bridges and trestles, with grades running to

a maximum of 4.49%, curves reaching 30 degrees.[8]

The contract for grading, bridging, and laying the rails fell to Orman and Crook of Pueblo August 13, 1897. They had four months to complete the work from date of beginning. This was not to include branches, only the main line from Boulder to Ward.[9]

The roundhouse and shops were to be located in Boulder, also the western offices of the company.

For some time rumors had been flying that the Pennsylvania men intended to build a big mill to handle ore from the Ward mines, also from other camps. In mid-August the Pennsylvania Mining and Milling Company filed papers with the Boulder County Clerk, listing a capital stock of $150,000. The incorporators were J. T. Blair, Charles W. Mackey, and S. A. Giffin.[10]

Orman and Crook set up a camp at Orodell, mining camp near the mouth of Four Mile Creek, four miles up Boulder Canon from Boulder. The crews began working each way from the camp, and by mid-September 600 men were on the job.[11]

The *Denver Daily News* of August 25, 1897, made a big spread of the story:

OPEN SEASAME
Colorado and Northwestern to
Open Boulder Treasure Vaults

Thousands of Tons of Ore Await
The Advent of the Locomotive

Dozen Camps Will Pour A Stream
Of Ore to Mill and Smelter

Work has been begun on the Colorado and Northwestern Railway from Boulder to Ward. . . .

The engines will be a special type, the three freight engines being very low geared and weighing 50 tons. The passenger will be a somewhat different type and calculated to make better speed. There

---

[7]*Ibid.,* July 20, 1897.

[8]M. C. Poor article in *Bulletin No. 65, Railway and Locomotive Historical Society.*
[9]*Daily Camera,* Boulder, August 14, 1897.
[10]*Daily Camera,* Boulder, August 16, 1897.
[11]*Ibid.,* September 10, 1897.

Sturtevant photo. R. H. Kindig Collection

Boulder after the flood of 1894. The buckled trestle of the abandoned Greeley, Salt Lake & Pacific is a short distance down Boulder Creek, almost opposite the low dark bulk of the Boyd Smelter with its tall smokestack. The big building in the center background with smoke and steam rising is the pioneer Sternberg Flour Mill. In the foreground the third rail track is in use.

Sturtevant photo. M. R. Parsons Collection

The Boyd Smelter, built in 1871, stood west of the present Boulder City limits, on the north bank of Boulder Creek. It was built by James H. Boyd, a Chicago casket manufacturer, who fell in love with gold mining and the Colorado Rockies. The smelter used both steam and water power. At the right of the building, in the background, is the fine stone bridge abutment of the narrow gauge railroads.

Sturtevant photo
University of Colorado Museum Collection

Mines on mountainside above the Switzerland Trail. Coal brought up by the railroad made steam for their power. The railroad hauled down their ore to concentrating mills and smelters.

Sturtevant photo
University of Colorado Museum Collection

Tunnel scene in a gold mine near Boulder. Note small mine railroad, candles in special miner's candlesticks hanging on tunnel walls and stuck into timber at mustachioed miner's feet.

Sturtevant photo
University of Colorado Museum Collection

Abandoned water-powered stamp (ore) mill along the Switzerland Trail. Water brought by wooden flume and ditch from upstream turned the big wheel, which raised the long vertical stamp shafts at right. At a certain height these were tripped automatically, allowing them to fall. Their steel bottoms or stamps struck ore fed in by the millmen, smashing it to powder fineness. The gold or silver could then be separated from the valueless rock dust.

has been ordered four passenger coaches of the size usual on narrow gauge lines though equipped with the conveniences common to the modern standard gauge coach. One hundred and fifty freight cars will be the balance of the rolling stock at present ordered. . . .

It is expected that a branch will ultimately be run to Gold Hill, Jimtown and Sunshine, and on to Caribou and Eldora. . . .

All along the line of the railway through Four Mile and Left Hand canons, mines are omnipresent. Ward camp at present is the principal camp in the district. . . . for 1894 and 1895 the output was over $1,000,000. . . . Within Ward camp are many propositions unequalled in the state. . . .

The camp has been admitted to be one of those lying within the great sulphide belt. Its riches are inexhaustible. Within its limits are billions of tons of low-grade ore, valued at from $10 to $25 (per ton). This ore it has been impossible to handle with the methods of transportation formerly used. The charge of $3.50 a ton on all grades shipped by teams rendered the handling of such ores impossible. The rate of $1 on low grades and $2 on high, to be charged by the railroad, will bring out unlimited quantities hitherto not looked at.

The matter of the expense of fuel in Ward camp alone has been no inconsiderable item. Wood sold at from $3.50 to $4.00 a cord. . . . Coal has not been considered as a practicable fuel at prices ranging from $6.50 to $9.50 a ton. The new road will bring coal from the Marshall banks at a maximum of $2.50, making the Ward price $4. It is estimated that at this price the consumption of coal in Ward alone will be 500 tons per day. It is further stated that one ton of coal is equivalent in value in the boiler to two and one-half cords of wood. . . .

In the other camps tributary to the road tellurium ore is prevalent. . . . An estimate is difficult, but one that may give some idea of the daily output has been placed as follows by the railway people:

Crisman, 20 tons; Sugar Loaf, 250 tons; Salina, 100 tons; Copper Rock and Sunset, 50 tons; Ward, 500 tons; Gold Hill, 200 tons; Sunshine, 100 tons; Summerville, 30 tons; Caribou and Cardinal, 50 tons; Eldora, 100 tons; Magnolia, 50 tons; Jamestown, 200 tons.

The road has been justly termed as the making of Boulder county. . . . Already investments are being made . . . and this beginning has unlimited possibilities.

Great hopes are held for the development of Eldora and Caribou.

The directors of the road have plenty of capital back of the enterprise and it is stated that they will not need to sell a bond for the construction of the road.

The men building the grade were not in on the big money. Ole Stromberg, who later became a farmer near Boulder, was a blacksmith for the Ryan Brothers, sub-contractors. He drew $100 a month, starting at 7 a.m., quitting when the work was finished. The muleskinners and shovel men worked 10 hours, drew $1.75 a day and board.[12]

Once again the old dream of a railroad through and across the Rockies fired men's minds. The *Denver Republican* reported that, as soon as the road to Ward was completed, in December,[13] the shrewd Pennsylvania capitalists intended pushing it on across the Continental Divide. It would tap the immense, almost untouched resources of timber, farm and ranch lands, coal and mineral deposits of Middle Park. Then on across Utah to the great Salt Lake.

For years a plucky little mining man named Robert Duncan, who had cut his eye teeth in the Leadville boom, had been studying the ore deposits at Ward. He and his brother John worked out a plan to tunnel in under them, at one stroke draining the troublesome water and taking advantage of gravity to bring out the ore. Robert Duncan went to New York and London and explained this plan to men of capital and vision. They promised support.

Late in September of 1897 Duncan announced the formation of the Big Five, a combination of five big mining companies in the heart of the Ward district, with over-all plans for development and production of ore. The Dew Drop Mining Company, Dew Drop Milling Company, Adit Mining Company, Adit Tunnel Company, and the Niwot Mining Company represented a capitalization of $5,750,000. The development plan called for

---

[12]*Boulder Daily Camera*, February 7, 1953, article by Forest Crossen.

[13]*Daily Camera*, September 13, 1897.

more than five miles of tunnels and laterals. It would open the entire wealth of the district.[14]

The officials of the Big Five expected an annual gold production of $5,000,000. They installed a ten-drill-capacity air compressor, the second largest ever brought into Colorado. Four new boilers of 100 horsepower each would furnish steam for a 125-horsepower engine. They planned to drive a double track tunnel 300 feet a month.

They planned to enlarge and improve the mill at the mouth of the Adit Tunnel to a daily capacity of 500 tons of ore. The new narrow gauge railroad would cross the mill yard, with a station and ample yard trackage.

The tunnel system would drive into the Niwot, at one time the greatest gold mine in Colorado. It would tap the fabulous Columbia vein of high-grade gold ore. Great success here could bring a boom to every mining camp in Boulder County.

Optimism began to snowball when the capitalists building the C&N planned a mill at Boulder with a capacity of 250 tons of ore a day. The Pennsylvania Mining and Milling Company had $100,000 with which to begin immediate construction. With a custom mill and a railroad to haul his ore to it, what more could a miner ask?

Sales of mines in Eldora, Ward, Gold Hill, Summerville, and other camps picked up. "There is no doubt but that the (Boulder) county will soon take its place in the front rank of mineral producing districts in the state," said the *Boulder Tribune* of October 8, 1897.

A few mornings later the regular Union Pacific, Denver & Gulf passenger train set out a car that made the eyes of the depot loafers go wide. The word flew and soon people began hurrying down to gape at the "Conneaut," private car of the Pittsburgh, Bessemer & Lake Erie Railroad.[15]

Presently in unhurried dignity down from it stepped Colonel Samuel B. Dick of Meadville, Pa., Chairman of the Board of Directors of the PB&LE, largest owner save Andrew Carnegie in that road; W. C. Culbertson, whose multi-million fortune had come from lumbering and land sales at the head of the Mississippi, now banker of Girard, Pa.; C. B. Culbertson, also of Girard; J. H. Dick of the powerful *New York Sun;* J. T. Blair, former President of the Pittsburgh, Shenango & Lake Erie Railroad and recently General Manager of the PB&LE, right-hand-man of Andrew Carnegie, and his wife of Greenville, Pa.; E. C .Thompson of Meadville and C. W. Betts, mining man of Boulder and Ward. They were men of substance, in broadcloth and fine linen, the beautiful woman in the latest Paris creations. Here walked envied wealth and power.

These gentlemen, so said the local press, had come to Boulder for an inspection tour of their Colorado & Northwestern. Somehow the rumor started that they intended to build a big luxury summer hotel in Boulder. Many people scoffed.

One week later the doubters had to swallow their words. The Boulder Development and Improvement Company filed incorporation papers with the Secretary of State, listing C. W. Mackey, prominent New York attorney and president of the Franklin Casting Company, President; J. T. Blair, Vice-President; T. S. Waltemeyer, Treasurer; R. T. Fulton, Secretary; W. C. Miller, General Manager, the latter three of Boulder. They set the capital stock at $250,000.[16]

Boulder tingled with excitement. The Fulton Brothers had converted part of the rock-strewn cow pasture west of the little University of Colorado into a fine residential district. Boulder would at last have a luxury hotel to attract rich tourists.

The officials of the Colorado and Northwestern announced plans for extensions of

---

[14]*Boulder Tribune,* September 24, 1897.
[15]*Boulder Tribune,* October 15, 1897.

[16]*Boulder Tribune,* October 22, 1897.

Sturtevant photo. University of Colorado Museum Collection

One of the gold mines perched high on a mountainside above the Switzerland Trail. Four-horse freight wagon has brought up coal, will take down ore.

University of Colorado Museum Collection

Ore haulers leaving one of the gold mines west of Boulder. They are the old-time four-horse teams hitched to a standard ore wagon. Each driver has his right foot on the brake lever, stopping the rear wheels with wooden brake shoes hard against the iron tires. These freighters hauled coal from sidings on the Switzerland Trail to steam-powered mines like this one, ore down to load onto railroad gondolas.

R. H. Kindig Collection

East-bound Colorado & Northwestern passenger train arriving at Sunset headed by a borrowed 2-6-0 diamond-stacker, which has lost her pilot or cowcatcher. Engine is evidently a C&S 2-6-0.

J. B. Schoolland Collection

C&N No. 1 ready to depart from the Boulder station with Combo No. 51 and coach. Logs in foreground have been shipped down from the mountains for the nearby McAllister sawmill.

69

the railroad as soon as it reached Ward. Their surveyors would begin running a line to rich Camp Albion before the end of December. Soon thereafter the crew would run a line from Ward to Buchanan Pass. From there the railroad would ultimately run into Middle Park, later perhaps to Salt Lake City.[17]

Work meanwhile was progressing rapidly on the bridges at the mouth of Boulder Canon. Soon track laying would begin. Once more Boulder would thrill to the beating exhausts of locomotives making a run for the canon.

On November 12, 1897, carpenters drove the last spikes into the bridge over Boulder Creek at Fourth Street. The next day the construction train moved over it, and track layers began spiking rails to the new ties that had been freighted down from the mountains.

These ties were of red spruce, with yellow pine the second choice, white pine the third. They were 7 feet long, 6 inches high, and 8 inches wide. Tie-makers hand-hewed them with a broadaxe, which had a blade about 8 inches wide, sharpened on one side, weighing 7 to 9 pounds. They used trees near the railroad right-of-way that were at least 10 inches in diameter at the small end. A good tie-maker could finish from 50 to 60 a day.

George Springsteel of Boulder, old-time freighter and timberman, furnished ties to the Switzerland Trail for many years. "I got as low as 33¢ a tie up to 65¢," he said. "It was all piece work. I paid the makers 13¢ a tie when I first started, later on 18¢. A good tie-maker could earn big wages—for that time."[18]

The *Daily Camera* printed a touching story headlined "An Old Friend Returns" about Locomotive No. 61, which had run between Boulder and Sunset on the old Greeley, Salt Lake & Pacific:

It will now be used in the construction of the new line to Ward and its lever will yield to a familiar

hand—that of Joe Monroe, who presided over it in former days as fireman. With No. 61 again with us, and in charge of Joe Monroe, the older time will be vividly brought back. Boulder welcomes them.[19]

There had been more excitement when the regular Union Pacific freight pulled in two days before. On a flat car stood a sleek black 2-6-0 locomotive, fresh from the Brooks Locomotive Works at Dunkirk, New York. She bore the number "1" on her sand dome, "C&NW" below the cab windows, "Colorado & Northwestern Ry." on her tender. She weighed 66,500 pounds on drivers, had 15 by 22-inch cylinders, 44-inch drivers, and a tall shotgun stack.[20]

The C&N lost no time in steaming up No. 1 and running her up and down the yards to limber up stiff bearings. Again the loafers had a field day. The *Boulder Tribune* said that "the engine is as fine a specimen of mechanism as any in the state."

Meanwhile faithful little diamond-stack No. 61 was pushing the construction train up Boulder and Four Mile Canons. The ties went down first in even spacing. Along them a line of men in rhythmical step carried a length of rail into place, spikers naked to the waist and with muscle rippling under bronzed skin, spiking it fast, their steel against steel ringing out on the clear mountain air. Then another rail down, another. On to Sunset!

The rails reached Sunset February 20, 1898. One year before, Chief Engineer Frankeberger and his corps of engineers had begun the survey of the line west from Boulder.[21]

The railroad celebrated by running an excursion train to Sunset. The guests—business and mining men—crowded the coach which the Union Pacific, Denver & Gulf had kindly lent. At Sunset the men watched the busy track-laying crew under the direction of Engineer F. R. Dungan push the rails up the grade that swung along the north canon wall

[17]*Boulder Tribune*, November 5, 1897.
[18]Interview, July 9, 1957, at Boulder.

[19]*Daily Camera*, November 12, 1897.
[20]*Ibid.*, November 10, 1897.
[21]*Daily Camera*, February 21, 1898.

Photo by Clint O. Dunn

DB&W No. 1 in the Boulder yards before she was equipped with turbogenerator and electric lights.

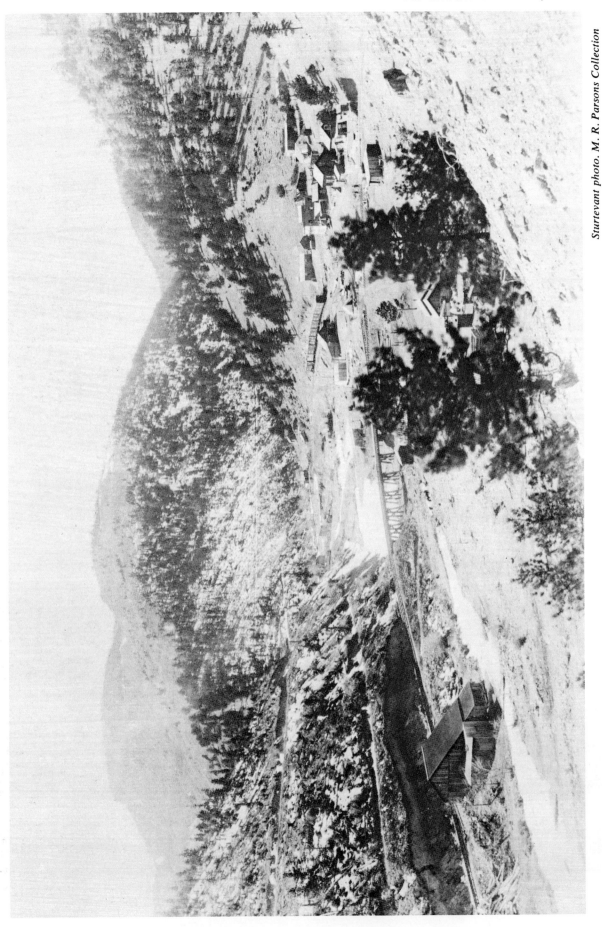

Sturtevant photo. M. R. Parsons Collection

Sunset not long after the arrival of the C&N. Only the Ward trestle is finished. The wye has been completed and the station is under construction. The two-story Columbine Hotel in row paralleling creek is not yet finished. Boxcars are on track that will later be the Eldora main line. Directly to left of mill building along the creek in left foreground will stand the water tank. Pipeline in ditch along mountain above creek will bring water to tank. Time: late winter or early spring, 1898.

72

Sturtevant photo. R. H. Kindig Collection

C&N No. 1 poses for picture on Sawmill Hill, probably in the spring of 1898.

Sturtevant photo. M. R. Parsons Collection

The Pennsylvania Mill, the largest at the time in Boulder County, was built to house 250 stamps. It measured 85 by 150 feet. The power came from two steam engines fed by four big boilers in boiler house at right.

Sturtevant photo. M. R. Parsons Collection ➤

Pennsylvania Mining and Milling Company's custom ore mill at Culbertson, four miles east of Boulder. In the foreground, at lower right, is the spur line of the C&N running west to gain elevation before looping back to the ore bins beneath shed at left. The two brick cottages on the shore of Owen's Lake were built to house executive personnel.

Sturtevant photo. M. R. Parsons Collection

Eldora was building feverishly when Joe Sturtevant made this photo shot in September, 1897. Looking northwest at Eldorado Mountain from the mouth of the Mogul Tunnel, at the foot of Spencer Mountain.

far to the east to gain elevation, then back to the west before heading northwest to Ward. They admired the wye, already in use, then turned to look at the grade of the old Greeley, Salt Lake & Pacific running along the south canon wall, a grade some six or seven miles long ending in the pines near Pennsylvania (Glacier) Lake. They repeated common talk that the Colorado & Northwestern intended using this grade to lay a track on to tap the riches of Eldora, already commencing to boom.

Their pulses whipped up as they identified themselves with this powerful concern, to which business was already rushing. On the way up, on a siding at Wall Street, they had seen a bright new red boxcar with "Colorado & Northwestern" on its sides. It had carried the first carload shipment of freight, billed to the busy Franklin gold mine.[22]

The next day four new coaches (two passenger, one baggage, and one combination) arrived at Boulder. They looked impressive, forty-six feet long and eight and a half wide, with beautiful interiors finished in oak and maple, painted Pullman green outside, fitted with steam heat and modern equipment.[23]

The Colorado & Northwestern had laid out its yards and was completing its facilities at Boulder. Originally it had bought a tract of land along the south side of Boulder Creek, west of the Fourth Street bridge. They erected a water tank and section house and built two short sidings here. One of its old-time employees said that the original plan was for the yards to be here.[24] Today this beautiful creek-side land beneath the great spruce and pine-covered foothills is part of the Eben G. Fine Park.

The C&N secured land from the Colorado & Southern and the Union Pacific east of the Fourth Street bridge north of Boulder

Creek and laid out their yards on this more level tract. It erected an engine house and shops and other necessary facilities.

Boulder bubbled with optimism. Four miles to the east, on a slope south of picturesque Valmont Butte, expert carpenters and millwrights were erecting the big Pennsylvania Mill, measuring 85 by 150 feet. Designed for an ultimate capacity of 250 stamps, it would be the largest ore mill in Boulder County and one of the largest in Colorado. It would soon be ready to receive the first ore. At last Boulder County mining men would have a modern reliable custom mill.

The Union Pacific, Denver & Gulf began laying track on the abandoned Colorado Central branch from Boulder Junction to Louisville, ten miles east. Hereafter all through freight would be routed via the shorter Louisville cut-off.[25]

The Colorado & Northwestern had made a deal with the Gulf road to lay a third rail on this line to a point four miles east of Boulder. From there a narrow gauge track would run north to the Pennsylvania Mill at Culbertson. Carloads of ore from the mountains could be shunted to the mill without transfer. Soon ore trains would be rumbling through Boulder.

This would be true if the proposition of the Big Five to supply the Pennsylvania Mill went through. The Niwot Company would furnish 100 tons a day for the first six months; 150 tons a day for the second six months; 200 tons a day the second year and 500 tons a day for a term of five years. The railroad's part would be transportation at $1 a ton, the mill's ore treatment charge $1 a ton.[26]

This schedule of ore shipments would render the big mill independent. It would keep the stamps dropping night and day.

There seemed to be no fading of the golden mirage; instead, there was a growing brightness. Rumor had it that the Pennsylvania Mill contemplated the immediate erec-

---

[22]*Daily Camera,* February 14, 1898.
[23]*Ibid.,* February 21, 1898.
[24]Interview with Oscar Bernsten at Boulder, November 4, 1955.

[25]*Daily Camera,* January 10, 1898.
[26]*Ibid.,* February 14, 1898.

tion of a smelter at Culbertson in connection with the mill. From Eldora came news of high-grade gold discoveries on Spencer Mountain, transforming the once quiet Happy Valley into a boom camp, complete with dance halls and gay women.

A few months before, a group from Texas had visited Boulder in their search for a site for a summer colony fashioned after the one at Lake Chautauqua, New York.

On February 23, 1898, the committee of this Texas-Colorado Chautauqua Association arrived in Boulder to make their decision. Enterprising businessmen of the town asked the Colorado & Northwestern to run a special to Sunset. They regaled their guests with sights of pigtailed Chinese placer mining in Four Mile Creek, gold mines clinging to the canon walls, and vistas of unsurpassed beauty.[27]

The Texans, who contemplated exiling themselves during the hot months from their beloved biggest state, were impressed. Less than a month later they formally selected Boulder as the site.

All seemed merry as a marriage bell, but, looking backward, the sober-minded felt a slight premonition of trouble. Two things had happened on December 10, 1897, that broke the pattern of success.

That morning No. 1 had steamed up for the hills, exhausts sharp as her fireman kept the safety valve slobbering at 150 pounds pressure. She came to the first 30 degree curve in Boulder Canon, started smartly around. Her pony truck wheels lifted, came off. She lurched. Only masterly control by her engineer kept her from heeling over into the creek.

Again the engineer tried the curve, slowly. Again the pony truck came off. Finally the crew gave up and backed down to Boulder. The officials hurried to examine this locomotive specifically designed to take tight curves, worry drawing their faces. If they

had to widen the curves, that would delay the rails' entry into Ward, cost a great deal of money. The mechanics finally installed an oscillating bolster on the front truck which permitted the wheels to follow the rails as the engine started around curves. That ended the trouble.[28]

That same day the Pennsylvania capitalists annouced abandonment of plans to build a luxury hotel. The knowing ones knew one good reason. The USS MAINE lay at the bottom of Havana harbor. War with Spain loomed. The money market was tightening

Instead of retrenching, however, the railroad opened two round-trips a day service to Sunset. At Sunset the passengers made connections with stages going to Eldora and Ward.

The railroad now had two new freight locomotives. One was a Shay, No. 25, with three-cylinder engine mounted vertically ahead of the engineer's side of the cab turning a long shaft whose beveled gears connected with all axles.[29] The other, No. 2, a Climax, had two inclined cylinders, one at each side, turning a center shaft that drove all axles through gearing.[30]

The loafers, small boys, and men who could get away from business watched them limbering up with eager eyes. They chuckled that these engines sounded as if they were doing sixty miles an hour when they were only doing about six. Slow they were—but they could pull heavy loads.

The morning of M a r c h 14, 1898,

[27]*Daily Camera*, February 23, 1898.

[28]*Boulder Daily Camera*, December 11, 1945, "People I Meet" column by Forest Crossen.
[29]*Daily Camera*, December 24, 1897.
[30]*Ibid.*, January 7, 1898.

Opposite Page

Courtesy of the Boulder Historical Society

Builder's photo of C&N No. 2 on her trial run in December, 1897, outside the erecting shops of the Climax Manufacturing Company at Corry, Pennsylvania. This 50-ton locomotive was built on special order for the Colorado & Northwestern to handle big-tonnage supply trains to Ward and ore trains down to the Culbertson Mill, four miles east of Boulder. It was the heaviest Climax built up to that time — and the only three-truck narrow gauge Climax built.

Climax Manufacturing Co.
Corry Pa.

Sturtevant photo. R. H. Kindig Collection

Fresh from her builders, No. 30 poses with her proud crew and admirers in the Boulder yards in 1898.

Sturtevant photo. Courtesy Elbert Hubbard

At lower right is William Hubbard of Wall Street, father of Elbert "Jimmie" Hubbard, later fireman and brakeman on the Switzerland Trail.

Proud and gallant, Colorado & Northwestern No. 31 stops on her trial run a short distance above mouth of Boulder Canon for this photo. She steamed easily but her bearings were so tight that she worked hard to surmount the grade.

79

Sturtevant photo. M. R. Parsons Collection

Street scene in Eldora during the mining boom days, looking southwest toward Spencer Mountain. Note six-horse freight teams.

Sturtevant photo. M. R. Parsons Collection

Visiting dignitaries at Camp Frances. We suspect this is Governor Alva Adams' party that stopped enroute to the big celebration of the C&N's entry into Ward June 28, **1898. The governor's party was taken on a tour of the Big Five Company, whose Adit Tunnel lay to left of photo.**

brought new excitement. The C&N passenger train pulled boldly into the new stone station on Fourteenth Street—over a track that the little railroad's men had laid shortly after midnight.[31] Now it was too late for the two big roads to secure an injunction against it. People laughed. The C&N men were nobody's fools.

On the heels of this move General Manager J. T. Blair made an offer to the committee of the Texas-Colorado Chautauqua Association. The C&N would run a branch line to its site for transportation of materials, later passengers.[32]

Up in the hills Chief Engineer Frankeberger and his crew began making a survey of a branch line from Sunset to Eldora.[33] Construction of this line was expected to begin at an early date.

One day early in April at Eldora, gamblers, gay dance hall girls, and businessmen began toasting each other in whiskey that had an extra punch at this 9,000-foot altitude. The Pennsylvania capitalists—C. W. Mackey, J. T. Blair, and T. R. Mann—had bought a big interest in the Mogul Tunnel.[34] They were going to drive the tunnel farther under Spencer Mountain. At 1,000 feet it would cut the rich veins of the Gold Fleece, Little Stranger, St. Louis, Protection, and others.

Instead of stagecoaches w a l l o w i n g through the snow, there would soon be a railroad to ride back and forth on in style. And out of the Mogul Tunnel would come strings of cars piled high with high-grade gold ore. Another round!

May came with its lovely days and nights. The big ore mill at Culbertson stood ready to run, the narrow gauge spur and third rail from Boulder completed. As soon as the C&N reached Ward, ore would come down in trainloads.

The *Ward Miner* reported a conserva-

tive estimate of 150,000 tons in the Adit-Dew Drop Tunnels of the Big Five blocked out for mining. The average value of smelting ore ran $80 a ton, the higher grades about $200.[35]

The first shipment of custom ore to the Pennsylvania Mill came May 23, 1898, from the Dorchester Mine at Caribou.[36] The powerful steam engines began running the stamps that crushed the ore to powder. The mill men smiled at the thundering jar of dropping stamps.

Up in Ward people impatiently awaited the entry of the Colorado & Northwestern. Day by day the rails inched nearer. Then on June 2nd it happened![37]

A little C&N special train swept around the curve and dashed up to the site of the station at Ward. Giant powder thundered, whistles of mines and mills shrieked, and cheers of citizens went up. The officials of the railroad and their Boulder guests stepped off into waiting arms. Now for prosperity unlimited!

In June Chief Engineer Frankeberger and his engineers ran a survey line from the mouth of Boulder Canon along the base of Flagstaff Mountain to the site of the new Chautauqua.[38] The committee had picked a spot of unparalleled beauty at the south edge of University Hill, near the base of the great reddish sandstone Flatirons. It commanded an inspiring view of Boulder Valley and the Rocky Mountain foothills. The local press reported that the C&N intended to finish the branch line in time for the opening of the Chautauqua.

Before the end of June, the little railroad received three engines, Number 30, 31, and 32, from the Brooks Locomotive Works at Dunkirk, New York.[39] They were impressive rod-type engines. No. 30 had flat valves, 31 and 32 piston valves. "The road is now better

[31]*Ibid.*, March 14, 1898.
[32]*Ibid.*, March 17, 1898.
[33]*Ibid.*, March 21, 1898.
[34]*Daily Camera*, April 4, 1898.

[35]*Ibid.*, May 16, 1898.
[36]*Ibid.*, May 24, 1898.
[37]*Daily Camera*, June 2, 1898.
[38]*Ibid.*, June 11, 1898.
[39]*Ibid.*, June 20, 1898.

equipped with powerful engines than any road of double or triple mileage in the country," the *Daily Camera* reported. Common talk declared that C&N had the biggest, most powerful narrow gauge engines in the world.

General Manager Blair returned from Pennsylvania with news. The C&N directors had decided to begin construction of the branch to Eldora at once. They had decided against building the Chautauqua spur; the cost of $13,000 was too great for a season of six weeks.[40]

Appreciation of the railroad's scenic beauty came swiftly. "One need not go to Switzerland, to Italy or to Spain for sublime mountain scenery, with such a magnificent array of Nature's wonderful beauties as you have here displayed within easy distance of your city," said Colonel Williams Jones, the representative of R. G. Dun's interests in the famous Caribou Mine. "The ride over the C&NW from Boulder to Ward is surpassingly grand and you may challenge any country to produce its equal."

People agreed. To reach Ward the builders had to twist and turn their rails, fighting altitude nearly every foot of the 26.1 miles. They had to make many fills, build bridges and trestles, slice through mountain shoulders. They drove no tunnels—a strange thing in that day. The open cuts proved both a blessing and a curse.

J. L. Frankeberger referred to the railroad as "My Monument" in his autobiography:

The road was 26½ miles long, but only 14 miles as a crow flies. From Boulder to Ward, the road climbs 4000 feet in elevation. . . . The average grade was 3½ per cent. In some places it was considerably more, as at Salina, where the grade for a short distance was 5 per cent and in others it was very light, as the Brainerds where the grade is practically level for considerable distance.

In the 26½ miles of road the longest tangent was only 1100 feet. . . .

From Sunset it began to ascend the mountains; on the opposite side of the canyon it approached Sunset. At the summit one could look down into the canyon, and see the railroad track beside the creek and count tracks on six different grades below. The point was named "Point Frankeberger" in honor of its chief engineer.

The railroad picked up the Switzerland theme, and in newspaper advertising began inviting people to "See the Switzerland of America."

The proud mining camp people of Ward planned a grand celebration June 28, 1898, in honor of the opening of the Colorado & Northwestern. They invited everyone to attend. The railroad announced a special round-trip fare of $1.30.

The morning of June 28th three special trains started to Ward. They carried over three hundred and fifty people, including Governor Alva Adams and his staff and prominent citizens of Denver.[41]

At Sunset proud citizens boarded all three trains and presented each passenger with a small bouquet of mountain flowers. At Camp Frances the train bearing Governor Adams stopped, so that he might visit the much-discussed Adit Tunnel. At Ward the passengers stepped down to the music of the Boulder band.

Ward had her proudest day there under the cloudless sky, the perfume of spruce and pine bracing on the high country air. The specials had rolled in to the thunder of dynamite explosions, shriek of steam whistles, hearty cheers.

From the speaker's rostrum, decked with spruce boughs, Governor Adams spoke feelingly of the importance of gold and silver mining, of transportation being the measure of the wealth of the mines. Ward now had a railroad that would bring great things.

And what a railroad! A rippling pride ran through the crowd. It was now common talk that the Colorado & Northwestern was

---

[40]*Daily Camera*, June 23, 1898.

[41]*Daily Camera*, June 28, 1898.

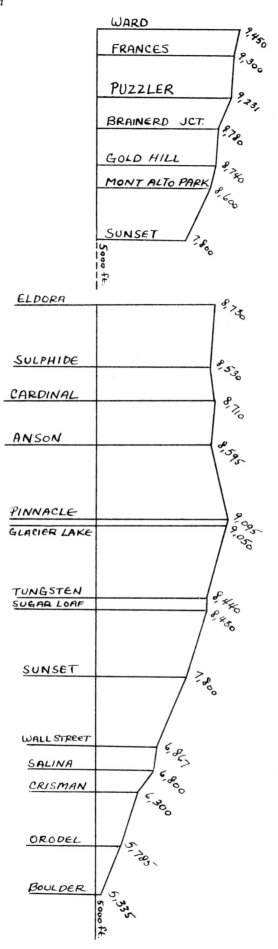

WARD — 9,450
FRANCES — 9,300
PUZZLER — 9,231
BRAINERD JCT. — 8,780
GOLD HILL — 8,740
MONT ALTO PARK — 8,600
SUNSET — 7,800

5000 ft.

ELDORA — 8,730
SULPHIDE — 8,530
CARDINAL — 8,710
ANSON — 8,595
PINNACLE — 9,095
GLACIER LAKE — 9,050
TUNGSTEN — 8,440
SUGAR LOAF — 8,430
SUNSET — 7,800
WALL STREET — 6,867
SALINA — 6,800
CRISMAN — 6,300
ORODEL — 5,785
BOULDER — 5,335

5000 ft.

Profile map of the Colorado & Northwestern shows why firemen seldom had a breather from Boulder to Sunset and even beyond.

the best narrow gauge railroad ever built in the United States. The Pennsylvania and New York capitalists had given it everything that money could buy. It had had the best engineering. Its roadbed and track with shining 56-pounds rails were at the top. When a man stood alongside one of the new 30-class locomotives, he forgot that it was a narrow gauge. They were far heavier and more powerful than any narrow gauge engines in Colorado, if not in the entire country.

There followed a banquet served by the Ward ladies. The eyes of the governor and the wealthy Denverites opened wide. Miners might live in log cabins but they had the best food. Hospitality was an everyday virtue.

In the early evening the trains departed for Boulder. The long, wonderful summer day faded into an equally wonderful night. The people of Ward had steel rails that could open a new world. Truly, the sky itself was the limit!

Sturtevant photo. M. R. Parsons Collection

Ward, Colorado, June 28, 1898, wears festive garb for the big celebration in honor of the Colorado & Northwestern's **entry. The railroad was the bright hope for prosperity for this sulphide gold mining camp.**

Chapter II

THE BRIGHT EARLY YEARS

Scarcely had the echoes of the Ward celebration stopped reverberating among the spruce and pine-covered mountains when Fortune smiled again on the Colorado & Northwestern. A long-talked-of smelter was to be built at the foot of Sawmill Hill near Ward. Its initial capacity would be 100 tons a day, to be increased as demands required. The Ward Pyritic Smelter Company would operate several nearby mines, producing their own ore.[1]

The Colorado & Northwestern's officials gave the company every support. The railroad's engineer made the survey for the plant site, lined out the spur and sidetrack. The C&N granted the smelter people a liberal freight rate.

Their hearts cheered by this news, the hill people proudly boarded the new cars for Boulder to celebrate the Fourth of July. They joined the four thousand who crowded into the new auditorium of the Texas-Colorado Chautauqua for the grand opening.[2] They agreed that it was a site of unrivaled beauty, that there was no place like it and the nearby hills for a summer vacation. Few understood the meaning of culture but they liked the idea of better things.

The next morning they had reason for elation.[3] As they waited in the bright sunlight outside the union station, the telegraph clicked out news of the destruction of the Spanish fleets at Santiago and Manila. They trooped aboard the regular train, filling the three coaches, turning to "guy" those left behind.

The latter felt their anger quickly evaporate when the C&N officials ordered a second section made up. They were important people.

On July 15th, Boulder had another big day, going all-out in celebrating the opening of a resort destined to become famous.[4] At the crest of the railroad's curving climb out of Four Mile Canon from Sunset the far-sighted officials had built a picnic resort. In a grove of big Ponderosa pines they had erected a rustic dancing pavilion, laid out grounds with picnic tables and a fountain of white quartz chunks down over which played clear spring water. It was a place of inspired beauty, the cloud-swept snowy peaks of the Continental Divide to the west, to the east the green-blue wooded hills rolling down to the great plains. They named it Mont Alto Park.

"The usually bustling town of Boulder did an unprecedented thing today when she closed down her business houses and banks," said the *Daily Camera,* "donned her picnic dress and hied herself away to the mountains. Never had such an unanimity of action characterized a popular move. The business and professional men one and all determined on celebrating 'Boulder Day' at Mont Alto. . . .

"Every train leaving Boulder, and there were four of them, was crowded to utmost capacity. It is stated that 350 tickets were sold to Mont Alto and other points on the road.

"Arriving at Mont Alto, the day was spent picnicking in the beautiful park at the crest of the summit. The Boulder band furnished music all day and will play for the dance in the pavilion tonight.

[1]*Daily Camera,* July 1, 1898.
[2]*Ibid.,* July 5, 1898.
[3]*Ibid.,* July 5, 1898.

[4]*Daily Camera,* July 15, 1898.

"The Colorado & Northwestern exhibited a get up and hustle in organizing the affair that demands the heartiest congratulations of the townspeople and its great success is a source of pleasure to the town."

All this must have brought smiles to the directors of the railroad meeting on July 17th.[5] They decided to make another thorough investigation of Eldora and its mines before embarking on the proposed branch. They elected the following officers:

President—Hon. W. C. Culbertson
Vice President—Col. Chas. W. Mackey
General Manager—J. T. Blair
Treasurer—Thomas R. Mann
Secretary—C. B. Culbertson
Directors—Hon. W. C. Culbertson, Col. S. B. Dick, Col. C. W. Mackey, J. T. Blair, and Thomas R. Mann.

The directors were happy to hear that Superintendent Davis of the famous Ward-Rose Mine at Ward had shipped a carload of gold-silver-copper-bearing sulphide ore to their big Culbertson Mill for treatment. If the saving was satisfactory, he intended to ship all ore there.[6]

Down in the yards the curious were looking at small cast iron plates recently screwed to cars and engines bearing the wording, "This car (or engine) is the property of the Pennsylvania Construction company." The railroad company explained that the construction company had furnished all materials and thereby retained ownership, the railroad merely leasing the rolling stock.[7]

The Chautauqua was making news and business for the C&N. "Chautauqua Day" on the railroad was a big success, with some 225 special excursion tickets sold to Ward and Mont Alto Park. Two sections left Boulder before the regular morning train, each crowded to the platform.[8]

At Ward the officials of the Newmarket Mine gallantly escorted a party of Chautauqua girls down the shaft to see the bodies of ore. We don't know whether the girls were more excited at this sight of raw wealth or the warm attention of the young miners.

The railroad's officials and employees felt a glow of pride when the *Daily Camera* reported that the work of transferring and shipping the machinery for the new pyritic smelter at Ward had been somewhat retarded by scarcity of narrow gauge cars, the entire rolling stock of the road being taxed at present.[9]

Editor L. C. Paddock of the *Daily Camera* had a warm spot in his heart for the railroad as he wrote, "Mont Alto—Possibly Manager Blair had an old flame named 'Alto' or 'Alta' and the name haunted him until he attached it to this delightful park set upon the crest of our foothills."[10]

In keeping with this romantic note the *Daily Camera* of the same issue reported that: "A midnight ride through beautiful Boulder Canyon, over picturesque Mont Alto and beyond is the plan of the C&N management . . . the moon will be full, the beauty and splendor of the canon will be at its height and the trip will furnish a ride of such fascinating beauty that none can resist it."

This was the first of the famous moonlight rides of the railroad. Conjure up, you quiet-living males, a picture of riding the swaying rear platform, holding tightly a pretty girl, the wonderful mountain night rising magnificently behind you.

There was brisk mining activity at Copper Rock, which had boomed briefly in Greeley, Salt Lake & Pacific days. Now nearly every placer claim in Four Mile Creek was taken up, and gold was coming out of the nearby hill mines.[11] The Camera Club of Denver went over the line to Ward, the crew

---

[5]*Daily Camera*, July 18, 1898.
[6]*Ibid.*, July 13, 1898. Newspapers and common usage changed the mill's name from Pennsylvania to Culbertson.
[7]*Daily Camera*, July 21, 1898.
[8]*Ibid.*, July 24, 1898.

[9]*Ibid.*, July 25, 1898.
[10]*Ibid.*, July 25, 1898.
[11]*Daily Camera*, July 26, 1898.

Crossen photo

Dining Hall at the Colorado Chautauqua, Boulder, still in use today. Behind this graceful, old-fashioned building rise the great Flatirons and Green Mountain.

Courtesy Mrs. John G. Oldaker

The Ward Pyritic Smelter, 1899. It is the big grey build-ing in the left foreground, standing on the south bank of Left Hand Creek and below the Sawmill Hill wagon road. The big building upstream is the Boston Mill, operated for many years by C. W. Strong. Near the top of the photo is the main line of the Colorado & Northwestern rounding Grassy Mountain at Alpine Point. The lower line to the right is the Big Five Branch.

Sturtevant photo. M. R. Parsons Collection

Mont Alto Park on a summer day. Today only the basin of the fountain remains. Thieves have carried off the red sandstones of the rim and the beautiful white quartz over which waters played.

Sturtevant photo. M. R. Parsons Collection

Picnic group at Mont Alto Park pavilion.

stopping to let members record beautiful views.[12]

The C&N officials needed a name that would bring out the romance and beauty of the railroad. They offered a cash prize for one.[13] It went to Professor Snooks, superintendent of schools in Weld County, for "The Switzerland Trail."[14]

The railroad capitalized on this publicity by having several panoramic views of the scenic points of the line framed for exhibition in leading Denver hotels.[15] These views may have been taken by Joseph Bevier Sturtevant, for he was the official photographer of the road.

Excursion trains were good business but year around hauling of supplies to the mines and ore on the return trip was what the railroad needed. In mid-September the C&N let a contract for construction of a siding to the mouth of the Adit Tunnel at Camp Frances. This was regarded as an important move in securing a big feeder to the new ore mill at Culbertson and as the beginning of sidings to mines along the railroad.[16]

The star of success rose ever higher for the Pennsylvania men. The Culbertson Mill was effecting a saving in treatment of ores never before equalled in Boulder County, reaching as high as 90 percent of the sulphide ores of Ward and Eldora.[17]

"With the building of new switches in the sulphide belt an increased amount of ores will be secured and it will be no distant period when this splendid institution is operating every stamp in the place," exulted the *Daily Camera*.

In September the railroad proudly issued a beautifully illustrated 32-page booklet, "Colorado and Northwestern—The Switzerland Trail of America." It is a collector's item today.

The Colorado & Northwestern closed a contract for carrying the mails to Ward and intervening points.[18] In November the Culbertson Mill was operating forty stamps. With the completion of the Bloomerville branch it was expected that the entire battery of fifty stamps would be dropping.[19] Engineer J. L. Frankeberger was engaged with his crew in surveying the proposed branch of the C&N to the B&M Mine at Ward.[20]

Late in November drifting snow blocked the railroad beyond Sunset, halting the evening train.[21] This was an evil omen, though few realized it at the time.

Snow continued to plague the road. The Culbertson Mill had to shut down temporarily because of lack of ore.[22] Only with the greatest difficulty did the C&N finally restore service to Ward.[23] It kept the line open by costly, almost daily bucking drifts by one or more locomotives coupled behind the snowplow.[24]

Nothing, it seemed, could break the pattern of high optimism of the frontier. President W. P. Daniels of the Big Five Syndicate announced the letting of the first contract for driving the Sunset-Frances-Ward Tunnel.[25] Although for only 50 feet, it marked the beginning of what was to be the longest tunnel in the state. From the mouth at Sunset it was to run 18,000 feet, cutting the Dew Drop vein at Camp Frances and the rich Columbia vein at Ward. It might take five years to complete, but who minded that? Once finished, cars filled with ore would be rolled out at Sunset and dumped into waiting gondolas for shipment to the Culbertson Mill.

Then, too, Boulder County stood proudly before the world. High-grade sylvanite ores

[12]*Ibid.*, July 30, 1898.
[13]*Ibid.*, August 10, 1898.
[14]*Ibid.*, August 15, 1898.
[15]*Ibid.*, August 20, 1898.
[16]*Daily Camera*, September 19, 1898.
[17]*Ibid.*, September 27, 1898.

[18]*Ibid.*, October 25, 1898.
[19]*Ibid.*, November 3, 1898.
[20]*Ibid.*, November 8, 1898.
[21]*Daily Camera*, November 28, 1898.
[22]*Ibid.*, December 6, 1898.
[23]*Ibid.*, November 30, 1898.
[24]*Ibid.*, December 10, 1898.
[25]*Ibid.*, December 20, 1898.

Sturtevant photo. R. H. Kindig Collection

Bunting-draped No. 30 with an early-day special to Mont Alto Park.

Sturtevant photo. M. R. Parsons Collection

Arrival of picnic special at Mont Alto Park. Note bunting-draped gondola and the many parasols. The latter may have been some protection against burning cinders.

Sturtevant photo. M. R. Parsons Collection

Spring-fed fountain at Mont Alto Park.

Sturtevant photo. M. R. Parsons Collection

Workmen excavating for scale track and siding in the C&N west yards in 1898. Note steep grade running east to Trestle No. 1 over Boulder Creek. Beyond are the main yards, with cars set out on various tracks. No. 30 is new, with link and pin couplers, oil headlight, cap stack, low running boards, and extended piston rods. If the well-dressed men in photo are officials, there as many chiefs as Indians.

from her mines had won prizes at the Omaha Exposition.[26]

The year closed with the *Rocky Mountain News* lauding the C&N for rescuing Ward from dry rot.[27] M. F. Leech of Boulder was planning to build about 20 miles of 2-foot gauge railroad from neighboring camps to a smelter in Nederland. The *Daily Camera* was jubilant about mining prospects for 1899.[28]

Superintendent J. T. Blair reported that the C&N people were pleased with business on their little line.[29] Plans were going ahead for snow fences and sheds. The future looked bright.

Boulder County smiled broadly at the gain in metal mining production for 1898. From 1,500 to 2,000 men were employed in the mines, mills, and placers.[30] The C&N had given a marked increase in trade between the mining camps and the valley towns.

The C&N, without giving any reason publicly, sold No. 2, its Climax center-geared engine.[31] The crews knew one reason — too many derailments.

Up in the mountains man's ancient enemy, winter, had flung down the gauntlet of battle. On January 21st a train reached Ward, unloaded and returned at once to Boulder with a few ore cars. The next day another train failed to reach Ward and had to back down to Sunset. Immense drifts swept along by winds howling down over the Continental Divide piled up on the tracks. Two, even three locomotives behind the snowplow could not break through.

The people of Ward watched daily for plumes of black smoke but none showed on the silent fields of white. Trains from Boulder did reach Puzzler, where freight was transferred to horse-drawn wagons a n d

sleds.[32] Ward did not lack food but it had to fall back on wood to keep warm.

The howling storms grew worse. By February 2nd traffic had to be abandoned beyond Sunset.[33] The snow at Ward, Eldora, Nederland, Caribou, and Cardinal was from 15 to 18 feet deep. Old-timers declared it the worst winter they had ever known. The only consolation the weary C&N crews and officials had was that most Colorado railroads were also snowbound.

April finally came with its promise of spring. Down in Boulder the C&N offered to build the spur from the mouth of Boulder Canon along the base of Flagstaff Mountain to the Chautauqua if the city would donate $1,000, private subscription another $1,000.[34] The city officials agreed. Citizens donated the money.

On April 13th the agent at Ward sent a jubilant message clicking over the telegraph wires. A passenger train had broken through, to everyone's great delight and relief.[35]

"The snow drifts in Left Hand canon near Ward," the *Boulder Tribune* reported, "vary in depth from twenty-five to thirty feet in places and the cuts through the drifts on the Colorado & Northwestern present scenes which are at once rare and novel. So as to permit everybody to view these wonders of nature, the Colorado & Northwestern management has arranged excursions on Saturday and Sunday."

With the stir of spring great things were once more in the air. On April 21st the Denver & Northwestern Railway was incorporated, with reported backing from German capitalists and the Gould interests. Construction was to begin within 30 days. The line was to run from Denver north to Lafayette, Erie, and Louisville and enter Boulder by way of the Chautauqua grounds over the Colorado & Northwestern track. From Boulder it would

[26]*Ibid.*, November 28, 1898.
[27]*Ibid.*, December 22, 1898.
[28]*Daily Camera*, December 28, 1898.
[29]*Ibid.*, January 3, 1899.
[30]*Ibid.*, January 3, 1899.
[31]*Ibid.*, January 21, 1899.

[32]*Ibid.*, January 31, 1899.
[33]*Daily Camera*, February 2, 1899.
[34]*Boulder Tribune*, April 7, 1899.
[35]*Ibid.*, April 14, 1899.

Sturtevant photo. J. B. Schoolland Collection

Excursion train on Ox-Bow Curve headed for Mont Alto Park.

Sturtevant photo. M. R. Parsons Collection

From the deep interest shown in the crowd behind the fountain, we guess that a keg of beer has been tapped. The "Dutch" picnics at Mont Alto Park were famous. All mountain people were welcome, and many flocked there from the nearby camps of Gold Hill, Sunset, and Ward.

THE CHAUTAUQUA, TEXADO PARK, BOULDER COLO. 1899. No. 11.

Sturtevant photo. M. R. Parsons Collection

The Texas-Colorado Chautauqua people enjoyed a magnificent view of Boulder Valley in this northeasterly direction. To the west they had an even grander view of the Rocky Mountain Foothills. Tents in foreground were later replaced by cottages similar to those at right. Big building is the Auditorium, which was built largely by public donation.

C&N No. 1 at Ward. Bill Tipps on pilot at left.

98

Sturtevant photo. R. H. Kindig Collection

Colorado & Northwestern No. 1 arrives with a flourish at Ward before construction of the station, probably sometime in June, 1898. To her right is a string of freight cars headed by a diamond-stack locomotive which may well be UPD&G No. 61, which assisted in the construction.

R. H. Kindig Collection

Rare photograph of Ward, the new Colorado & Northwestern terminus, taken in 1898. Station is under construction. The long string of freight cars is headed by No. 2, the Climax geared locomotive. It was the first three-truck locomotive built by the Climax Manufacturing Co., and the only one of its class for narrow gauge operation.

run to Ward over the C & N and from Ward the company would build boldly on to Steamboat Springs.[36]

When the news reached Boulder, Superintendent Blair shook his head in puzzled surprise. This was the first he had heard of it.

At the end of April Boulder learned that an electric line was to be built from downtown to the Chautauqua grounds. C. B. Culbertson assured the city council that if the electric line was not built, his railroad would put in the spur from Boulder Canon.[37]

The private cars "Bessemer," of the Pittsburgh, Bessemer & Lake Erie Railroad, and the "Ottawa" arrived in Boulder with a party of capitalists. They rode up to Ward, then to Eldora. Their inspection, so it was announced, had practically decided them in building the much-discussed Eldora branch.[38]

The stockholders and directors of the C&N held their annual meeting July 21st. W. C. Culbertson was reelected President. The Vice President was J. T. Blair, and C. B. Culbertson took over as Secretary-Treasurer and General Manager.[39] The Culbertsons owned nearly all the stock and bonds, and they were maintaining tight control.

C. B. Culbertson established residence in Boulder and built a big two-story brick house on Mapleton Hill, the swank section. He took part in civic affairs and at once became popular.

The annual meeting of the Pennsylvania Mining and Milling Company saw Colonel S. B. Dick elected President. W. B. Hayes became Secretary. Directors were Col. S. B. Dick, C. W. Mackey, J. T. Odell, T. R. Mann, and C. B. Culbertson.

The railroad's excursion business picked up. A delegation of druggists, meeting in Denver, took the trip to Ward. The Wood Mountain Tunnel officials chartered a special, giving some 200 people the opportunity to see practical demonstrations of mining.[40] A Ward and Bald Mountain excursion was well patronized by Chautauqua people. Texas Day at the Chautauqua featured a special trip to Ward. Judge Aldrich of Dallas stated that the Switzerland Trail was the most magnificent bit of scenic railway line on the globe.[41] A C&S special of 7 coaches brought in 200 Denver Tramway employees and their families bound for Mont Alto Park.

Additional feeder business seemed looming up for the C&N. J. L. Frankeberger completed the preliminary survey for a 28-inch gauge tramway from Nederland to the junction of Four Mile Creek and Boulder Canon. It was designed to haul ore. Construction was to begin at an early date.

The Spanish-American War was over, and Boulder's troops were soon to return. For their heroism they must be appropriately welcomed home. Boulder merchants again closed their stores and boarded specials for Mont Alto Park. The proceeds of the excursion went into a fund for the coming celebration, which took place September 22, 1899.

A short time later, Colonel Dick, after an inspection of mines, said that he was pleased with Boulder's growth, business along the C&N, and the promised increased tonnage for the Culbertson Mill.[42]

The mill was handling 60 tons of ore a day, mainly from the Wood Mountain Tunnel. The Pennsylvania Mining and Milling Company was now operating that property.[43]

The *Boulder Tribune* of December 1st carried a story that made hearts warm toward the railroad Boulder regarded as its own:

The Colorado & Northwestern railroad company remembered its employees in this Thanksgiving season in a substantial manner. Superintendent Hill gave Euler & Voegtle, proprietors of the City Market, orders to furnish each one of their employees with a large, fat turkey—the best of that market's fine

[36]*Boulder Tribune*, April 21, 1899.
[37]*Ibid.*, April 28, 1899.
[38]*Ibid.*, May 19, 1899.
[39]*Ibid.*, July 21, 1899.

[40]*Boulder Tribune*, July 28, 1899.
[41]*Ibid.*, August 18, 1899.
[42]*Boulder Tribune*, October 6, 1899.
[43]*Ibid.*, October 20, 1899.

R. H. Kindig Collection

Mouth of the Adit Tunnel of the Big Five, Camp Frances. Track is the 0.7-mile spur from Big Five Junction to Big Five. Stone building dead ahead is the powder house, which was carefully roofed with sheet metal to make it fire-proof. Long building to the right is the mill, which was later enlarged. Beyond it is the power house with its tall smokestack. To left of smokestack may be seen the big "5" on office building. Colorado & Northwestern main line to Ward angles high up along mountainside to the right.

The Bright Early Years

Courtesy A. A. Paddock

An early snowstorm has left its blanket on the foothills. The ornate building in the right foreground is the Boulder County Courthouse.

The Texas-Colorado Chautauqua (in the far background) and the Colorado & Northwestern were new when this photograph was made in the autumn of 1898.

Sturtevant photo. M. R. Parsons Collection

No. 1 at Ward with one of the two cabooses owned by the C&N. Behind her is one of the 30-class engines with one coach. Conductor Fred Conrad is second from left. No. 1 has been bucking through snowdrifts.

Courtesy Library, State Historical Society of Colorado

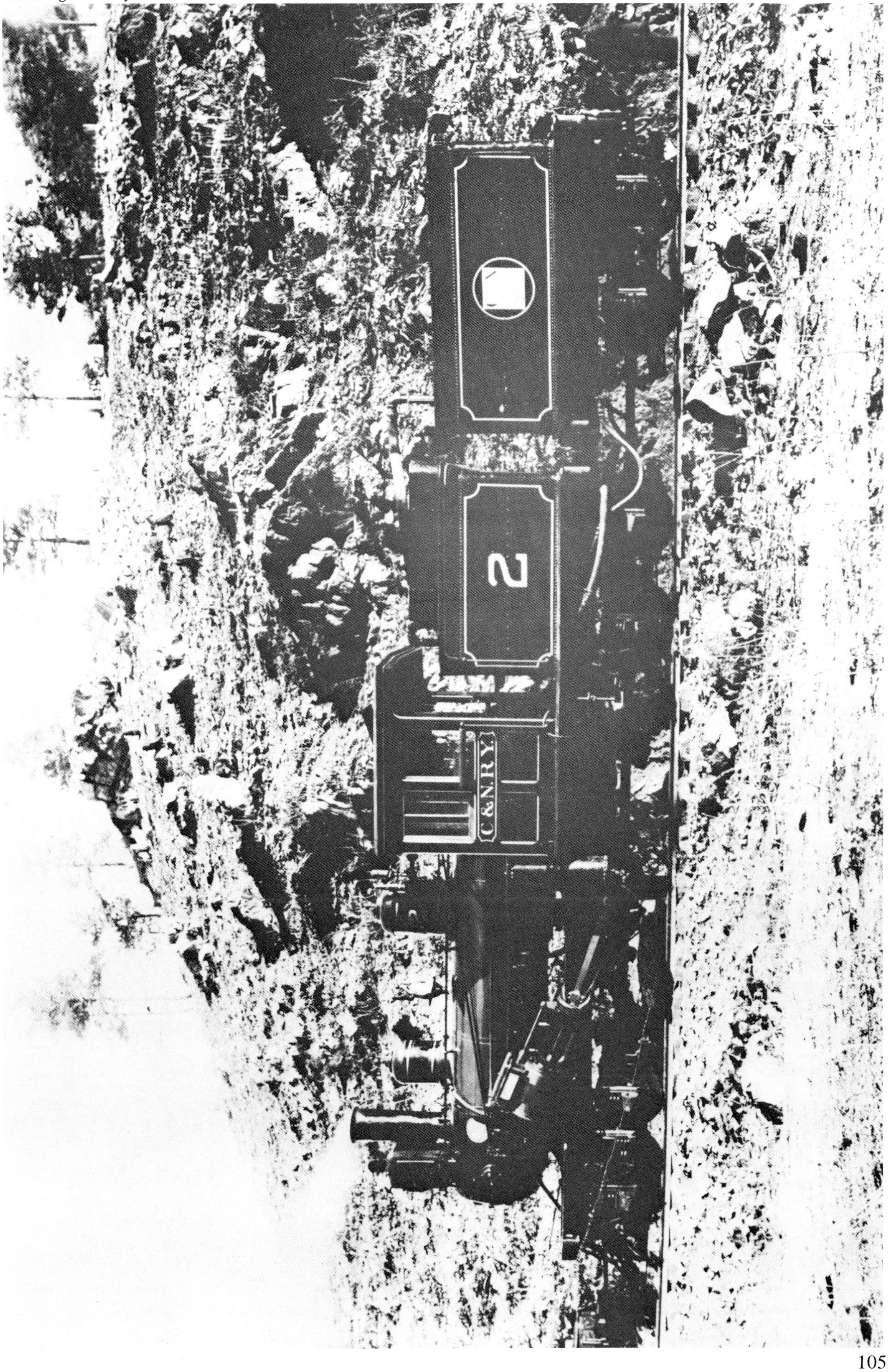

C&N Climax No. 2 pauses in her work of pushing a train. This may be a construction train or she may be acting as a helper. Note long link and pin coupler on the pilot connected with the flatcar on which man is standing.

Sturtevant photo
University of Colorado Museum Collection

C&N No. 2 locomotive stands beside the stone powder house at the Big Five, having backed her train down from Big Five Junction, 0.7 miles. This is at the mouth of the Adit Tunnel, which was to open the fabulous riches of the Ward district's gold ores.

R. H. Kindig Collection

C&N No. 2, the Climax center-geared engine, steaming up in the Boulder yards preparatory to going out. No. 2 is minus her shapely pilot, evidence of trouble on the new track.

R. H. Kindig Collection

C&N locomotives ram snowplow through drift at edge of Ward.

Sturtevant photo. R. H. Kindig Collection

Special snow train in last big cut short of Ward. To the right, in the Ward yards, may be seen new boxcars of the Colorado & Northwestern.

line—and the order went down the line to each section hand even on the road. Not only this, but the company sent a turkey to every one of the C&S employees here, in acknowledgement of courtesies shown and services rendered during the year.

Organization of the Denver, Boulder & Northern Railway December 12, 1899, promised fast, frequent commuter service to Denver. Electric cars were expected to start making the run by June of 1900. They would bring more people to Boulder who would be encouraged to view the scenic wonders of the Switzerland Trail.

As the year closed, the famous Melvina Mine at Salina, with a record of nearly $1,000,000 production, was again shipping ore on the C&N.[44]

The Boer War, which was raging as a new century came to a tired world, caused only a little stir in Boulder.[45] South Africa was too far away to affect people much. There were too many things to think about at home.

On January 23rd, a disastrous fire at Ward wiped out most of the town.[46] The crowded frame and log buildings and cabins burned with a fury that chilled all hearts. People shivered in the mountain winter night. They needed help.

It came swiftly. "Mayor Whiteley received the following message from Supt. F. W. Hill of the Colorado & Northwestern road who left for Ward early in this morning:

" 'Please say to the merchants and papers that the C&N Ry. Co. will haul free to Ward all provisions donated by Boulder merchants.'

"Mr. Hill returned with his special about 2:30 this afternoon. He said that what was wanted was enough staple articles of food to tide the citizens of Ward over for two or three days and that he had handed a list of these to Mayor Whiteley." — The *Daily Camera*, Jan. 24, 1900 .

The response was immediate and generous.

Out of this response came a news story that reflects the humor of the frontier. "Chairman Willis rather played it over 'Honest Tom' Butler and good old 'Saint Nick' Herival of the board of county commissioners at Ward Thursday. The commissioners went up to investigate what they could do to alleviate the sufferings of the people and 'Billy' found a woman, so Tom says, that seemed to need a little cheering up. So he failed to hear the whistle for the returning train and was compelled to run all the way to Sawmill hill. He covered the road in four minutes and eighteen seconds, so Tom and Nick say, and caught the train and a severe cold in his joints at the same time."[47]

So spectacular was the destruction that the C&N ran a special train to Ward on the Sunday following the fire for the curious.

The C&N and people of Boulder felt their pride soar a few weeks later. "One of the Northwestern's big geared engines is proving effective in bucking snow on the South Park branch of the Colorado & Southern, where all the snow plow engines had failed," reported the *Boulder Tribune* of February 23, 1900.

This was No. 25, the Shay, with Bill Tipps at her throttle.

A touch of foreboding came in February with the announcement that the Adit Mill had been completed and would now treat Big Five ore.[48] The railroad and the Culbertson Mill would lose this tonnage.

Rumors kept cropping up of extension of the C&N over the Continental Divide. Colonel S. B. Dick stated that the Eldora line would probably be built in 1900 and that the road might be extended over into Middle Park.[49]

June with its soft warmth saw a big ex-

[44]*Boulder Tribune*, December 29, 1899.
[45]*Daily Camera*, January 2, 1900.
[46]*Ibid.*, January 24, 1900.

[47]*Daily Camera*, January 26, 1900.
[48]*Ibid.*, February 27, 1900.
[49]*Daily Camera*, March 6, 1900.

Sturtevant photo. R. H. Kindig Collection

Had these people known the menace of snowdrift at left they would never have posed for this photo. Two years later, No. 30, bright and shiny new here, was to be swept down at this spot in a tragic slide. Time is spring of 1899.

Sturtevant photo. R. H. Kindig Collection

Gold Hill Cut west of Mont Alto Park. This cut through ridge dividing Four Mile and Left Hand watersheds, originally known as Gold Hill Pass, was later renamed Culbertson Pass. This cut was one of the longest on the railroad and was roundly cursed by all trainmen in winter.

A. A. Paddock Collection

The snowdrift ahead of photographer stands between train and Ward.

Sturtevant photo. University of Colorado Museum Collection

The gods of winter must have been been angry at the Colorado & Northwestern's invasion of their territory. They threw everything they had at the new railroad during its **first winter's operations. This Dew Drop Cut, shoveled and rammed through at great expense, was at the north edge of Frances, 1.5 miles south of Ward. Time: April 10, 1899.**

111

Spring has come again to the Switzerland Trail but this huge drift on the north side of Grassy Mountain remains as grim evidence of a terrible winter. To left, below, is Big Five Spur.

Sturtevant photo. R. H. Kindig Collection

Picnic party boarding special train on the Wood Mountain spur above Wall Street. Below may be seen the new mine and mill buildings, with a gondola loaded with coal spotted beside the mill. The locomotive is No. 32. Cap stack denotes first days of the C&N.

University of Colorado, 1899. Buildings, left to right, are Engineering (torn down to make room for Norlin Library), Woodbury Hall, Old Main, Hale Scientific Building, President's house.

Set-out boxcar at left served as station for Wall Street when Joe Sturtevant made this photograph in 1899.

cursion season shaping up. The Boer War ended with the surrender of the Boers in Pretoria, and in China the Boxers were killing foreigners—but that was far away.[50] The big free gold strike in the Mogul Tunnel at Eldora was far more important.[51]

Near the end of June something happened in Boulder that began to shape destiny for the Switzerland Trail of America.

"The first automobile seen on the streets of this city was brought here today to advertise a bicycle house having a Denver connection. Its perambulations over the city excited gaping wonder."—*Daily Camera,* June 23, 1900.

That summer the Colorado & Northwestern operated two daily trains each way between Boulder and Ward. Tourists who had come out to Denver and Boulder flocked to these trains. Fares were low.

Of all the people who rode over the Switzerland Trail none loved it more than honeymooners. To a young husband like Brad Denny it was an experience unforgettable . . .

It's a wonderful morning, the great foothills of the Rockies sharp and blue against a cloudless sky. Pat—the most beautiful black-haired Irish girl in the world—and I are taking Train No. 2 of the famous Switzerland Trail of America to Ward.

No. 32 stands waiting, her air pump throbbing, at the head of five little coaches. Engineer Bill Tipps is oiling 'round, and the way she shines you know she's his darling. On top of the headlight is a pair of deer antlers.

Before we know it the train from Denver is in. Baggage and mail are transferred. Passengers hurry over and are helped aboard by broad-shouldered Conductor Jap Reed. His smile goes warm at sight of Pat, and he gives her extra help up the steps.

We roll easily up through the yards,

pass the engine house and shops of the C&N. There stands No. 30, ready to go out.

A rumble whips up under our feet. We look out at the clear rushing waters of Boulder Creek as we cross Bridge No. 1.

The exhausts of the 32 are sharper now. It's upgrade all the way to Ward. We pass the water tank and section house, rumble across Bridge No. 2.

Then we shout, for we glide between cliffs that go up hundreds of feet. We are in the mouth of Boulder Canon.

On we go, hugging the canon wall on a shelf above the roaring creek. We cross another bridge beneath the famous Maxwell Pitch of the old stagecoach road. Then on to the mouth of Four Mile Creek, passing the old Hunt and Barber Smelter, gaunt and hard looking, the windows all knocked out.

After a brief stop at the little mining camp of Orodell, we commence to see piles of gravel beside the stream.

"Old Chinese placer mining," Jap Reed tells us. "A little farther on we'll see some Chinamen mining."

Next stop is Crisman, huddled in the narrow canon. A sack of mail goes off and a few pieces of express and on we go.

We come to Salina station, pull past it. Later we learn that the grade is so steep here —5 percent or more—they have to pull past to more level ground to get started again. Several people get off, for there's a big camp up the side gulch, which they call Gold Run. These fascinating names!

We pull on strongly, the exhausts bouncing back from the canon walls. We see more and more mines. Jap tells us this is rich gold country.

At busy Wall Street we see wagons loaded with gold ore on the narrow roads.

All at once Jap stops beside us and points.

There are the Chinese, dressed in baggy blue cotton pants and loose blue blouses, round blue hats on their heads. Two have

---

[50]*Ibid.,* May 28, 1900.
[51]*Ibid.,* June 4, 1900.

C&N No. 32 in the early days of railroad poses at the Wood Mountain Mine above Wall Street with two pretty girls. The excursionists who have ridden this special are inspecting the mine.

Welcoming Co. F. Home from War

Sturtevant photo. M. R. Parsons Collection

Crowd at the Boulder station gathered to welcome Co. F., Boulder's own troops, returning from the Spanish-American War, Sept. 15, 1899. Whistle of diamond-stack Colorado & Southern No. 100 is screaming. At left of No. 100 is rear coach of a C&N train about to start to the mountains.

Crowded lower section of downtown Ward prior to fire of Jan. 23, 1900.

Sturtevant photo
Courtesy Library, State Historical Society of Colorado

Business section of lower Ward after disastrous fire of Jan. 23, 1900.

Copy photo by Hildreth Studio, Longmont, Colo.
from J. B. Schoolland Collection

Rare photograph of C&N No. 25, the Shay geared engine. Photo taken at Breckenridge, Colorado, on the South Park line of the Colorado & Southern, early in 1900. Engineer Bill Tipps, dapper as ever in white shirt and bow tie, took this engine over to the South Park to buck snow. He was there two months or longer on one of the "lend" courtesies that the C&S and C&N practiced.

queues down their backs! They're shoveling gravel into a sluice box. Jap says they're cleaning up plenty of gold.

We're still talking about them when we reach Copper Rock. On our right a high cliff with greenish streaks, bored here and there with tunnels, gives the camp its name.

Every time we stop I hear the blower go on the engine, see black smoke shooting up from the stack. The fireman has to work hard here to keep up steam, shoveling coal most of the time.

Soon we creak and grate to a stop. "Sunset," Jap tells us. I lean out the open window, see the 32 spotted under the water tank. Pat and I swing down to watch the fireman fill the tender tank. Bill is oiling 'round. He tells us we'll stop at the station ahead for several minutes.

Pat and I cross the curving trestle, watching our steps. A little breathless, we stop at the other end.

Sunset, at the head of the canon, is a charming spot. There's a row of business houses, cabins here and there. The ones we like best are log. The air is almost like champagne, which we drank on our wedding night. What it did to Pat!

From Sunset we turn right and start boldly up the side of the mountain to the east. Soon we can look down on the track we just came up. We round curves, always going higher, wheel flanges screaming. More glimpses of Four Mile, the creek tiny now, the track two little lines.

At last we screech around a great high curve, head west. "Ox Bow Curve," Jap announces. "We'll soon be at Mont Alto."

Mont Alto Park is the most beautiful place we've ever seen, a grassy flat set amongst big tall pines. There's a rustic pavilion with a big stone fireplace chimney. Nearby is a fountain with circular pool around it. And the view. . . .

To the west Arapaho Peak with its great white glacier sweeps the sky. To the east the bluish mountains roll to the plains and out to the horizon, maybe a hundred miles away.

West from Mont Alto the train hugs the mountainside. Jap Reed comes along again. "I want you to see this. You can look down on six levels of track. There!"

We gasp.

"Point Frankeberger. Named in honor of the engineer who laid out the railroad."

A minute or two later we slip through a long cut. "This is Culbertson Pass, though some people still call it Gold Hill Pass. It's the divide between Four Mile and Left Hand Creeks."

We continue on easily through a beautiful wooded hilltop country, pause at Gold Hill station. Then on until we round a sharp curve.

"Klondike Point. Down below is Left Hand Canon and Camp Brainerd. They get out lots of gold ore."

We stop at Brainerd, little station from which a steep wagon road leads down to the camp. Then on once more, the track clinging to the mountain. Some of the women scream, but not my Pat. Her grey eyes sparkle as she looks down nearly a thousand feet.

Puzzler is next, a little camp in a lovely side canon. How green the grass is, how tall the stately spruces beside the cabins. We cross a trestle and head west once more.

At Bloomerville we make a complete loop and start east up along Grassy Mountain, which has only a few wind-twisted pines at its top. We round sharp Alpine Point, where a spur runs down to the Big Five mines.

Camp Frances is a pretty camp in a gentle gulch. Farther on we cross California Gulch and start up east along the opposite mountainside. Below are the big tunnel workings of the Big Five. A two-track tunnel runs in under the mountains, cutting the veins of the famous Niwot, Columbia, and Dew Drop.

We round a couple of curves, come within sight of Ward. How exciting it looks there on the mountainside and in the little gulch!

Sturtevant photo
University of Colorado Museum Collection

Station at Salina, looking east. Not drop in grade. J. L. Frankeberger, location engineer for the C&N, gave it as 5%. F. R. Dungan, who had charge of the surveying from Salina to Sunset, gave the short piece here at the station as 7%.

Sturtevant photo
University of Colorado Museum Collection

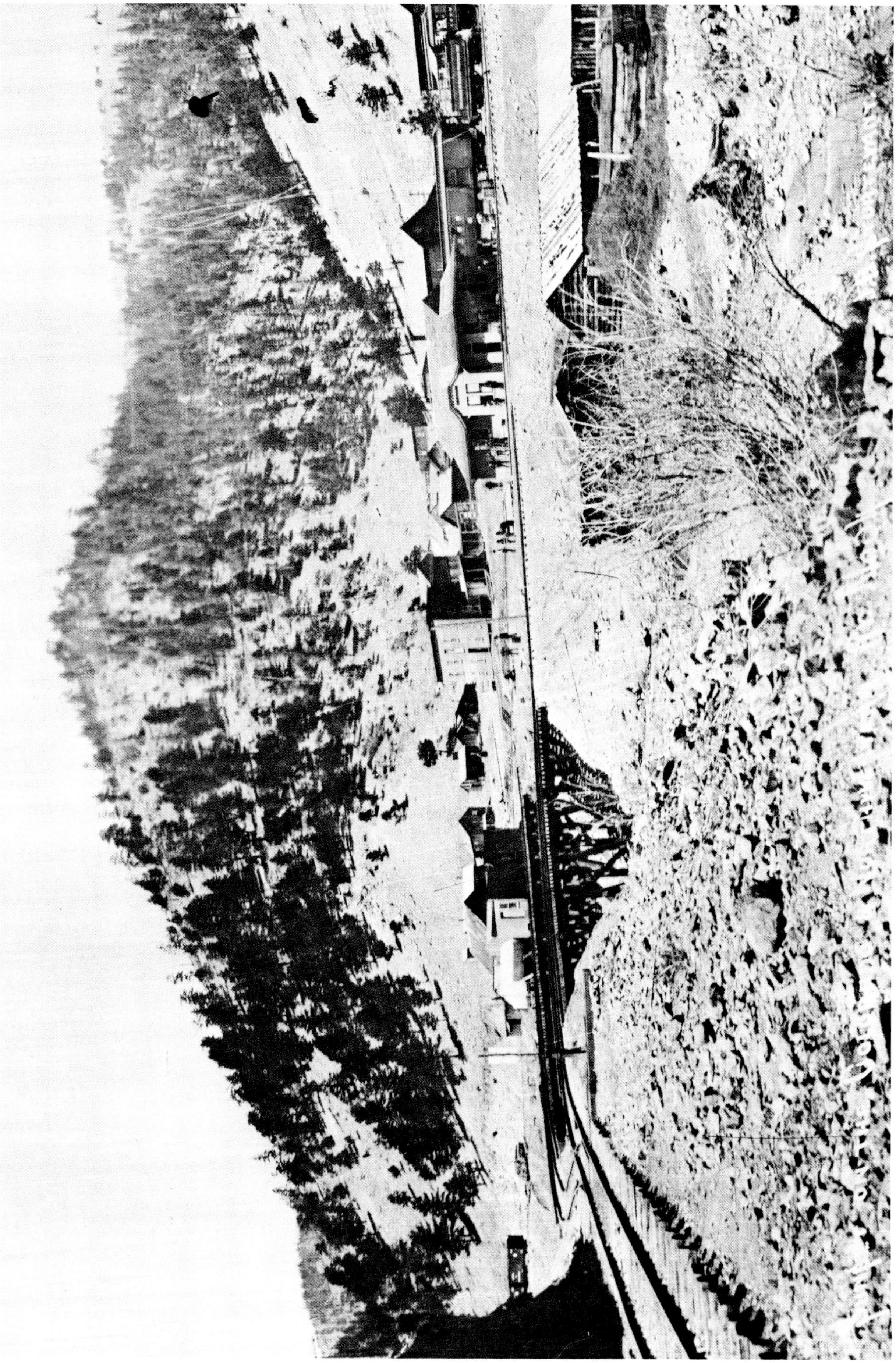

No. 1 at the newly finished Sunset station. Two-story building at left is the Columbine Hotel, as yet unpainted. Switch in foreground is set for the Ward main line. In a later day, after the Eldora branch was built, the switch was always locked open on the Eldora or left trestle.

Sturtevant photo. M. R. Parsons Collection

Point Frankeberger, west of Mont Alto Park. Visible are six levels of track on the Ward and Eldora branches. Far below is Four Mile Canon with main line of the C&N.

Herb O'Hanlon Collection

West-bound mixed train crossing the trestle at Puzzler headed for Ward. Locomotive is either C&N No. 31 or 32.

C&N No. 32 at Ward with happy excursionists, July 14, 1901.

Bill blows his whistle long and loud, pulls up smartly at the long red frame station. Jap jokes with the people getting off, those at the station. He knows everybody.

He tells us we can have dinner at the nearby C&N Hotel, either take the 2:10 train back or stay overnight.

We look at the mines on the hills with their great yellowed dumps, stacks pouring out black smoke, steam rising from their engines. Teamsters are pulling up to the station with ore to ship. Others are unloading freight. The station crowd looks friendly . . . and the air is even more like champagne.

"We'll stay over."

Jap grins, shakes hands, holding Pat's long. "I would too if I were you," he says to me.

In addition to specials for tourists and honeymooners, the railroad ran one special after another for the home people. Odd Fellows and Rebekahs, Parson Tom Uzzel's annual picnic party with 800 adults and children of Denver, and the basket picnic to Mont Alto of the Society Norden.[52] Then came the big annual picnic of the Retail Grocers' Association of Denver, requiring five trains to Mont Alto.[53]

"We carried yesterday 4,900 to 5,000 people," said Supt. Hill of the C&N this morning. "That is to say we moved about 2,500 people both ways between Boulder and Mont Alto. It called for a great deal of sacrifice and good service and loyalty to our road for our trainmen, but they got there. Crews made three trips in the same day. They had no time to eat—they were getting business for the C&N—and the management is glad to have the fact recorded. Less loyal men would have 'balled' things up so that but half the crowd that came from Denver could get to the mountains. We appreciate our men and believe we can point with pride to the record

of our little road on this excursion day." — *Daily Camera*, Aug. 10, 1900.

A little earlier, at the annual meeting of stockholders, Colonel Samuel B. Dick advanced to the office of Vice President. He became President of the Pennsylvania Mining and Milling Company.[54] These were significant moves.

Gold and silver mining were picking up. The Melvina began running a tunnel from Wall Street to the main shaft, thus providing a direct connection with the C&N.[55] The B&M at Ward struck ore on the 800-foot level running $100 a ton.[56] The Culbertson Mill was busy night and day.

Momentum built up behind the move to extend the railroad to Eldora. The Mogul Tunnel at Eldora cut a vein of gold ore running $10,000 a ton. One report said that the people of Eldora intended to have a railroad, whether the C&N built it or some other company.[57]

The golden days of autumn came to the hills. Here and there amidst the brief vivid beauty the smokestacks of mines poured out the greenish-blue of wood or black of coal fires. Steam puffed upward from hoisting engines' exhausts, and the pant of air compressors carried on the clear air. Gold and silver were coming out of the mines, and the people of the hills were happy. So were the people of the Switzerland Trail.

Again there was a happy Thanksgiving for the employees of the Colorado & Northwestern, the railroad providing the turkeys.

The first year of the new century ended on a happy note. More and more good ore was being blocked out in mines along the C&N. The railroad was busy hauling coal, machinery, and supplies — everything that people needed up to the mining camps. From the day the little railroad reached Ward these had been bright happy years.

[52]*Daily Camera*, July 11, 1900.
[53]*Daily Camera*, August 9, 1900.
[54]*Ibid.*, July 18, 1900.
[55]*Ibid.*, July 16, 1900.
[56]*Ibid.*, July 27, 1900.
[57]*Daily Camera*, August 7, 1900.

Part II

Chapter III

THE FACE OF TROUBLE

The year 1901 opened with two events that seemed of little significance but which were to affect mightily the destiny of the Switzerland Trail. Charles G. Hickox, prosperous former livery stable operator of Central City, bought a one-half interest in a leading Boulder stable.[1] Colonel S. B. Dick arrived from Meadville, Pa., and expressed himself vigorously on his project of extending the C&N over the Continental Divide. He would run the extension through Eldora.[2]

Treasure was pouring out of the hill mines. A special train of eight boxcars came down, banners proclaiming it as the first shipment by the Big Five Company from its recent big strike in the famous old Niwot Mine at Ward.[3] Much of the ore, thought to be worth $8,000 and $10,000, was consigned to the Culbertson Mill.

The B&M Mine at Ward was steadily producing smelting ore, and the Slide near Gold Hill struck tellurium ore running $40 a pound.[4] The C&N was shipping coal and supplies to these mines and taking down their ore.[5]

Colonel Dick pressed his demand for an extension from Sunset to Eldora. The Culbertson interests were reported ready to extend—if they could secure a steady 50 tons of ore a day haulage. The manager of the Mogul Tunnel at Eldora said that this was easy.[6]

The Culbertsons insisted that a commis-

sion of three competent mining engineers check the tonnage output of mines along the proposed extension.[7]

In due time the commission made its report: the ore in sight ran to several times more than the required 50 tons a day.

Spring came with its treacherous weather. On April 6th the editor of the *Ward Miner* reported his town snowed in, the C&N train stalled by huge drifts near Puzzler.

Two locomotives coupled behind the snowplow (the road never owned a rotary) went out to clear the tracks. The crews broke through but more snow fell and the wild winds piled it high over the line. Then a story ran through Boulder that chilled every heart. A stark headline in the *Daily Camera* of April 18, 1901, read:

BOULDER MEN KILLED
LANDSLIDE AT FRANCES TAKES
OVER TWO C&N CREWS

Two locomotives (No. 30 and No. 31) of the C&N road lie at the bottom of the gulch at Camp Frances, near the Big Five tunnel. They were hitched double-headed and were pushing the snow plow, when they went over the hill at 2:00 o'clock this afternoon.

Just before the accident, S. O. Clark, agent of the road at Ward, had wired Manager Culbertson that the snow was too hard to buck and Mr. Culbertson had ordered, "Tell them to stop then, and to come down." Hardly had he given the order when Clark wired that the locomotives had gone over the hill and it was reported some men were hurt.

Manager Culbertson summoned a physician, ordered an engine steamed up and thought he could get away for Frances at 5:30 o'clock.

---

[1] *Daily Camera*, January 5, 1901.
[2] *Ibid.*, February 15, 1901.
[3] *Ibid.*, January 7, 1901.
[4] *Ibid.*, January 12, 1901.
[5] *Ibid.*, February 16, 1901.
[6] *Ibid.*, February 18, 1901.

---

[7] *Daily Camera*, February 23, 1901.

These are the dead:—W. J. Hannan (engineer), 35, married, has family residing in Boulder; F. M. Milner (fireman), 30, family in Boulder; E. B. Fitzgerald (fireman), 26, single; W. H. Blair (conductor), 45, married.

Mr. Culbertson at once sent messengers to the homes of the afflicted families to break the news gently. Sam Mackey, his messenger, broke down but resolutely started for stricken homes in Boulder on his sad errand. . . .

Many of the residents of Camp Frances saw the tragic accident. Forty years later, the *Boulder Daily Camera* published the following story in the column "People I Meet" by Forest Crossen:[8]

The young wife watching the two locomotives bucking snow suddenly gasped. High up on the stark white mountainside, above the blockaded narrow-gauge Colorado & Northwestern railroad, she saw the avalanche start. Fascinated with horror, she could neither move or cry out as it swept the locomotives off the track. They tumbled over, down, down. . . .

"We lived at the Big Five Mine," she (Mrs. Maude Willis) began in her calm even voice. "My husband, J. J. Willis, was superintendent. It was a bad spring; the snow lay several feet deep on the level. We'd had no train for days."

She had lived in constant dread deep in the winter-locked mountains. At night she shivered as the winds roared and shrieked, for each new blizzard meant more snow piled in the deep rock cuts through which the trains must come. They were marooned— at the mercy of fire, accident, epidemic, gaunt hunger itself.

"When the locomotives with the wedge snow-plow broke through that afternoon and started west towards Camp Frances, we felt happy. But they still had the cut right above the mine to go through before trains could reach us."

She had known that this cut—one of the most exposed on the railroad—was packed full of snow. It would be hard to open.

Mrs. Willis' eyes brightened with the sheen of remembered excitement. "I couldn't take my eyes off those locomotives. They came down on the cut full speed. The plow just slammed into the snow! Then they stopped and had to back out for another run."

She had quickened to the two powerful locomo-

tives, black smoke intertwined with white steam shooting high, small drive wheels revolving furiously. She saw them careen into the hard-packed snow, laughed as the plow flung great chunks up and aside. Then anxiety seized her as they slowed down, down, their drivers spinning, smoke raging against the clear sky. Their baffled roaring penetrated even the stout cabin walls.

"I was afraid they'd get stuck."

She would have been more afraid had she known that the engineers also had this fear, that they crowded their engines as far as possible, then, with the help of firemen, reversed them.

"They were coming down full speed on the cut when I saw the avalanche." Her voice quickened, and into it there sprang a gasp. "Right above them. It knocked them off the track!"

The horror of it had been a vise on feet and tongue. With breath suspended she saw the locomotives plunge downward, hit the deep snow, bound out and down again. Then shoot down until they brought up hard against the switch of the Big Five, 400 feet beneath the main line.

"There they were—almost level with our cabin. I was sure everybody was killed."

She had drawn back, ears ringing from the roar and crash of destruction. What had been, but a short minute before, proud creations of steel and fire now lay in hissing death.

"The whistle at the mine began to blow, calling every man out. Men began running by our cabin to the wreck. They started to dig."

For an instant she had shuddered at the rending shriek of disaster. Then she resolutely turned, for Tragedy lay on her very doorstep.

"The miners dug out Engineer James Marks. He was beneath the tank of the rear engine. They brought him into our cabin and laid him on the bed. He had one arm broken, and an iron rod had run through one foot. But he was still breathing."

She had ministered to him, fighting back death, who had descended into the gulch.

"He recovered all right." Mrs. Willis shook her head sadly. "But all the rest were dead. . . ."

In 1957 Roy M. Adams of Spokane, Washington, was visiting his old boyhood friend, Elbert Hubbard of Wall Street. The talk swung around to the Switzerland Trail and the wreck at Camp Frances.

"I was attending school at Frances when that wreck occurred," said Roy. "The schoolhouse sat on a ridge where we could see the

---

[8]*Boulder Daily Camera*, December 4, 1941.

Sturtevant photo
University of Colorado Museum Collection

Special train of eight boxcars filled with high-grade gold ore from the famous Niwot Mine at Ward, Jan. 7, 1901, at Sunset, enroute to Boulder.

A. A. Paddock Collection

The snow has melted away from locomotives and snow-plow which were stopped on their avalanche-borne slide down Grassy Mountain by Big Five Siding. No. 30 lies in the foreground. Beyond her is No. 31. Still coupled to No. 31 is the snowplow mounted on the head end of a flatcar. Shortly afterward Conductor Fred Conrad and picked crew rerailed locomotives and plow with help of No. 25, the Shay.

Cut through drift on north side of Grassy Mountain, April 13, 1899. Beyond is Frances.

130

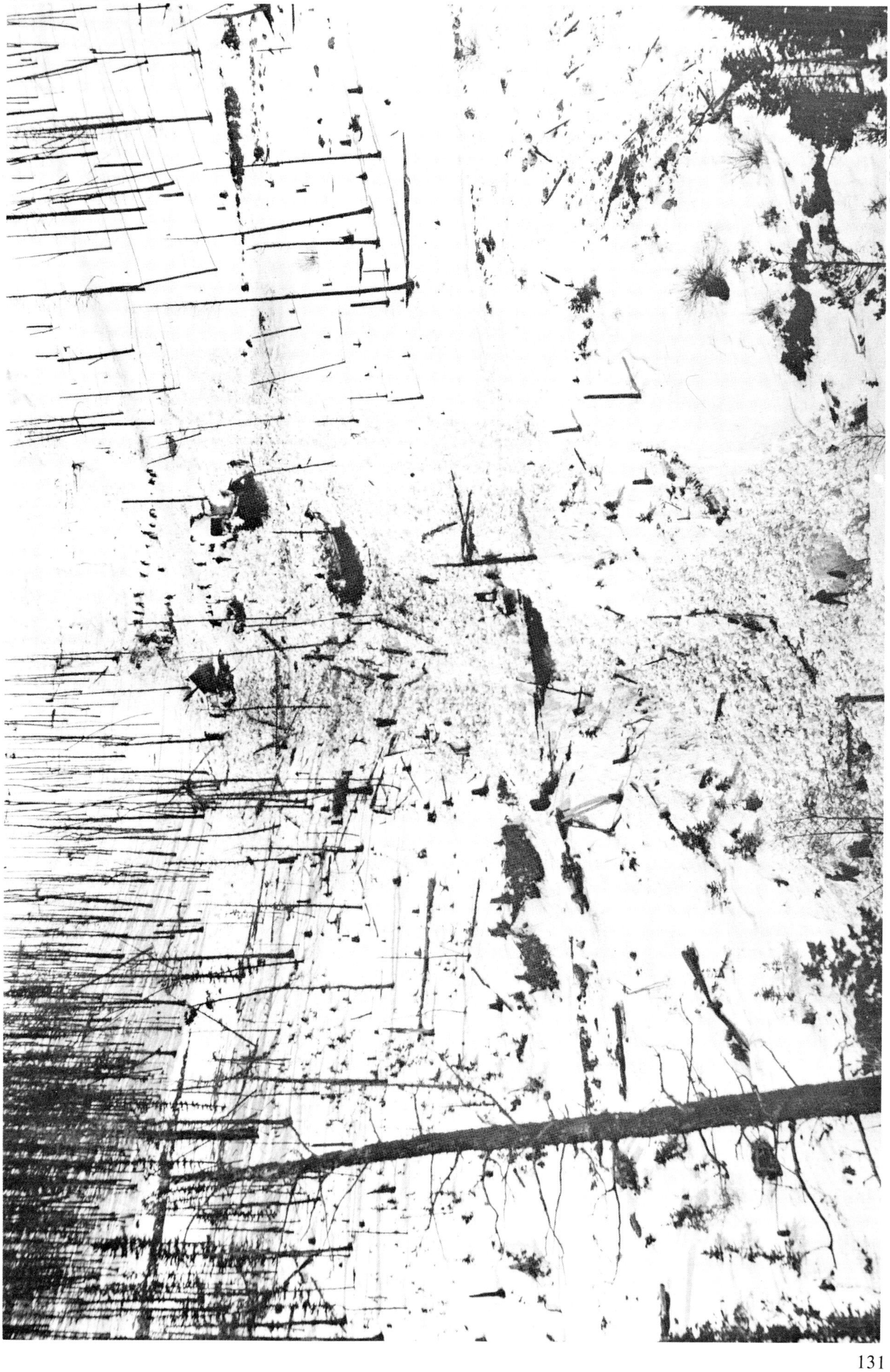

Spectators and workmen around two locomotives swept down north side of Grassy Mountain near Frances, April 18, 1901. They were bucking through huge drift with plow on main line (near top of photo) when snowslide hit. Locomotives lie on siding from Big Five Junction to Big Five.

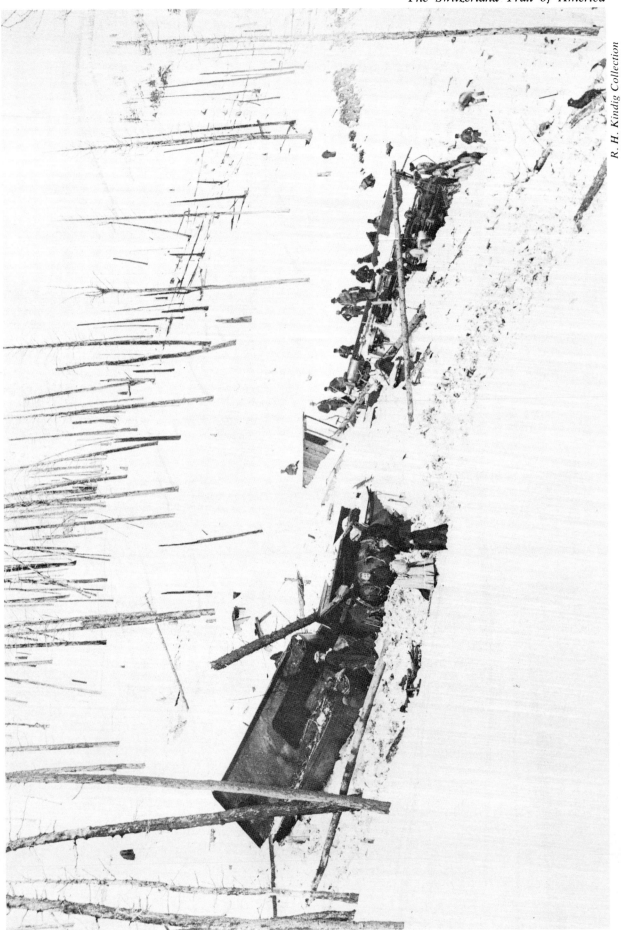

No. 30, No. 31, and snowplow lie on Big Five Siding near the mouth of the Adit-Dew Drop Tunnel after avalanche hit them on main line 400 feet above.

Close-up of No. 30 after she had been swept down Grassy Mountain 400 feet by snow avalanche.

train come around the shoulder of Grassy Mountain. The teacher let us out to watch them plow snow. It was nice and clear and not very cold.[9]

"There had been an awful storm a short time before. The snow used to drift so bad there, and the train hadn't been in for several days. There was about four feet of new snow piled up on the old drifts, which went 'way up the side of the mountain.

"Here they came around the curve, black smoke shooting up from the two engines pushing that big blade plow. (It was mounted on the head end of a gondola filled with gravel.)

"The road went back into the hill a ways on a bend. The timber was heavy there and it was dead from a fire years before. On came the plow, shoving the snow to one side, down the mountain.

"When the plow hit there, we could see it jar loose the snow up above about a hundred feet. Down it came—all that new snow and maybe some more. It just mowed the timber off like you'd cut it with a mowing machine."

The locomotives fared better than the men who drove them. The wrecking crew under Fred Conrad had to wait for the rapidly melting snow to clear away and the ground dry before they could begin operations.[10] They planted "dead man" timbers and with No. 25, the Shay, pulling on block and tackle lines, set No. 30 and 31 up on the Big Five spur track.[11] Their damage was confined to pilots and smokestacks.

Mining continued to look up. In May the tungsten deposits of Boulder County were termed the biggest in the world. This black metal, once contemptuously called "black iron" by prospectors, was now e a g e r l y sought.[12] Alloyed with steel, it could be forged

into machine tools that would continue to cut well even when hot. Its great use was still to come, a sudden intense demand for it to change the life of Boulder and its mining hinterland.

The Boyd Smelter at Boulder was operating at capacity. The Culbertson Mill was handling mill dirt from the B&M Mine at Ward.[13] The superintendent of this mine was petitioning the C&N to lay track on the grade already built to the property.[14]

General Manager C. B. Culbertson bought a handsome Mobile steamer, the first automobile in Boulder.[15] Could he have known what steamers would do to the Switzerland Trail, it is doubtful if he would have had any pleasure in it.

The Switzerland Trail had a great tourist year, excursion after excursion running to Mont Alto Park and Ward.[16]

One day in early August came an announcement that rocked the C&N.[17] A new Intermountain Railroad had let a contract to J. R. DeRemer of Pueblo to grade twenty-five miles of railroad from Superior to Eldora by way of South Boulder Canon. Members of the new company were M. F. Leach, President; John R. Wolff, Secretary; Raymond L. Wright, George C. Kirby, and Walter S. Lee.

The C&N officials recovered quickly. Superintendent Hill rounded up surveying instruments and a crew and headed for South Boulder Canon to head off the interlopers.[18] Some Boulder people saw a possible clash of desperate men and partisans of the two roads.

Colonel Dick stamped onto the scene, announcing that he had bought controlling interest in the C&N.[19] If anybody was going to build the Eldora line, it was going to be he. He had a surveying party between Nederland

[9]"People I Meet" column by Forest Crossen in *Boulder Daily Camera*, September 10, 1957.
[10]*Boulder Daily Camera*, April 9, 1938.
[11]*Ibid.*, September 10, 1957.
[12]*Daily Camera*, May 15, 1901.

[13]*Ibid.*, May 16, 1901.
[14]*Ibid.*, July 24, 1901.
[15]*Ibid.*, July 24, 1901.
[16]*Ibid.*, August 1, 1901.
[17]*Daily Camera*, August 6, 1901.
[18]*Ibid.*, August 8, 1901.
[19]*Ibid.*, August 19, 1901.

R. H. Kindig Collection

Snow shovelers were glad to pause in their work of clearing away around wrecked C&N No. 31. Man at right has bucketful of hot coffee to cheer the boys.

Sturtevant photo. R. H. Kindig Collection

New Colorado & Northwestern rolling stock proudly displayed on main and side tracks near the mouth of Boulder Canon. String of special dump ore gondolas is being switched. Over gondolas, to left of boxcars, are piles of new ties for the railroad. The cathedral-like formation of reddish sandstone is the Red Rocks. To their right, in far background, is the new Colorado Sanitarium. The first permanent settlers, arriving October 17, 1858, camped on the north side of Boulder Creek at right of photo.

Photo courtesy of Lloyd E. Parris
Denver, Boulder & Western switch padlock No. 23.

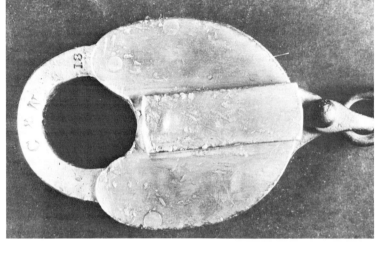

Photo courtesy of Herb O'Hanlon
Colorado & Northwestern switch padlock No. 13.

Courtesy of Jewell and Frank Black
**View from fireman's side of No. 32 on Mont Alto Park
siding at the Elks Picnic, August 14, 1902. Photo made
by T. C. Black, Jr., fireman on the C&N.**

A. A. Paddock Collection

The first automobile in Boulder, a Mobile steamer, was owned by C. B. Culbertson, General Manager of the C&N. Photo taken in 1901. Car steered with tiller bar. Note exhaust steam at right.

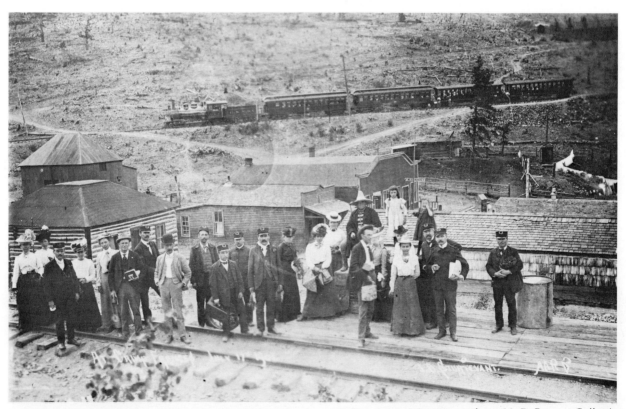

Sturtevant photo. M. R. Parsons Collection

Band members, probably of some fraternal organization, and their families wait on station platform at Frances July 17, 1901, for excursion train. C&N No. 30 heads the eastbound train.

and the Boulder County Mine. Two miles behind it came Frankeberger's engineers for the Intermountain.

Colonel Dick bristled with energy. His million-dollar fortune had come from building and operating railroads; he had promoted the Pittsburgh, Bessemer & Lake Erie. He was heavily interested in Boulder County mining property and the Culbertson Mill. W. C. Culbertson had held him off from building the Eldora branch, but now Colonel Dick was in the saddle.

At once his troubles began. The valuation of the Colorado & Northwestern jumped from $138,875 to $385,000.[20] A contract for grading the Intermountain Railroad was reported signed, work to begin in one week.[21]

On the last day of August Colonel Dick stated that the C&N would be extended to Salt Lake City.[22]

That day ground was broken for the Intermountain. The contractor had a crew at work at the mouth of rugged South Boulder Canon.

In October Colonel Dick announced that the C&N would extend its line from Sunset to Eldora, 22 miles, tapping a rich mining district.[23]

Boulder County mines were booming. New developments at Wall Street, Sugar Loaf, Salina, and Gold Hill were going strongly ahead.[24] There had been an immense new strike in the Concord, west of the famous Melvina at Salina, on the line of the C&N. The ore ran as high as $10,000 a ton.[25]

The winds of November chilled some of the fervor. Colonel Dick did not take up the option on W. C. Culbertson's stock in the Colorado & Northwestern.[26]

At the year's end two new mills of large capacity stood ready to operate. One was the

Wall Street Gold Extraction Company's plant, a great stone and wood structure hugging the north wall of the canon at Wall Street. It would handle 125 tons a day and could easily double that figure. The Big Five Mill at Frances would begin treating ore with the new year.[27]

This meant that ore which might feed the stamps at the Culbertson Mill would now be processed at the mines. The Colorado & Northwestern would have to content itself with bringing up coal and taking down the concentrates.

Boulder's spirits rose as 1902 began. There was an oil boom going to the northeast.[28] New strikes were reported in the gold and silver mines in the hills.[29] The Colorado & Northwestern was battling snow, the eternal enemy of the winter months, but going through.[30] Down at the narrowest point in the Western Hemisphere plans were going ahead to build a canal across the Isthmus of Panama.[31] David H. Moffat, Denver banker and railroad builder, was ready to start building a railroad west to Salt Lake City.[32]

The tourist season started off with the Third Annual Basket Picnic of the Deutcher Verein of Boulder to Mont Alto Park.[33] On the Fourth of July the C&N ran excursions in connection with the Colorado & Southern. The Elks held a big picnic at Mont Alto Park in August, three special trains filled to the platforms.[34] After that came the annual Grocers' Picnic. Business was good for the Switzerland Trail.[35]

The mining picture was not so bright. The Big Five was practically shut down, Frances almost a dead camp. High smelting charges were blamed for retarding mining in Boulder County.[36]

[20]*Ibid.*, August 19, 1901.
[21]*Daily Camera*, August 20, 1901.
[22]*Ibid.*, August 31, 1901.
[23]*Ibid.*, August 10, 1901.
[24]*Ibid.*, October 22, 1901.
[25]*Ibid.*, November 4, 1901.
[26]*Ibid.*, November 11, 1901.
[27]*Ibid.*, December 31, 1901.
[28]*Daily Camera*, January 10, 1902.
[29]*Ibid.*, April 2, 1902.
[30]*Ibid.*, February 4, 1902.
[31]*Ibid.*, January 10, 1902.
[32]*Ibid.*, March 22, 1902.
[33]*Ibid.*, July 17, 1902.
[34]*Ibid.*, August 12, 1902.
[35]*Ibid.*, August 14, 1902.
[36]*Ibid.*, September 22, 1902.

Huge mill of the Wall Street Gold Extraction Company at Wall Street was still under construction when this photo was taken, probably in 1901.

Sturtevant photo. M. R. Parsons Collection

C&N No. 31 with trainload of important-looking people at Frances. No. 31 looks factory-new, still has her cap stack, so photograph must have been taken in 1898. Joe Sturtevant took shot from atop the boxcar station. On siding are two of the special dump cars to haul ore down to the Pennsylvania Mill at Culbertson, four miles east of Boulder.

Sturtevant photo. M. R. Parsons Collection

Locomotive of excursion special takes water at Sunset tank. The plume of smoke shooting upward shows that blower is on full, building up steam pressure for the hard run to Mont Alto Park. Observation coaches are ordinary gondolas and couplings are link and pin.

142

Courtesy of Waldo Bliss

No. 25 in the company yards west of 9th Street, Boulder. Ahead of it is a dump gondola built for hauling ore. Photo taken by Waldo Bliss of Boulder about 1902. His sister, Miss Gertrude Bliss, is standing in the gangway.

Sturtevant photo. M. R. Parsons Collection

Two of the new Colorado & Northwestern's dump gondolas loaded with ore on the siding at Salina immediately west of the station. Station stood at point of mountain to left of cars.

The C&N regular trains began running half empty to the mining camps. Often there was no ore to haul back down. The losses mounted. Then came the first black shadow on the little road.

On November 1st C. B. Culbertson surrendered the management. He was succeeded by H. D. Milton, former General Agent of the Colorado & Southern at Colorado Springs. The arrangement was made between President W. C. Culbertson and Colonel S. B. Dick.[37]

Culbertson owned the controlling interest; Dick was the heaviest minority stockholder, also owner of the Logan and Monongahela Mines and heavily interested in the Mogul Tunnel at Eldora. Culbertson had opposed Dick on building a branch to Eldora. Dick had applied for a foreclosure and receiver. Culbertson had turned the railroad over to Milton for six months, during which time Milton was to thoroughly investigate the feasibility of the Eldora extension.[38]

A battle was shaping up. Colonel Dick insisted that the C&N would have to connect with the new Moffat Railroad near Eldora, build to additional mines to secure ores to keep the Culbertson Mill operating. It would have to develop mines if it wished to stay in business. Dick had the backing of John T. Odell, President of the Lima (Ohio) Railroad, who was interested in the Mogul Tunnel and the Culbertson Mill. Odell was considered a considerable mogul in New York, Ohio, and Pennsylvania.[39] Culbertson was tired of seeing year after year only the red ink of losses.

Not long after this, public confidence in the Colorado & Northwestern received another jolt. A dispatch from Lockhaven, Pa., told of the suicide of Thomas R. Mann:[40]

. . . For some years he was manager and principal owner of the Logan Mine. . . . He had invested heavily in the ill-starred Culbertson Mill and was an owner in the Colorado & Northwestern road. Neither of these have been sources of profit to their owners as yet, though they may become so if the railroad can be connected with other mining districts or with the proposed Moffat road—plans which Col. Dick has under consideration. . . .

Some hearts lifted, however, at news of the big mill of the Wall Street Gold Extraction Company. The Nancy Tunnel could furnish 75 tons a day, with 1,000 tons ready for treatment. The mill was operating on the electrolysis process, already successfully used by the great Camp Bird Mining Company and others.[41]

On the heels of this came the resignation of F. W. Hill as Superintendent of the C&N, a position he had held from the start of the road.[42] General Manager Milton appointed no successor, but would handle the duties himself. Many people shook their heads solemnly, saying that good men do not quit going concerns.

[37]*Daily Camera,* October 14, 1902.
[38]*Ibid.,* October 14, 1902.

[39]*Ibid.,* October 14, 1902.
[40]*Daily Camera,* November 17, 1902.
[41]*Ibid.,* December 11, 1902.
[42]*Ibid.,* December 30, 1902.

Part II

Chapter IV

ELDORA EXTENSION AND THIRD RAIL

The Eldora extension was a great hope and a move of desperation. The mines at Ward, particularly the Big Five combine, had failed to deliver their promised production. The Culbertson Mill lay idle on the north shore of Owens Lake east of Boulder. The tourist business was growing more popular, but it lasted only during the summer months. The nightmare of expense came when winter roared down, and snowplow crews were out day after day. Something had to be done to keep the Switzerland Trail of America operating.

Colonel Samuel B. Dick was a doughty warrior. He was ready to fight to the last ditch for extension of the line from Sunset to Eldora to tap the great potential production of the new gold camp. The thought of ore rolling out of the Mogul Tunnel always excited him.

W. C. Culbertson stood fast against him. Culbertson was obviously disillusioned by the failures of the Colorado & Northwestern. As 1903 began he apparently had no intention of throwing good money after bad into the railroad's maw.

The big mill of the Wall Street Gold Extraction Company became a factor in the decisions. It was the first big mill in Boulder County to attempt the reduction and conversion of gold ore into bullion.[1] If it succeeded it would stimulate mining as nothing had done or could do. It could mean the extension of the C&N to Eldora, where Colonel Dick and associates had thousands of tons of ore in the Mogul Tunnel that would not pay

present smelting and transportation charges. They would become profitable if reduced in a mill nearby. General Manager Milton of the C&N was watching the mill with great interest.[2]

Today this mill is a spectacular ruin hugging the north wall of the canon, its weathered stone foundations resembling some robber baron's stronghold in the Middle Ages. Nearby is a handsome stone house that was the office and assay office.

As March waned the C&N was battling snow. Trains were stalled at Camp Frances, but they were still running at Puzzler.[3] General Manager Milton was working like a Trojan with a large force to relieve the trains. All this meant big expenses.

The Wall Street mill continued in the news. Colonel Dick, J. A. Gilfilian of the Mogul Tunnel, Joseph Luxon, Captain Hanbury—probably the sporting English remittance man whose exploits are still laughed about in Boulder—Manager Milton and Manager Hayes of the Logan Mine, and other notables went up to Wall Street on a special train. After a tour of the mill they regarded it as a great success.[4]

The mill continued to run steadily, the C&N hauling ore to it from Crisman, Salina, Sunset, and Ward.[5] Everyone who investigated it regarded it as a success.

On the heels of this optimistic note came news of the pending receivership of the C&N.[6] Many regarded this as an evil sign.

[1]*Daily Camera,* July 7, 1903.

[2]*Daily Camera,* February 2, 1903.
[3]*Ibid.,* March 24, 1903.
[4]*Ibid.,* April 18, 1903.
[5]*Ibid.,* May 5, 1903.
[6]*Ibid.,* May 16, 1903.

The country had been plagued by too many railroads going into receivership.

Judge Moses Hallet of the U. S. court at Denver was asked to appoint Captain Harry P. Gamble, a Boulder attorney, master in chancery, pending the application for a receiver of the road and a sale under receivership. Gamble, satisfactory to both Culbertson and Dick interests, would make an inventory of the company's assets preparatory for the turn-over to the receiver.

Culbertson, worth $20 million, wanted the road sold. He owned three-fourths of the C&N's stock, $390,000 of its $500,000 bonds, $96,000 of the $120,000 floating debt. He had a mortgage of $100,000 on the rolling stock—and he was firmly opposed to any extension.

Colonel Dick, a millionaire, wanted a receiver to manage the business. He wanted to extend the railroad to Eldora, to connect with the Moffat (Denver, Northwestern & Pacific), then a-building, and on to Middle Park. The Colonel owned the Logan Mine, which was making him money. He owned $50,000 of the C&N bonds and had some money in the Culbertson Mill, which had long been idle. He demanded the right to secure ore for the mill and tonnage for the railroad. He had a very high opinion of the Wall Street Gold Extraction Company's mill, believing that the railroad's future depended on the success or failure of the mill's chlorination system.

As if to bolster Colonel Dick's side, Superintendent S. G. Knott of the Nancy Mine was supplying big tonnage of the mine's low-grade ores to the Wall Street mill and reporting good returns.[7]

Summer came again, the snowdrifts that had caused so much agony mercifully gone. Only a few remained deep in the timber and of these the C&N made up some of its losses by organizing snowball specials. Here

tourists who had never faced a blizzard pelted each other in high glee.

Excursions rolled out of the Boulder station: the Elks, the Methodists, Christian Endeavors, Moonlights to Mont Alto,[8] wild flower specials where the train stopped to let people pick bouquets of fragile and lovely mountain flowers, the Presbyterian Sunday School that drew over 900 persons by its low rate of 40 cents for adults, 15 cents for children.[9]

Now and again something happened that whipped up the excitement and reminded people that this was mountain railroading. Take this story in the *Daily Camera*:[10]

The passengers on the Colorado & Northwestern train this morning were horrified to hear and see coming and thundering behind them a box car, which with the speed of lightning was flying down the main track between Wall Street and Salina, following the train. Instant death seemed sure, for the speed of the run-away car was terrific. Men and women paled and grew sick. The situation was intense yet there was nothing that could be done. Within 200 feet of the rear coach, the car's velocity proved too much for the descent of the rails on the sharp curve of the "Switzerland Trail." It struck a projecting rock and reared back, falling a mass of kindling wood across the track. The car had escaped from the siding at Wall Street.

In the background of this pleasant summer interlude, the struggle to keep the railroad operating continued. In July the First National Bank of Boulder placed in its windows two gold bricks weighing 425 ounces valued at $7,000.[11] They were part of the clean-up of the Wall Street mill, now under lease to the Nancy Gold Mining Company.

Manager Knott said that the saving at the mill had been all that could be desired. They were treating 25 to 30 tons a day, purchasing some custom ore. The treatment charge was lower than anywhere in northern Colorado.[12]

[7]*Daily Camera*, May 23, 1903.

[8]*Ibid.*, June 8, 1903.
[9]*Ibid.*, June 30, 1903.
[10]*Ibid.*, June 26, 1903.
[11]*Daily Camera*, July 10, 1903.
[12]*Ibid.*, July 10, 1903.

Sturtevant photo. Courtesy Elbert Hubbard

Mill of the Wall Street Gold Extraction Company at Wall Street. Note tramway which carried coal and supplies from railroad siding across creek to top of the mill. In the foreground is the steam-powered pump house.

Sturtevant photo. David S. Digerness Collection

C&N No. 1 on the Ox Bow Curve with combo coach.

S. S. Sleeth photo. A. A. Paddock Collection

Making the last run for Ward April 5, 1903. C&N No. 32 and 30 ram snowplow mounted on head end of flatcar through big drift that has kept the mining camp isolated. Over cab of No. 30 may be seen the wide front of the C&N Hotel.

Black photo. A. A. Paddock Collection

C&N No. 31 at the Boulder station ready to pull out for Mont Alto Park or Ward. At rear of train are two open observation coaches, where one got his money's worth of scenery — and cinders. Bill Tipps, who was to hold his rights as engineer to the end of the railroad, is at left. His fireman is Pat Dinley, who was shortly afterward promoted to engineer.

SECTIONS CREW ON THE COLORADO & NORTHWESTERN RY.

M. R. Parsons Collection

The C&N was new when Joe Sturtevant made this fine shot of section crew on a curve west of Puzzler. At upper left is the cut at Alpine Point, east of Frances. In the far middle background is the line headed for Ward.

150

Colonel Dick was further encouraged by the August report that his Logan Mine had netted him $4,519.70.[13] Also, the United States Tungsten Company leased a mill at Nederland and was preparing for big operations. It would need rail transportation.

The colonel had the sale of the C&N postponed until February 3, 1904, tight money conditions in the East prompting this move.[14] He went ahead resolutely gathering data on ore tonnage, etc., to show investors.

Late in November Colonel Dick announced the first moves in building a smelter at the Culbertson Mill. He would hire three well-known mining experts to examine and report the feasibility of a smelter and extension of the Switzerland Trail to Jamestown and Left Hand Canon, also Eldora.[15] The Jamestown miners were again in the news, producing high-grade ores and reviving the old dream of a boom in that camp.

As 1904 opened people in Boulder and the mining country were so much interested in the proposed smelter at Culbertson and the extension to Eldora and Jamestown that news of the outside world largely fell on deaf ears.[16] It meant little that the Japanese and Russians were preparing for war in the Far East.[17]

Optimistic reports of mining revival came in almost daily. There were some adverse reports too. The Nancy Tunnel and the Wall Street mill were shut down for weeks. The arrival of Manager Knott from the East with money permitted operations to resume.[18]

The sale of the Colorado & Northwestern was again postponed, this time for 90 days. Colonel Dick's experts had reported favorably on mining and smelting conditions, and his people were reported as desiring to acquire the railroad.[19] The reason for the delay was Colonel Dick's health; he had been ordered to Florida by his physicians for a rest.

Another jarring note came with a court order granting application for a receiver for the Big Five Company and the appointment of Thomas J. Sipple, sheriff of Boulder County, to take charge of all property of that once so promising concern.[20]

Despite these troubles, the Switzerland Trail went bravely ahead with a guide book for excursionists. They asked owners of resorts to furnish information about their places —all to be inserted free.[21]

The C&N reported a minor victory in the battle with winter. Master Mechanic Fitzgerald turned out at the shops a snow plow that General Manager Milton said was superior to anything used by the company.[22]

The deadline drew near for the sale of the C&N. On May 4th the *Daily Camera* carried a front page headline that drew all eyes: " 'Switzerland Trail' Bought In By W. C. Culbertson And Colonel S. B. Dick And Will Be Extended To Eldora Sure."

What had happened was rather typical of financial manipulations of that day's capitalists. "The entire road was knocked down at the upset price of $100,000. . . . The transaction required but $15,000 cash and the deposit of some bonds. As a matter of fact the gentlemen were simply buying from themselves for themselves the road their money paid for. . . . The transaction wipes out some small stockholders and was necessary in order that debts shall be paid and the control established in the hands of men responsible for the debts. . . . Mr. Culbertson and Col. Dick retain their interests unimpaired and the way has been made clear by an agreement between the two parties for Col. Dick to reorganize the company and take over control."

Colonel Dick was jubilant. "Then comes printing of bonds so as to get money for

[13]*Ibid.*, September 18, 1903.
[14]*Ibid.*, November 18, 1903.
[15]*Ibid.*, November 21, 1903.
[16]*Daily Camera*, January 6, 1904.
[17]*Ibid.*, January 28, 1904.
[18]*Ibid.*, February 3, 1904.
[19]*Ibid.*, February 4, 1904.

[20]*Ibid.*, February 20, 1904.
[21]*Ibid.*, February 23, 1904.
[22]*Daily Camera*, April 7, 1904.

these Boulder county extensions. It means $500,000 or $600,000 to be expended in this county and I think the money will be forthcoming. My friends will reorganize the company and adopt a progressive policy. I think Boulder county can yield 1,000 tons of ore a day for the road to haul, if we build a matte smelter here and I am told by all smelter men that such a smelter is feasible. If so, we shall extend to Eldora, down Left Hand past the Slide and Prussian and go after ore. The road is nothing as it is—we must have tonnage."

A short time later came the announcement that The Colorado & Northwestern Railway Company would be known hereafter as The Colorado & Northwestern Railroad Company. The new company had filed its articles of incorporation May 19th with the Boulder County Clerk and Recorder.

Things began to stir. Robert Sumner, son of the Chief Engineer of the Denver, Northwestern & Pacific (Moffat), began making a survey for the proposed extension between Sunset and Eldora. All efforts would be made to miss points subject to frequent snowdrifts.[23]

Mining activity at once picked up at Eldora and in Left Hand Canon.

Colonel Dick imported Robert Law to be local head of the C&N. Some years before Law had made a report on the road for Colonel Dick. For a young man he had gone far: Roadmaster on the Union Pacific at Cheyenne, later General Roadmaster, Superintendent, and General Superintendent. He later became General Manager of the northwestern lines of the Burlington. He was to spend about one million dollars on the extension, the matte smelter, and in developing mines along the route of the railroad.[24]

The American Smelting and Refining Company sent one of its experts to Eldora to investigate the field and report on the feasibility of building a $250,000 smelter at Boulder and assisting the C&N.[25]

Colonel Dick ordered a formal reorganization of the new company. Samuel B. Dick was elected President; Vice President, Robert Law; Secretary and Treasurer, W. B. Hayes; General Counsel, Richard H. Whiteley. The directors were W. C. Culbertson, C. F. Webster, J. T. Odell, S. B. Dick, Robert Law, W. B. Hayes, and Richard H. Whiteley.[26]

The published report showed capital of $500,000 — $500 cash, $499,500 by purchase of property. Indebtedness ran to $27,439.36.

The report was as follows:

Main line	26.5 miles.	Value......$26,500.00
Sidings & Spurs 2.39 miles,		Value...... 717.00
Total	28.89 miles	......$27,217.00
5 locomotives and tenders		......$ 6,250.00
9 coaches		1,800.00
4 observation coaches		600.00
2 combination cars		300.00
29 box, 35 gondolas, 4 flat cars		5,900.00
30 dump, 2 caboose		2,600.00
		$17,450.00
Real estate		540.00
Buildings		610.00
		$ 1,150.00 [27]

The total value came to $45,817, a paltry figure for a railroad that cost so much.

The company rented offices in the fine stone National State Bank Building, a suite of seven rooms on the second floor. From there the Switzerland Trail of America was to be directed to the end.[28]

The bristling energy of Colonel Dick shot new life into the Colorado & Northwestern. Orman and Crook of Pueblo, builders of the Ward line, received the contract for

[23]*Daily Camera*, May 24, 1904.
[24]*Daily* Camera, June 1, 1904.

[25]*Daily Camera*, June 14, 1904.
[26]*Ibid.*, June 28, 1904.
[27]*Bulletin No. 65, Railway and Locomotive Historical Society*.
[28]*Daily Camera*, June 13, 1904.

The COLORADO & NORTHWESTERN RAILWAY

BOULDER TO WARD

West Bound Trains			Stations and Passing Places.	East Bound Trains		
6 Local	**2**	Distance from Boulder		Altitude	**3**	**7**
Daily P. M.	Daily A. M.				Daily P. M.	Local A. M.
4:30	8:20	......	Leave........ Denver ....Arrive	5,147	5:45	9:30
5:50	9:40	......	.... Boulder	5,400	4:10	8:10
6:05	9:54	2.9	.... Orodell		3:57	7:48
6:28	10:12	6.2	.... Crissman	6,300	3:43	7:31
6:40	10:20	7.5	.... Salina	6,800	3:35	7:23
6:50	10:30	9.0	.... Wall Street	7,100	3:27	7:12
7:08	10:43	11.6	.... Copper Rock	7,550	3:10	6:51
7:20	10:55	13.3	.... Sunset	7,800	3:00	6:39
.....	11:15	16.4	.... Mount Alto Park	8,600	2:44	.....
.....	11:23	17.8	...... Gold Hill	8,750	2:38	.....
.....	11:39	21.9	.... Puzzler	9,000	2:19	.....
.....	11:48	23.0	.... Bloomerville		2:14	.....
.....	11:54	24.6	.... Frances	9,300	2:07	.....
.....	12:00	26.1	Arrive........ Ward ....Leave	9,450	2:00	.....

Take Colorado & Southern Ry. from Denver.

OFFICIAL ROSTER C. & N. RY. CO.

Hon. W. C. Culbertson, President, Girard, Pa.
Col. Sam'l B. Dick, Vice-President, Meadville, Pa.
Frank May, Secretary, Girard, Pa.
Chas. B. Culbertson, Treasurer, Boulder, Colo.
H. D. Milton, General Manager, Gen'l Frt. & Pass. Agt., Boulder, Colo.
S. Robinson, Auditor, Boulder, Colo.
M. Fitzgerald, Master Mechanic, Boulder, Colo.
J. J. Laton, City Pass'r Agent, 1025 17th St., Denver, Colo.
Hon. R. H. Whiteley, Gen'l Counsel, Boulder, Colo.
General Offices, Boulder, Colo.

COLORADO & SOUTHERN RY.

Denver to Boulder, Ft. Collins and Greeley

Ft. Collins District.

*35	*23	*21	M	STATIONS	*24	*22	*36
10:50	4:30	8:20	....	Lv..... Denver .....Ar	5:45	9:45	1:05
....	4:36	8:25	2	.... Argo	5:38	9:40	....
**11:11	**4:55	** 8:45	9	.... Semper	**5:22	** 9:21	....
11:59	5:52	9:43	29	.... Boulder	4:28	8:35	12:05
....	6:20	**10:10	37	.... Ni Wot	**4:01	8:08	....
....	6:33	10:21	43	.... Longmont	3:50	7:58	....
....	**6:45	**10:35	49	.... Highland	**3:35	** 7:43	....
....	6:56	10:45	54	.... Berthoud	3:25	7:33	....
....	7:12	11:00	60	...... Loveland	3:12	7:20	....
....	7:45	11:27	74	Ar.. Ft. Collins ..Lv	2:42	6:49	....
....	8:11	11:52	86	.... Windsor	2:15	6:23	....
....	8:35	12:20	98	Ar..... Greeley Lv	1:50	6:00	....
*10:50	4:30	8:20	....	Lv..... Denver .....Ar	5:45	9:45	1:05
11:40	5:30	9:20	16	.... Louisville	4:49	8:50	11:30
11:50	5:40	9:30	23	Ar..... Lafayette Lv	4:40	8:40	11:20

Courtesy of A. Joe Bell

Timetable published in the May, 1904, issue.

Courtesy of A. Joe Bell

The Switzerland Trail Guide Book, issued monthly by The Swiss-Trail Publishing Company of Boulder and Denver, carried this ad in the May, 1904, issue. It is listed as a "Tourists and Excursionists Pocket Guide Book of The Colorado & Northwestern Ry. and Northern Colorado."

Black photo. Courtesy Jewell and Frank Black

Baseball game at Mont Alto Park, June 28, 1904.

Eldora Extension and Third Rail

Well

I'm from Missouri and they are going to SHOW me the famous Switzerland Trail next Sunday.

Denver to Ward and return $2.25

Denver to Mont Alto and return $2.00

Via Colorado and Southern Ry. from Denver. Secure tickets at office "Colorado Road," 17th and Curtis Streets, or at Union Depot.

Train leaves Denver at 8:20 a. m. Returning arrives Denver 5:45 p. m., just in time for dinner.

J. J. LATON,
City Passenger Agent,
1025 17th Street, Denver

Courtesy of A. Joe Bell

Inside back cover ad in The Switzerland Trail Guide Book of May, 1904.

the Eldora extension. It was to use the old Greeley, Salt Lake & Pacific grade to the Washington Avenue Mine, then on twelve miles to Eldora.[29]

The railroad began to advertise. The *Daily Camera* of August 12, 1904, carried an ad two columns wide and ten inches deep, "The Switzerland Trail of America—Round Trip Rate, One Day Limit: Mont Alto Park, $1.00, Ward, $1.75. The Finest Scenery on Earth. L. R. Ford, General Passenger Agent, Boulder."

L. R. Ford was to wield great influence on the Switzerland Trail. He began railroading in 1883 in Cincinnati and in 1889 came west for his health. He joined the Colorado Midland and was in charge of construction of the line from Divide to Cripple Creek. He then went over to the Florence & Cripple Creek Railroad, where he was Vice President and Traffic Manager as late as December, 1903.

An ad in the August 16th *Daily Camera* showed the circle emblem of the C&N, along with a new time table and notice of a moonlight excursion to Mont Alto Park.

In September the Switzerland Trail announced a "Dollar Round Trip to Ward — The Cheapest Ride Ever."

In October General Manager Law announced rates of $1.50 a ton on ore not exceeding $20 a ton value from any point on the line to the Denver smelters. Ore above a $20-value would command a fair rate.[30] These were far better rates than Boulder County mining men had ever had.

A promise of greatly increased summer business came with the incorporation of the Denver & Interurban Railroad Company. It was to electrify the Colorado & Southern line between Denver and Boulder and provide swift, frequent transportation.[31]

An ad carrying a nostalgia for those

quieter days appeared October 5th: "Autumn Leaf Excursion, Sunday, October 9, via Colorado & Northwestern. Ward Round Trip, $1.00. Train leaves Boulder Depot 9:30 a.m. The train will stop to permit passengers to gather autumn leaves."

The aspens were in their full golden glory; the mountainsides that had been burned or cut over were unforgettably beautiful. Over the hills hung a slight blue haze, said by the Indians to be smoke from the fires of the departed spirits. In the air was the crispness of the nearby Continental Divide peaks.

The completion of the C&N to Sugar Loaf and Eldora was to bring immediate help to mining men. The Colorado & Southern would cooperate in new low rates to the smelters at Argo and Denver.[32]

Boulder eagerly awaited news of the new branch's progress. When the rails reached Sugar Loaf Mountain, many people boarded the railroad's first excursion to that point.[33] From Sunset their nerves tingled as the train climbed along the south wall of Four Mile Canon. As they slipped through cuts and swung around curves, the views of the nearby Continental Divide made them cry out with delight.

The rails crept nearer Eldora, the line running west from Pennsylvania (Glacier) Lake, then southwest to Cardinal, south to Sulphide Flats, and west up the Middle Boulder Valley through touching scenic beauty.

Many of the old-timers in the Cardinal-Caribou district looked at the line with tight lips; they had seen terrible blizzards pile great snowdrifts here.

On December 29th the first train to Eldora reached a point 6,000 feet below the camp shortly after one o'clock. The one hundred-odd guests of the railroad walked good-naturedly up to the camp. They had been impressed by the speed over the new line, they

[29]*Ibid.*, June 19, 1904.
[30]*Ibid.*, October 5, 1904.
[31]*Daily Camera*, September 20, 1904.
[32]*Ibid.*, October 25, 1904.
[33]*Ibid.*, October 25, 1904.

C&N No. 1 has rounded Ox Bow Curve and is headed for Mont Alto Park. The few remaining snowbanks indicate that spring has come again.

Sturtevant photo. M. R. Parsons Collection

Refreshment stand for one of the many picnics at Mont Alto Park.

A. A. Paddock Collection

C&N No. 1 passes Lover's Leap (on left) in Boulder Canon on a sparkling summer day with a mixed train. Hooked behind is a push car. Officials and some favored passengers will ride the car down. To the right is the wooden flume of the Silver Lake irrigation ditch hugging the mountainside.

Gosha photo. A. A. Paddock Collection

First train to Eldora, December 29, 1904. The train did not actually reach Eldora; the end of steel was 6,000 feet short of the camp. The party of railroad officials, businessmen, bankers, and crew pause for photograph before hiking up to a big turkey dinner at the Gold Miner Hotel. No. 30 has pushed train from Sulphide Flats.

Freighters at New Market Extension above Ward unloading coal, mining machinery, and supplies in the early days of the C&N.

160

had been awed by startling vistas of the great peaks. They were joined by the hilarious citizens of Eldora, who escorted them to the Gold Miner Hotel, where they enjoyed a turkey dinner. The big dining room buzzed with happy talk of new and great prosperity.

General Manager Law had big hopes for a reopening of the Culbertson Mill. He had turned down offers to buy or lease it. He said he was astonished by the unfolding of facts day by day indicating promise of increased tonnage of ore all along the C&N.[34]

The skeptics shook their heads. They hoped it would come true, the golden dream that would not die. They had to face reality, however. The big mill at Wall Street, upon which high hopes had been placed, was idle. The Nancy Gold Mines and Tunnel Company had recently been sold by the sheriff for a judgment of $4,026.02.[35]

Then came a new development.

"General Manager Law and Freight and Passenger Agent Ford of the C&N have returned from Chicago, where they closed a contract with the Colorado & Southern road to lay a third rail for use of C&N narrow gauge cars into Union depot at Denver. Manager Law said the contract calls for completion of the work by May 1."—*Daily Camera*, February 7, 1905.

Again hopes soared. Cars loaded with ore could roll down from the hills directly to the smelters at Argo Junction, even out to Golden. Excursionists could board trains in Denver, roll speedily over to Boulder, then on to the mountains without change of cars. It looked like the Switzerland Trail under Colonel Dick was going to make the grade.

Prospects for increased mine tonnage looked brighter. There was even talk of shipping dump ore, hitherto discarded as too low grade to handle profitably.

All was not good on the new Eldora branch, however. The old battle with winter

continued. On February 22nd the C&N track was still snow-bound between Washington Avenue and Eldora, despite relays of snow shovelers and as many as four engines behind the plow.[36]

On March 27th the snow at Eldora and Ward was three feet deep on the level. The drifts of the past week had raised it to enormous heights. The C&N had been practically out of business west of Sunset for a week.

With the spring the snows retreated. The railroad ran its first excursion to Eldora Sunday, April 30th, the round-trip $1. A newspaper ad advised people to "View from the Eldora Line the Continental Divide."

In the same issue was another ad that probably seemed of little significance then: "Come down and see our 1905 Rambler. 20 horse power. Models from $650 to $3,000—Boulder Bicycle Co."

In Russia the 1905 Revolution was in full swing. It did not seem very significant either.

The Colorado & Northwestern was in the news. It was to run solid passenger trains into the Denver Union Depot June 1st. The headquarters of the road would be in Denver, using C&S terminal and shops. The road probably would be taken over by the C&S. Work was to begin about May 15th on the third rail laying. Pennsylvania Lake was to be made a big summer resort. Just beyond the lake, a New York banker was to build a hotel and establish a resort for Eastern millionaires. The railroad was to build several hotels and put in picnic grounds.[37]

At Boulder, Superintendent Hayes said that all this was practically correct.

The excursion business boomed as never before. General Freight and Passenger Agent L. R. Ford reported that the following excursions were booked:[38]

National Association of Stationary En-

---

[34]*Daily Camera*, December 13, 1904.
[35]*Ibid.*, November 5, 1904.

[36]*Daily Camera*, February 22, 1905.
[37]*Daily Camera*, May 6, 1905.
[38]*Ibid.*, May 22, 1905.

A. A. Paddock Collection

C&N No. 1 west-bound up Boulder Canon with combo and observation car. To the right is the wagon road.

Courtesy Mary E. Wirtz

Charles M. Williams, right, when he was station agent at Sunset in the early days of the Colorado & Northwestern.
Jimmie Rose at left.

The mountain people were proud of their railroad, and photographer Joe Sturtevant was quick to record the fact.

gineers of Denver, 500 strong. Eldora, July 16th.

Walther League, May 30th.
Hurlbert's Grocery Clerks, June 18th.
Iron Molders, July 30th.
Boulder Presbyterians, June 5th.
Epworth League, five special trains through to Eldora or Ward, as delegates select, July 8th.

The company had men at work at Glacier Lake preparing a resort for the expected business. They took down the pavilion at Mont Alto Park, transported it in sections on flat cars to Glacier Lake, and set it up again.[39]

Boulder eagerly awaited completion of the third rail to Denver. On Saturday, June 17th, the last rail was spiked down in the Boulder yards. At once the C&N officials ordered all coaches available sent to Denver for two big excursions scheduled for the next day.[40]

The Hurlbert Grocery Clerks and the Eagles went up in four special trains. One group went to Glacier Lake, the other to Mont Alto Park. Their expressions of pleasure made the C&N officials beam.[41]

The crowds that flocked to the Boulder station that morning gaped at an unusual sight. A Colorado & Southern standard gauge locomotive came in from the east on the Louisville cut-off dragging a long train of narrow gauge coaches loaded with people. The locomotive was equipped on tender and pilot with a special coupler to take narrow gauge car and coach couplers.[42]

At 15th Street the C&S engine stopped and uncoupled. One by one, four C&N locomotives backed down, switched out the coaches into equal trains, and took off for the hills. When they returned that evening, the C&S engine made up the coaches into a train and departed for Denver.

The operating agreement of the Colorado & Southern and the Colorado & Northwestern was that no through individual C&N trains would be operated between Boulder and Denver, no C&N locomotives pulling trains between these points. This was the reason for the special coupler.

Colonel Dick arrived in Denver from the East, to the great delight of the press boys. They reported that the President and principal owner of the Colorado & Northwestern owned controlling interests in several valuable tungsten deposits along his road. The colonel said that Pennsylvania capitalists, representing U. S. Steel, had inspected the field several times. He hinted that they intended to secure control of it.[43]

Colonel Dick rolled up to Boulder in a private narrow gauge car lent by the Colorado & Southern, then on to Eldora. He and his guest, Durban Horne, wealthy and prominent merchant of Pittsburgh, expressed great satisfaction over the ride. Their refusal to admit they were here on tungsten business quickened the pulses of mining men.[44]

Denver was planning a big Fourth of July celebration. The Colorado & Northwestern announced that it would sell round-trip tickets from Ward, Eldora, Sunset, and Salina to Denver for the regular one-way fare. Colonel Dick wanted his coaches pulling into the Union Station jammed to the platforms.

The colonel and his men decided to take their old enemy, Cold, by the throat and make it pay. They organized the Glacier Lake Reservoir and Ice Company, capital stock $25,000, incorporating with the Secretary of State. M. Herbert, Phillip Feldhauser, R. Law, W. B. Hayes, and S. B. Dick were the incorporators.[45]

They proposed to build a big reservoir in the natural basin known as Pennsylvania Lake near North Boulder Creek. The name

---

[39]*Daily Camera,* May 22, 1905.
[40]*Ibid.,* June 17, 1905.
[41]*Ibid.,* June 19, 1905.
[42]*Ibid.,* September 4, 1952.

[43]*Daily Camera,* June 26, 1905.
[44]*Ibid.,* June 27, 1905.
[45]*Daily Camera,* July 13, 1905.

THE

COLORADO AND NORTH WESTERN RAILROAD

COMPANY

EMPLOYES' TIME TABLE

NO. 7.

IN EFFECT SUNDAY, OCTOBER FIRST, 1905, AT 1:00 A. M.

MOUNTAIN TIME

This Time Table is for the use and government of Employes only, and is not intended for the information of the Public, or as an advertisement of time of any train. The Company reserves the right to vary from it at pleasure.

STUDY THE RULES WELL AND BE SURE THAT ALL UNDERSTAND THEM ALIKE.

IMPORTANT CHANGES HAVE BEEN MADE.

ROBT. LAW,
Vice President and Gen'l Mgr.

C. M. WILLIAMS,
Chief Train Dispatcher.

ELDORA LINE

Time Table No. 7
October 1, 1905

WEST BOUND TRAINS							EAST BOUND TRAINS	
SECOND CLASS 27	FIRST CLASS 35	Distance From Boulder	Altitude	Length of Sidings in Feet Between Head Blocks	STATIONS	Coal, Water and Turning Station / Station No. / Distance from Eldora	FIRST CLASS 36	SECOND CLASS 28
Accommodation Mail and Express P.M. DAILY	Mail and Express A.M. DAILY						Mail and Express P.M. AR. DAILY	Accommodation Mail and Express A.M. DAILY
1 00	8 00				DENVER .... AR. LV.		5 45	11 59
2 00	9 17	0		13380	BOULDER .... AR. LV.		4 25	11 00
2 30	9 25	0	5400		COLO. & SO. CROSSING	C-W-Y-S 0 33 4	4 15	9 00
2 50	f 9 39	2 9			ORODELL No Siding	3 30 5	f 4 03	8 40
3 02	f 9 49	4 7		565	LANGDELL No Siding	5 28 7	f 3 56	8 29
3 12	x 9 57	6 2	6300	304	CRISMAN	6 27 2	x 3 48	8 19
		7 4		665	BLACK SWAN	W A 8		
3 21	x 10 05	7 5		396	SALINA	A 8 25 9	x 3 40	8 10
		8 5			TAMBOURINE	A 9 24 9		
3 32	x 10 15	9 0	7100	638	WALL STREET	9 24 2	S 3 32	8 00
		9 2		1084	WOOD MOUNTAIN	B 9		
	f 10 28	11 6		581	COPPER ROCK	12 21 8	f 3 21	
		11 8		174	SHELTON'S MINE	A 12 26 1		
3 48	x 10 35 / 10 45	13 3	7800	500	SUNSET	W-Y 13 20 1	x 3 15	7 44
	f 11 05	17 3	8430	200	SUGAR LOAF	E 17 16 0	f 2 54	7 35
	f 11 09	17 9		150	TUNGSTEN	E 18 15 4	f 2 50	
	f 11 30	22 4	9050	300	GLACIER LAKE	C-W-Y E 22 11	x 2 30	
	f 11 33	22 8	9054	700	PINNACLE	E 23 10 6	f 2 27	
	f 11 37	23 5		400	SILVER LAKE	E 24 9 9	f 2 24	
	x 11 57	27 3	8595	60	ANSON	W E 27 6 1	x 2 02	
	f 12 10	29 4		100	WOLFRAM JUNCTION	E 29 4 0	f 1 51	
	x 12 14	30 0	8710		CARDINAL-CARIBOU No Siding	E 30 3 4	x 1 48	
	x 12 24	32 1	8530	200	SULPHIDE	C-W-Y E 32 1 3	x 1 36	
4 00	12 30	33 4	8730	900	ELDORA	E 33 0	1 30	
P.M. ARRIVE DAILY	P.M. ARRIVE DAILY						P.M. LEAVE DAILY	A.M. LEAVE DAILY

Passengers will be carried on Nos. 7 and 8.   All trains will stop on signal at platform west of Wood Mountain, to receive and discharge passengers.

D—Day Telegraph Office.   C—Coal.   W—Water.   Y—Turning Station.   F—Stop on Signal.   S—Regular Stop.   S—Scales.

WARD LINE

Time Table No. 7 — October 1, 1905

WEST BOUND TRAINS 27 SECOND CLASS Accommodation Mail and Express P.M. DAILY	ALTITUDE	Length of Sidings in Feet. Between Head Blocks.	Distance From Boulder	STATIONS	Distance From Ward	Station No.	Coal, Water and Turning Station.	EAST BOUND TRAINS 28 SECOND CLASS Accommodation Mail and Express A.M. DAILY
4 00	7900	500	13 3	DR......SUNSET.....SU	12 9	13	W-Y	7 35
4 20	8600	362	16 4	MONT ALTO PARK	9 7	16		7 15
4 29		603	17 8	GOLD HILL	8 3	17		7 06
4 42			20 0	BRAINERD, No Siding	6 1	19		6 53
4 53		608	21 9	PUZZLER	4 2	22		6 41
4 59		550	23 0	BLOOMERVILLE	3 1	23	W	6 35
5 03		3525	23 2	BIG FIVE JUNCTION	2 9	25		
5 20	9300		24 6	FRANCES No Siding	1 5	25		6 25
P.M. AR. DAILY	9450	532	26 1	DR......WARD......WA	0	26	Y	A.M. LV. DAILY
		523	26 5	NEW MARKET	4	26	Y	

SPECIAL INSTRUCTIONS

ENGINES AND TRAINS will come to a full stop and two distinct blasts of the whistle sounded before proceeding past stop posts at Sunset and Boulder.

CONDUCTORS WILL EXAMINE BULLETINS daily at Dispatcher's office, Boulder, and at Terminal Points.

SPEED OF EXTRA OR IRREGULAR trains will not exceed the schedule time of regular trains.

CONDUCTORS WILL PROTECT their trains by flag when using Y at Ward.

WEST BOUND TRAINS have right of track against east bound trains of the same and inferior classes.

WATER TANKS will be treated as regular stopping places and trains approaching them must be under control.

CONDUCTORS WILL BE HELD personally responsible for the proper adjustment and care of all switches used by themselves and crews.

THE STANDARD CODE OF RULES adopted by the American Railway Association will govern, except where they conflict with special time card rules.

TRAIN AND ENGINEMEN, as well as car inspectors, must examine the running gear and test the air at terminal and other points where opportunity affords and know that everything is right before starting.

IN COUPLING, utmost care must be taken to guard against accidents, as drawbars, cars and engines vary in size, heighth and kind. Employes must personally examine and make sure that the appliances are alright before attempting to make couplings Coupling by hand is positively forbidden, and the Company absolutely declines to be responsible for accidents growing out of negligence of its employes or others.

MAILS must not be allowed to remain upon trucks or platform unguarded or where they will be liable to depredation or to damage by the elements and they must be dispatched to the post office or placed aboard the proper trains without delay. Agents will be held personally responsible for their proper care at stations. Do not receive pouches unless properly locked and correctly labeled.

THE HANDLING OF UNITED STATES MAILS will take preference over express and baggage.

TRAINS WILL NOT LEAVE INITIAL or starting point without clearance card or orders from Dispatcher.

THE CLOCK IN DISPATCHER'S OFFICE, BOULDER, is standard time. Conductors and Engineers will compare their watches with it daily. When this is impracticable, comparison will be made by telegraph.

CONDUCTORS WILL REGISTER their trains in books provided for that purpose at Boulder, Sunset, Eldora and Ward. Trains originating at and destined to Boulder yard will register at Boulder shops.

BRAKEMEN, and as necessary, CONDUCTORS, are required to be on the platform of passenger cars and on top of freight cars in proper place and position to insure control of trains in descending grades.

NO TRAIN will exceed a speed of six miles per hour within Yard Limits.

TRAINS MOVING in the same direction will keep not less than five minutes apart.

In the event of a person being injured such as having an arm or leg run over by a car, or any other severe injury to an extremity, attended by loss of blood, the following instructions should be observed in order to arrest bleeding and support strength until assistance of a surgeon can be procured:

In the absence of a proper instrument, called a "tourniquet," a small strap or rope about the size of a clothesline, should be tied loosely around the limb, if possible about a foot above the injury; and then by placing a short stick beneath the ligature sufficient pressure can be easily made to prevent the loss of blood by twisting the stick, care being taken to not tighten the rope too much, as it might injure the safe parts, but merely twisting the stick enough to prevent bleeding, and thereby place the person out of immediate danger. An injured person should be placed lying upon the back, and if weak from the effect of the shock and loss of blood, pillows should be removed and head put on a level with the body. Should there be coldness and shivering, warm drinks, such as tea, should be given; and if there is great prostration and weakness from loss of blood, stimulants, such as brandy, whiskey or wine, may be administered in moderation.

E. B. QUEAL, Chief Surgeon,
Boulder, Colo.

Phones—Office 2332 Black, Residence 152 Boulder.

W. W. REED, Surgeon,
Boulder, Colo.

Phones ...

FOLLOWING INFORMATION FOR THOSE INTERESTED. THE RAILROAD COMPANY ASSUMING NO RESPONSIBILITY.

Stage lines operate from points on this line as follows:
Between Salina and Gold Hill 3½ miles, daily service.

(Connect with No. 1.) Leave Salina 10:10 a. m., arrive Gold Hill 12:00 m.

(Connect with No. 7.) Leave Salina 5:50 p. m., arrive Gold Hill 7:10 p. m.

Leave Gold Hill 6:30 a. m., arrive Salina 7:15 a. m. (Connect with No. 8)

Leave Gold Hill 2:25 p. m., arrive Salina 3:25 p. m. (Connect with No. 2.)

Between Ward, Gresham and Allen's Park.

Tuesdays, Thursdays and Saturday.

Connect with No. 1, leave Ward 1:00 p. m. arrive Allen's Park 5:00 p. m.

Leave Allen's Park 7:00 a. m., arrive Ward 11:00 a. m.

Ward to Gresham, 6 miles.

Ward to Allen's Park, 14 miles.

Between Cardinal-Caribou station and towns of Nederland and Caribou, daily service connecting with trains 1 and 2.

The following mines are accessible by good roads from the stations on this line named below:

Crisman—Logan mine, New Enterprise mine.

Salina—Emancipation mine, Gardiner mine, Little Johnny mine. Richmond mine, Ingram mine, Golden Eagle mine, Victoria mine. Cash mine, Black Cloud mine, Cold Spring mine, (Gold Hill, Colo.) Slide mine, (Gold Hill, Colo.) Black Swan mines and mill, Bell mine.

Wall Street—Nancy G. M. Co. mines and mill, Tambourine mine, Wood Mt. mines and mill, Lucky Star mine.

Frances—Big Five mines and mill including Ni-Wot, Columbia and Madeline.

Ward—Ward Struggler mines and mill, San Blas mine. Myrtle mill, Baxter. new Market, Utica, Colorado. B. & M, U. P. Worth, Morning Star, Boulder County.

Sunset—Lee. S. mine, Golden Chest. Shelton's mine. Governor Routt, Ruby mine and mill.

Puzzler—Walters. Ward Rose. Puzzler, Pennsylvania, Ruby. Milwaukee.

McClure photo. R. H. Kindig Collection

No. 33 at Glacier Lake with a train of seven borrowed Colorado & Southern observation cars. James Peak, under which was later to run the 6.2-mile Moffat Tunnel, stands proud and aloof to the west.

would be changed to Glacier Lake and it would draw water from North Boulder Creek.

The manufacture, storing, and selling of ice was the main purpose of the company. It would also store flood water and sell it for irrigation and even power purposes.

The excursions rolled out of Denver, into Boulder and up the Switzerland Trail almost in a steady stream that summer. One of the largest was the Denver Grocers to Glacier Lake, 1,200 strong.[46]

In September General Granville M. Dodge, chairman of the board of directors of the Colorado & Southern, General Manager J. M. Herbert, and General Superintendent J. H. Young made an inspection of the Switzerland Trail. General Dodge was a personal friend of Colonel Dick and he was in Denver to attend the Grand Army of the Republic encampment.[47]

The Switzerland Trail continued its advertising campaign, the local newspapers now publishing reproductions of scenic photographs taken from the track.[48]

New rich strikes were reported in mines along the Switzerland Trail. In October Simon Guggenheim and other notables visited the mining district of Eldora, Caribou, and Albion. They were said to be looking for fluxing ore for their smelters.[49] Here and there in the hills ore mills were resuming operations.

On November 10th Colonel Dick arrived in a special car on another of his inspection, though some people now called them promotion, trips. He was accompanied by George F. Davenport of Meadville, Pa., General Attorney for the Erie Railroad, and Charles F. Mackey, New York attorney and promoter.[50]

Editor L. C. Paddock of the *Daily Camera* saw great hopes in Colonel Dick's

efforts. The Caribou district alone should revive and employ as many as 1,000 men, thanks to low smelter charges of $7 a ton for $50 ore, as against $42.50 at the time the Caribou silver mines were shut down. Colonel Dick promised shipping charges of $1.50 as against $10 in the old days.

"Experts estimate that there is more ore in sight in the Boulder County district than there is now or has been taken out of the Cripple Creek district, and from present indication next year will be the banner year for mineral production of that county," said Colonel Dick in Denver.

He was trying to persuade the heirs of the R. G. Dun estate to reopen the Caribou mines, which had produced $7 million to $8 million. They would make good returns again if worked.

The newspaper boys loved Colonel Dick.

The bustling colonel returned to Boulder to address the Commercial Association. "The American Smelting company experts tell me there is more merchantable ore in Caribou hill than in Cripple Creek. I want you to help me go after that ore. I want tonnage for the railroad. You want a great city here supported by a mining population to the west of you. Can't we work together and bring these things about?"[51]

Again hearts lifted to the magic lure of gold and silver within the rock. Reports came in of low-grade ores being profitably treated by cyanide at Cripple Creek, with equally good results elsewhere.[52] Ten feet and four inches of solid gold ore had been opened near the famous Potato Patch strike at Sugar Loaf. Ward was going to outdo itself in the coming year. The Pennsylvania Mining and Milling Company, so long in hard luck, now had good ore in one if its Wall Street mines. The rich Mogul Tunnel strike some weeks before had been followed by even higher-grade ore.[53]

[46]*Ibid.,* August 21, 1905.
[47]*Ibid.,* September 2, 1905.
[48]*Daily Camera,* October 3, 1905.
[49]*Ibid.,* October 4, 1905.
[50]*Ibid.,* October 10, 1905.

[51]*Daily Camera,* November 14, 1905.
[52]*Ibid.,* November 25, 1905.
[53]*Daily Camera,* November 28, 1905.

Chapter V

THE DENVER, BOULDER & WESTERN

Colonel Samuel B. Dick was a driving man, but not even his drive and high optimism could hide the facts that the Colorado & Northwestern was in bad condition financially. For the fiscal year ending June 30, 1905, it had carried 42,171 paying passengers at a gross profit of $23,216 and 25,835 tons of freight at a gross profit of $31,680. Charged against these gross profits were operating expense, taxes, and interest on bonds. The Colorado & Northwestern lost $32,897.[1]

The management cut expenses to the bone. In January of 1906 it was running one train a week to Ward, having the mail carried daily to the camp by wagon or sled from Sunset. Ward was practically a dead camp, the big mines that had promised enormous tonnages of milling ore shut down or doing only a little development work.[2] A receiver was appointed for the huge mill of the Wall Street Gold Extraction Company.[3] It too had been shut down, its great rooms ghostly echoing the lonely watchman's tread. The Mogul Tunnel, darling of Colonel Dick, was sold by a deputy United States marshal at the Boulder County courthouse.[4]

Even with the fortunes of the C&N at this low ebb, Colonel Dick called his General Manager, Robert Law, back to Pennsylvania and New York to talk about extension of the railroad.[5]

Shortly afterward came the announce-ment that Robert Law had been chosen President of the new electric interurban line linking Boulder and Denver.[6] On Robert Law, Colonel Dick had counted much.

Then the people of Boulder and the hills plagued by the Colorado & Northwestern's troubles forget them temporarily. In the early morning of April 18, 1906, an earthquake shattered San Francisco. Fire broke out, the destruction of life and property making the nation shudder. Appeals for help went out, and Boulder responded with a railroad car filled with clothing, food, and necessities.[7]

The Colorado & Northwestern went gamely on. On the first pleasant week-end of the new spring it advertised a trip to Eldora for $1.25, with stopoffs at Glacier Lake, $1.00, and at Sugar Loaf, 75 cents.[8]

These trips were a bargain, even with the prices of that day. Potatoes sold for $1.00 per hundred pounds; ham, medium size, was 12 cents a pound; coal, $4.00 a ton; W. L. Douglas union made shoes, $3.50 a pair; Hart Schaffner & Marx suits, $16.50 to $27.50, a chicken dinner at a good restaurant, 25 cents.

With the death of W. C. Culbertson, whose money had largely built the Colorado & Northwestern, Colonel Dick mounted to the seat of power. He began inspecting mines along the railroad. He looked over the work of shipping the immense dumps of the silver mines on Caribou Hill.[9] The returns so far had been disappointing but they might show

[1]*Bulletin No. 65. Railway and Locomotive Historical Society.*
[2]*Daily Camera*, January 22, 1906.
[3]*Ibid.*, January 26, 1906.
[4]*Ibid.*, February 2, 1906.
[5]*Ibid.*, March 31, 1906.

[6]*Daily Camera*, April 5, 1906.
[7]*Ibid.*, April 21, 1906.
[8]*Ibid.*, May 5, 1906.
[9]*Ibid.*, June 4, 1906.

better values later. The colonel had options on the Caribou and adjoining mines and he planned to drive a tunnel from Eldora or Cardinal to cut the big veins at the 1,500-foot level.[10]

Shortly after this, the Switzerland Trail received some bad publicity, through no fault of its own. The Iron Moulders of Denver held a picnic at Glacier Lake. They took up an express car loaded with beer and they had a big supply of liquor.

Well along in the afternoon William Fortier started staggering around looking for trouble. He picked on Louis Glore and a fight started. More sober ones stopped it. Fortier went off, muttering. When the train started back the trouble began afresh. In the scuffle Fortier fell off the coach platform and was dragged to death. The fight occurred about a quarter-mile above the Wood Mountain Mill in Four Mile Creek.[11]

A coroner's jury in Boulder found that "no one is responsible for William Fortier's death but himself and whiskey."[12]

More people were riding the excursions, but more and more were turning to the new automobiles. Bids were called for proposed new roads in the mountains.[13]

The Switzerland Trail was doing more and effective advertising, with panorama views of "The Most Spectacular Scenery in the World." Few, if any, ever disputed the claim. "Coasting on the Crest of the Continent—Above the Clouds in Open Observation Cars Over the Switzerland Trail of America," read another enticing ad.[14]

The Switzerland Trail excursion business was booming, and General Passenger Agent L. R. Ford was happy.[15] If this frail but resolute little man could have had his one wish, it would have been for a summer nine

months long instead of a short three. August was nearly ended. Soon the first snow would sift down and the weary battle would resume.

Nothing could down Colonel Dick. He reported the C&N's income for the past year as $89,046, operating expenses and taxes $82,122, with net earnings of $6,924.[16]

"During the last fiscal year we have rebuilt the entire equipment and purchased one new engine at a cost of $37,000," he said, "all of which has been charged to operating expenses. Earnings increased 46.86 percent and operating expenses 24.13 percent. The prospective increase for the coming year bids fair to enable the company to earn interest and make it valuable property."

The new locomotive was No. 33, a 2-8-0 built by the Brooks Locomotive Works.[17] It was the heaviest and most powerful engine on the Colorado & Northwestern and it arrived July 23rd. The 33 had 16 by 20-inch cylinders, 37-inch drivers, and weighed 102,000 pounds. The operating steam pressure was 200 pounds, in contrast to the 180 and the 150 carried by the other engines. She sang a new song of power in the hills.

The 33 quickly became the darling of the Switzerland Trail. Wherever she stopped admirers encircled her. Proudly they repeated that she was the largest narrow gauge engine in the world. She was bought for the new Eldora branch. They tried her on the Ward line, but she was too long to swing around the tight curves.

The Colorado & Northwestern was in the news again as 1906 drew to a close. The U. S. Government had sought to punish the railroad for failing to install the new automatic couplers. Judge Lewis of the U. S. District Court held that the road was not engaged in interstate commerce, hence the law could not touch it.[18]

[10]*Daily Camera,* June 21, 1906.
[11]*Ibid.,* June 25, 1906.
[12]*Ibid.,* June 29, 1906.
[13]*Ibid.,* July 5, 1906.
[14]*Ibid.,* August 18, 1906.
[15]*Daily Camera,* August 18, 1906.

[16]*Ibid.,* September 28, 1906.
[17]*Bulletin No. 65, Railway and Locomotive Historical Society.*
[18]*Daily Camera,* December 20, 1906.

The Denver, Boulder & Western

J. B. Schoolland Collection. Courtesy Herbert O'Hanlon

Special trains at Glacier Lake during one of the big picnics. Locomotive at left is standing beside ramp built to load ice cut during the winter. Square boat house is at right of ramp. People had fun at Glacier Lake. Note beer drinkers in boat in foreground.

Postcard from A. A. Paddock Collection

The main Eldora line is to the left. Frame pavilion beyond tent was formerly at Mont Alto Park. Glacier Lake is to the right of the big tent. Meals were served during summers in two-story house to left. In distance was highest point on this branch, Pinnacle.

173

Sturtevant photo. R. H. Kindig Collection

Four-coach train struggling to round Ox Bow Curve east of Mont Alto Park.

A. A. Paddock Collection

C&N No. 31 leaving Sunset with an excursion train on the Ward line. Boxcar on ground at right is probably a Colorado Central.

Nelson photo. J. B. Schoolland Collection

"Boulder Canon, Colorado — On Time." No. 1 blasts up Boulder Canon on a fine summer day with her two-coach train headed for Ward. This is below present rock slide that blocks grade.

R. H. Kindig Collection

Shining in her newness, No. 33 awaits her adventures on the Switzerland Trail.

Not long afterward the C&N installed automatic couplers on all its cars. The management well realized the advantages of the new coupler over the old link and pin. Railroading on the heavy grades was hazardous at best; no safety device or practice was neglected.

The new year blew in with terrible storms in the mountains. By the middle of February the Modoc Mine at Ward was compelled to shut down for lack of coal. When the C&N crew finally broke through the drifts, the first carload of coal was for the Modoc.[19]

This was one of the last trains through for a while. The railroad, because of bad weather, light traffic, and heavy expenses, abandoned service to Ward. It began running two mixed trains a week to Puzzler. It again contracted with a stage line to run between Sunset and Ward, giving daily service via the Eldora trains.

There was one bright spot in this picture of cold—the ice business at Glacier Lake. The pure water from the Arapahoe Glacier froze into beautiful blue-white ice two feet thick. For weeks crews sawed it into blocks and floated them over to the shore, where a conveyor run by a steam engine loaded them on the cars. As soon as 10 cars were filled, a crew made up a train and brought it down to Boulder. Here the ice was transferred to Colorado & Southern cars for shipment to Denver. The Maddux Ice Company received part of their supply from Glacier Lake,[20] storing it for summer use. The Crystal Springs Brewing and Ice Company of Boulder contracted for ice.[21] Because of its purity and beauty it was in big demand.

George Hughes of Boulder, who was born and raised at Washington Avenue, little mining camp near Glacier Lake, recalled this ice cutting.

"It was good while it lasted—but that

was only four or five years. The wind used to blow something terrible there across Glacier Lake. It would get so strong it'd blow the men down. They finally had to quit cutting ice on account of it."[22]

The weary battle with drifting snow went on and on. The officials sent out No. 33 coupled behind the snowplow to clear the Eldora line. She went through minor drifts with ease, and the crew began to grin exultantly. Then they came to a long cut drifted nearly full.

The engineer backed up, started the 33 cautiously, quickly increased the speed. She bore down on the cut with a fury of sound and motion, slammed into the snow so hard she nearly knocked her crew out of the cab. Then she stuck, the drivers spinning furiously, the staccato exhausts bouncing off the winter-locked hills. The engineer tried to back out. She refused to budge.

Anxiously the crew spilled out of the cab and caboose. The story was all too clear; the rails had spread under the 33, letting her down to the ground.[23]

With sulphurous language they set to work righting her, a hard task made doubly hard by the snow and cold. Finally they had her back on her drivers. The engineer backed her down to Sunset, turned and headed for Boulder. The officials received the report solemnly. She was too heavy for such work.

The people of Boulder and the mountains had much to talk about these winter days. Down in Panama the U. S. Government under Teddy Roosevelt was digging a canal across the Isthmus. William Jennings Bryan spoke in Boulder, big crowds of miners fav-

[22]Interview with George Hughes, February 12, 1960.
[23]Interview with Oscar Bernsten, October 4, 1952.

Opposite page

Original painting by Howard Fogg

Colorado & Northwestern Train No. 35 enroute to Eldora on a summer day in 1907. No 32 is conquering the grade east of Sunset along the south wall of Four Mile Canon. In the background Arapaho Peak and its glacier and other Continental Divide peaks loom against the sky. At the train's rear is an observation coach.

[19]*Ibid.,* February 15, 1907.
[20]*Bulletin No. 65, Railway and Locomotive Historical Society.*
[21]*Daily Camera,* November 9, 1906.

oring his 16 to 1 silver ratio coming down to join the throngs hearing him. Many came down to hear Eugene V. Debs, the great Socialist leader. Harry K. Thaw was on trial for his life for killing his wife's lover, Stanford White, the famous architect. On the stage of the Curran Opera House in Boulder a company was playing "Monte Cristo," with the new motion pictures between acts.

With the spring came a new surge of hope. Up at Sulphide Flats west of Nederland sixty men began preliminary work for building a high dam across Middle Boulder Creek, to store water for a power plant far down Boulder Canon. The force would soon be increased to 600. The dam would be 135 feet high, 500 feet long, the core 80 feet wide at the base. It would be made of concrete, and this would require 150 carloads of cement.

In addition, there was to be another higher dam constructed at the Barker Meadows, a lovely stretch of grasslands cut through by the silvery waters of Boulder Creek just east of Nederland.

Total cost of the project would run to $1,500,000. It would generate power for all northern Colorado. The concern backing this great enterprise was the Hydro-Electric Company of Colorado Springs, which rumor said had been absorbed by the Central Electric Power Company. Big money was behind the venture, including the Camp Bird silver millions of Thomas F. Walsh and the Leadville, Creede, and railroad millions of David H. Moffat.[24]

The Colorado & Northwestern people down to the newest section hand breathed a big sigh of relief. They began to flex their muscles. Every car and every engine would have to be used far more than ever before. At last the Switzerland Trail had a chance to make money.

General Manager Hayes was called to Colorado Springs to consult with the power company superintendent on freight rates and

the speedy delivery of materials. Three construction locomotives of the saddle tank type, 65 special cars, and several miles of track would be used on the dams. Additional machinery to be transported included a big sawmill, a railroad type steamshovel like the ones used on the Panama Canal, and two aerial tramways.

The C&N promised to begin at once building one mile of spur line to the upper dam site. From there on the construction company would build their own tracks to the jobs.

Even as the spring breezes lightly touched the hills, old Winter growled and in his death agony struck once more.

"Robert Cook, faithful engineer of the Colorado & Northwestern road, was instantly killed while pluckily serving his employers at 5:26 Sunday afternoon (April 28th). This is the minute when his watch stopped mashed flat in his vest pocket by the pressure of the heavy locomotive which rolled over his body and pressed it deep in the snow and ice of Slide point near Frances. . . .

"The locomotive had gone ahead to buck snow, leaving the train which left Boulder at 12:30 p.m., so as not to involve passengers in this always perilous work. The rear wheels of the tender had got off the track and the train crew, by aid of a frog, were attempting to get the wheels on again. To do this necessitated backing a little and Cook from his seat in the cab opened the throttle, pushed the locomotive back a couple of feet — not enough to right the tender but enough to cause the wheels to slip on the ice beside the rail and the tender to careen down the hill. The weight was such as to pull the locomotive with it and Cook went to his death. Four hundred feet below, a battered thing deeply imbedded in the snow lies the wreck, while Cook's broken body was nearer the top. . . .

"Cook's tragic death was nearly the sixth anniversary of the death of three (four) of a snow-bucking crew of the same road. . . .

---

[24]*Daily Camera*, April 15, 1907.

177

Cook came here to take the place of one of the dead engineers."—The *Boulder Tribune*.

The locomotive slid down Grassy Mountain near the same spot where the four crewmen met their deaths in 1901.

Fate was to hurl another body blow at the Switzerland Trail that same month of May. Colonel Samuel B. Dick died at his home in Meadville, Pa., after an illness of three days. He was 75 years old but hale, hearty, genial, and up-to-date, so ran the news account. He had served through the Civil War as Captain and later Colonel of the Ninth Pennsylvania Reserves. As head of the great Phoenix Iron works, he had built the Pittsburgh, Bessemer & Lake Erie Railroad to haul iron ore from the Great Lakes to his furnaces. Andrew Carnegie and associates took over the railroad, Colonel Dick making a million dollars.[25]

Faces went pale as people in Boulder and the mountains read this news. Colonel Dick had been expected in Boulder in June to take up the question of the Nederland extension. It was anybody's guess what would happen to the railroad now.

W. B. Hayes was appointed Receiver of the Colorado & Northwestern as well as of all the Culbertson-Dick interests in Boulder County.[26] Under his able management things began to roll. The resort house at Glacier Lake opened under Mrs. M. F. Thompson, proprietor of the C&N Hotel at Ward. A spur line was begun at Salina to serve the new Pollock Mill.[27]

On February 1, 1907, Hayes had been appointed by Colonel Dick as Acting General Manager in place of Robert Law.

At the annual meeting in June J. T. Odell of New York was elected President; W. B. Hayes, Vice President; L. R. Ford, Traffic Manager and Auditor; C. M. Williams, Sup-

erintendent; M. Fitzgerald, Master Mechanic; and C. F. Tracey, General Foreman.[28]

Hayes went bravely on with the big work of transporting machinery and supplies for the big dam project at Sulphide. Elbert Hubbard, who was raised at Wall Street and who later worked as brakeman and fireman on the road, said,

"I remember when they took up the big railroad type steam shovel. The 25 (Shay) was pulling it. That's all it had, except the caboose. The 25 was slow and it was going extra slow that day. That steamshovel was very heavy, and I think they were afraid of the rails spreading."[29]

The tourist business was good that summer and all seemed well when tragedy struck again. It was early morning of August 10th.[30]

Fire broke out in some freight cars, both narrow gauge C&N and standard C&S, at the Boulder freight depot. Volunteers rushed down to put out the fire and a big crowd gathered. Suddenly a terrific explosion sent men and debris flying. Three men were killed.

The police were not long uncovering the cause. John W. Reeves, a boomer brakeman hired only a week before by the C&N, confessed setting the fire. Whiskey and his hatred for non-union railroadmen had made him do it.

Reeves stayed at Mrs. Kiser's boarding house at 9th and Walnut Streets, a favorite stopping place of railroaders. The Colorado & Southern had a switchman's strike on, and it was using Pinkerton Agency scabs to break it. Some of them stayed at Mrs. Kiser's and this started Reeves off. He made the rounds of the saloons with Frank Kiser, young son of Mrs. Kiser, also his boss on the run from Sunset to Ward. He persuaded Frank to accompany him and set fire to a caboose

[25]*Boulder Tribune*, May 10, 1907.
[26]*Ibid.*, June 14, 1907.
[27]*Boulder Tribune*, May 31, 1907.

[28]*Ibid.*, June 3, 1907.
[29]Interview with Elbert Hubbard, November 30, 1959.
[30]*Boulder Tribune*, August 16, 1907.

The shapely and powerful No. 33 with two girl friends at Glacier Lake.

C&N snowplow rams through drift at edge of Ward in fine flurry of action. Flatcar had one-foot high sidings to hold **sand for extra weight. House on rear had controls for flanger, which were operated by two men.**

R. H. Kindig Collection

Steam conquers snow in violent action near Ward.

R. H. Kindig Collection

Snow shovelers clearing station platform at Ward.

Sturtevant photo. R. H. Kindig Collection

No. 30 proved far better adapted to bucking snow that the more powerful No. 33. She seems to have attracted pretty girls as well as the admiration of men who loved steam power. Conductor Jap Reed is standing between girls.

A. A. Paddock Collection

Special train has brought crew of snow shovelers to open cut on north side of Grassy Mountain near Frances. It was here that the tragic snowslide of 1901 was to wipe out lives of four trainmen. Part of snow-blockaded Camp Frances, as the miners called it, may be seen in the background. Here Engineer Bob Cook lost his life May 3, 1907.

No. 30 has been bucking snow to reach Puzzler in the early days of the Colorado & Northwestern. Coach and boxcar are on siding east of trestle. Engineer Bill Tipps at left.

First station at Wall Street, May, 1898. Man on roof with legs dangling over edge is Charles M. Williams, agent, later Superintendent of the C&N-DB&W. Man reclining is Phillip Gonneley, section foreman, later Roadmaster. After the DB&W quit operating, he returned to his native Italy with enough money to end his days as a rich man.

where some scabs were sleeping. Burn the b........ up! was his idea of bringing victory.

Some boys who had been up in the mountains on a beefsteak fry came along and put out the fire. Reeves and Kiser saw them, so they set fire to a C&N car that Kiser said had merchandise in it. It had—2,400 pounds of dynamite.

The dynamite had been consigned to the Boulder County Mine at Cardinal. It should have gone out on the afternoon train, but it lay in the yards from Thursday until Saturday because only mixed trains had pulled out for the hills.[31] No powder could be shipped on them.

Reeves and Kiser were tried and found guilty of murder in the second degree.[32] They were sentenced to from 10 to 15 years in the Colorado State Prison.[33]

The C&N officials braced themselves for damage suits. Nearly all the plate glass windows in the Boulder business district had been blown out, along with several doors and much minor damage.

But the road must go on. At the end of August the U. S. Gold Corporation purchased the mill of the Wall Street Gold Extraction Company. It dismantled it, shipped the machinery to Sugar Loaf on C&N cars, and set it in another huge mill.[34]

Summer's bright days ended, the aspens in the hills turned to gold, and the first snows of the season came sifting down. Then came an announcement more chilling than the first frosts.

The construction of the big dam at Sulphide was shut down, about 500 men paid off and sent on their way. The reason: financial stringency in New York. There had been many bank failures.[35] We know it now as the Panic of 1907.

It was a dreary winter for the Switzer-

land Trail. There was little business but there was much snow. Month by month the losses mounted.

Not until late June, 1908, did the Eastern Colorado Power Company announce that it would resume work. Barker Dam east of Nederland was to be constructed first. From it a 36-inch concrete pipeline would be run to Kossler's Lake, high in the mountains southwest of Boulder.[36] From there it would drop 1,835 feet to the power house in Boulder Canon.[37]

The first car of the new interurban line reached Boulder from Denver June 25th.[38] This project of hourly service to and from Denver looked good to the officials of the C&N.

On August 20th spruce and pine-framed Glacier Lake had its largest picnic so far. On this day something happened that made Boulder people even prouder of their little railroad. The *Daily Camera* tells it as follows:

Evidently steam engines as well as people have to become acclimated. Yesterday the Colorado & Northwestern borrowed several narrow gauge engines from the Colorado & Southern in order to assist in taking the Denver grocerymen's excursion to Glacier Lake. The Colorado & Southern engines were the ones usually running on the Clear Creek and Platte Canon division of the road, but they had either been standing in the shops too long or were not accustomed to the grades for several of them stuck on the hills and had to be rescued by the regular Northwestern engines. One Northwestern engine pulled three dead Colorado & Southern engines into Boulder this morning and they were coupled on a freight train and taken on to Denver for repairs.

Traffic Manager Ford of the Northwestern says that the picnic was certainly a record-breaker for his road. Over 2,700 tickets were sold from Denver and in addition, a number of Boulder people spent the day in the mountains. Rain in Denver kept many others from going but the weather at the lake was ideal and the picnic a grand success.[39]

---

[31]*Boulder Tribune*, August 23, 1907.
[32]*Ibid.*, November 22 and December 3, 1907.
[33]*Ibid.*, June 3, 1908.
[34]*Boulder Tribune*, August 20, 1907.
[35]*Ibid.*, November 1, 1907.

[36]*Ibid.*, June 19, 1908.
[37]Interview, L. A. Sweeney, Supt. of Boulder Canon Hydro Plant, Public Service Co. of Colorado, February 12, 1960.
[38]*Boulder Tribune*, June 25, 1908.
[39]*Daily Camera*, August 21, 1908.

Courtesy Mary Elizabeth Wirtz

Charles M. Williams, later Superintendent of the C&N, pauses on the Ox-Bow Curve with push car party coasting down from Mont Alto Park, August 23, 1902.

W. L. Cox photo. J. B. Schoolland Collection

Hole blasted out by explosion of 2,400 pounds of dynamite in a C&N boxcar at the old U. P. station near 10th Street in Boulder, August 10, 1907.

184

Courtesy Mary Elizabeth Wirtz

Agent Charles M. Williams and his sister, Miss Sara Williams of Grove City, Pa., on the steepest grade of the C&N below Salina station. They are using the tricycle that could be pedaled upgrade, if one were man enough.

R. H. Kindig Collection

Special train with sightseers arrives at Boulder to look over damage caused by dynamite explosion August 10, 1907.

Sturtevant photo. R. H. Kindig Collection

Four-wheel caboose of the new C&N on industrial spur at west edge of Boulder. At left is big Delano ore mill. Derby-hatted trainmen looks like he has been places and seen many things.

McClure photo
Denver Public Library Western Collection

Four trains heading out from Sunset, two on Ward branch to the right, two on Eldora branch to left. At lower right may be seen the main line, Four Mile Creek, and the wagon road opposite, which largely followed the grade of the abandoned Greeley, Salt Lake & Pacific.

187

Herb O'Hanlon Collection

Glacier Lake on a busy summer excursion day. The pavilion at the right was moved from Mont Alto Park, the square building at the extreme right put up later. The lake is to the right. The dark building beyond the locomotives is the lunch room, that in background the section house. The locomotive at the left is Colorado & Southern No. 39, formerly Denver, South Park & Pacific No. 43, a 2-8-0 built by Cooke in 1883. No. 42 at right is former DSP&P No. 46, a 2-8-0 built by Cooke in 1883. Both were borrowed from the C&S to haul picnic specials from Denver. The Eldora main line continues west.

Ives photo. A. A. Paddock Collection

The contractor's spur line from Sulphide ran down to and beyond face of Barker Dam during the earliest construction, July 20, 1908.

In September the property of the Pennsylvania Mining and Milling Company was sold by the sheriff of Boulder County.[40] Fate was kind to W. C. Culbertson, for whom the mill and station were named, and to Colonel Dick, who held to the last that he could make the complex pay. They did not live to see this day.

The traffic that the railroad had enjoyed to the dam site was halted in October. The preliminary work of digging down to bedrock was completed, ready for the concrete pouring. No concrete, however, could be poured in freezing weather.[41]

Things had never looked darker for the Switzerland Trail of America than at the bleak beginning of 1909. Everywhere in Boulder and the hills, men, at mention of the little railroad's plight, shook their heads solemnly. The *Boulder Tribune* expressed the general gloom with this story:

Trying To Preserve Relic

The Colorado & Northwestern railroad company receivership is about to be wound up and Receiver Hayes is going to turn the interests and property of the company over to Special Master Bartlett of the U. S. Circuit Court. Meanwhile Mr. Hayes will operate the road under the court's orders. The road will shortly fall to pieces unless someone buys the special master's order. Unless it has already gone to pieces.[42]

The gloom deepened on February 12th with this story:

Colorado & Northwestern Railroad At A Forced Sale

A notice of the sale of the Colorado & Northwestern railroad is being published. Special Master George F. Bartlett, Jr., will offer the road and equipment to the highest bidder for cash on March 29, no bid to be less than $250,000, and a cash deposit of $20,000 by the bidder as an evidence of good faith is required. The sale is for the purpose of paying principal and interest on the bonds.

The option which the Colorado & Southern has held on the road is thought to have expired, though it is possible that the road will be the purchaser. . . . It has been under the management of Receiver W. B. Hayes for the past two years. The road cost three-quarters of a million, mostly the money of the late W. C. Culbertson of Girard, Pa. The late Col. Dick put in $38,000 and went broke. It has never had intelligent railroad management.

In Boulder, Ward, Eldora, and Sunset people forgot the terrible earthquake in Calabria and Sicily that had killed 100,000 and wiped out the city of Messina from the earth.[43] They discussed again and again who would buy the Switzerland Trail, trying to bolster their hopes. The C&S option had been allowed to expire. Maybe the Burlington would buy it. It was one of the best scenic railroads in the country. There were promising gold mines along its route, and the tungsten deposits were the most valuable in America, if not the whole world.

The crews took out the trains with no lift in their hearts. Their gloom deepened when Roadmaster C. F. Tracey resigned.[44] They did not blame him for not wanting to go down with a sinking ship.

At last came the news of the sale.

"The Colorado & Northwestern, generally known as the 'Narrow Gauge' or 'Switzerland Trail' was bought at forced sale today by Charles B. Culbertson of Detroit, Michigan, and W. M. Culbertson of Girard, Pa., representing the reorganized bondholders, known as the United States Trust company of New York. Receiver Hayes expects the sale to be confirmed at once and the road to be operated under the new name, Denver, Boulder & Western by April 1st."[45]

The next day, incorporation papers of the Denver, Boulder and Western were filed by M. J. Fields, Robert H. Widdicombe, W. B. Hayes, F. E. Guy, and A. S. Brooks. The capital stock was placed at $300,000.[46]

[40]*Boulder Tribune*, September 18, 1908.
[41]*Ibid.*, October 16, 1908.
[42]*Ibid.*, January 8, 1909.

[43]*Boulder Tribune*, February 19, 1909.
[44]*Boulder Tribune*, February 26, 1909.
[45]*Daily Camera*, March 29, 1909.
[46]*Boulder Tribune*, April 2, 1909.

No. 30 has backed her train of three Colorado & Southern observation cars nearly to end of siding along south shore of Glacier Lake.

Courtesy M. C. Trent

Switching at Sunset on a summer day. No. 33 is pulling a Florence & Cripple Creek boxcar and a gondola loaded with coal. Ahead of the 33 is another locomotive pulling up to get in the clear.

Copy photo by Hildreth Studio, Longmont, Colorado
Courtesy Boulder Daily Camera

Railroad type steamshovel, mounted on rail trucks and moving on sections of track, loading dump cars at Barker dam site, June, 1908. Only the boom (high fore end) of this shovel swung, a separate crane man operating the engines that moved dipper sticks in and out. This shovel used chain for hoisting, so the noise was terrific. This narrow gauge steamshovel came up to Boulder from Denver on the third rail track, then to Sulphide on the Colorado & Northwestern, No. 25, the Shay, pulling it very slowly. From Sulphide the 0-4-0 saddle-tank locomotives took it to the dam site on the construction company's spur line. This type shovel dug the Panama Canal.

Copy photo by Hildreth Studios, Longmont, Colorado
Courtesy Boulder Daily Camera

Close-up of railroad type shovel digging down to bedrock for foundations of Barker Dam, June, 1908. The flow of Boulder Creek in foreground is being diverted around dam site through ditch at left.

Sunset was a delightful place this summer afternoon, ready to spring to life at the arrival of trains. The long building at the right of far trestle is at the mouth of the Sunset-Frances-Ward Tunnel. It was to be driven 18,000 feet, cutting the high-grade gold Dew Drop vein at Camp Frances and the Columbia Lode at Ward. Ore from these veins was to roll out of the tunnel and be loaded onto cars. The tunnel was driven 50 feet, then abandoned— another of the bright hopes of the Switzerland Trail that faded in the thin mountain air.

Black photo. Courtesy Jewel and Frank Black

No. 32 at the Boulder station ready to pull out on a snowy morning with mixed train. Bill Tipps, veteran engineer, is in the cab. Conductor Jap Reed, wearing high laced boots, is on the ground at left. No. 32 has an automatic coupler but still retains her extended piston rods and oil headlight. Steam hose is coiled around sand dome and ash pan rakes hang over smokebox number plate.

At once new life flowed into the Switzerland Trail. Trainloads of cement and other supplies began to go out to Sulphide. Here the DB&W crews cut off locomotive and caboose and turned over the loaded cars to the construction men, who hauled them down their track to the Barker Dam site.

By this time the upper dam had been abandoned and all efforts were concentrated on the high Barker Dam east of Nederland. So down the line went single cars bearing the newly painted name, Denver, Boulder & Western, pulled by little saddle tank 0-4-0 locomotives, which rolled and bucked on the rough track.

These were happy days for the Switzerland Trail. Oscar Bernsten, who was a fireman, always had a happy light in his eyes when he talked about them.

"When they were building Nederland (Barker) Dam, we used to go out of here at 6 o'clock in the morning with twelve cars of cement and the caboose. Twenty tons in each car, and, brother, we sure had to scratch between here and Sunset to make it."

The water grade in Boulder and Four Mile Canons was heavy, running from 3.78% upward. One short stretch below Salina was very heavy. One authority gave it at 5%, another at 7%. The latter figure was usually quoted by the train crews and officials.

"One time I was on the 25 (the Shay) with Fred Wilson, double-heading with Henry Gormley on the 33, with Greenley as fireman. We stopped at Langdell, there at the foot of Poorman Hill in Four Mile (Creek), for Greenley to blow her up. I guess he had too much green coal in her."

Here was a scene: the two hard-pulling locomotives grating to a stop, the roar of the blower going on the 33, black smoke boiling up from her stack as the too-thick bed of coal blazed up gradually to a white blinding glare. In the cab the needle of the steam gauge moved upward to 200 pounds. Then with a mighty effort the engineers started the heavy train, the 33 spinning her drivers a couple of times, the engines of the 25 going like mad, thrusting her ahead foot by foot. On up the canon, the fireman on the 33 careful where he threw the coal.

"After we got to Sunset we could couple on a couple of coal cars—40 more tons anyway. Then, when we got to Glacier Lake, the 33 took 'em on. We came back light with the 25.

"Gormley would go on to Sulphide and then on down to Camp No. 1, above Nederland about a mile. The power company took the cars with dinky engines down to the dam."[47]

The dam under construction was a stirring sight. The railroad ran excursion trains to Sulphide, the construction company taking the coaches down to the dam. Today at low-water stages in Barker Reservoir one may see the grade of this temporary railroad.

The excursion business brought more happy days to the Switzerland Trail's people. Seven excursions went out before June 24th. Thirteen more were scheduled as follows:

Thursday, June 24th—Baptist Young People's Union, Denver.

Sunday, June 27th—National Stationary Engineers, Denver.

Saturday, July 10th—Chautauqua Snow Ball Excursion to Ward.

Thursday, July 15th—Special Excursion from Northern Colorado.

Sunday, July 18th—United Brotherhood of Leather Workers, Denver.

Saturday, July 17th—Order of Maccabees, Denver.

Saturday, July 24th—Sechrest Mfg. Co. employees, Denver.

Saturday, July 24th—Chautauqua Wild Flower Excursion to Eldora.

Sunday, July 25th—Team Owners' Association, Denver.

Sunday, August 1st—Danish Societies, Denver.

[47]*Boulder Daily Camera,* December 13, 1956.

McClure photo. Courtesy Boulder Daily Camera

Barker Meadows showing spur line running down from Sulphide, contractor's camp, and equipment. In the foreground are three of the vertical-boiler steam hoists that moved the heavy materials.

Sturtevant photo. R. H. Kindig Collection

C&N Shay No. 25 with mixed train at Mont Alto Park.

Denver Public Library Western Collection
Courtesy L. Arend and M. C. Poor

Denver, Boulder & Western observation car No. 15 in the Boulder yards.

The Denver, Boulder & Western

Ives photo. Courtesy Boulder Daily Camera

Orodell railroad yards of the Eastern Colorado Power Company were busy during construction of the hydroelectric power plant a short distance up Boulder Canon. Big steel pipe on flatcars and ground are for the penstock, which dropped 1,835 feet from Kossler's Lake to the plant. Triangle frame in foreground served as crane to unload pipe, a steam hoist furnishing the power.

199

Section of the 1,835-foot steel penstock that dropped water from Kossler's Reservoir to hydroelectric plant of the Colorado Eastern Power Company in Boulder Canon. Note tramway up which special cars loaded with materials were pulled by cable and steam hoist. The pipe was 52 inches in diameter in upper sections, narrowing to 44 inches above the plant. The 52-inch pipe was one-fourth inch thick, the 44-inch stock ran from three-sixteenths to three-fourths inches.

Courtesy Boulder Daily Camera

Conductor Jap Reed on east leg of wye at Sulphide. Coach is Colorado & Southern No. 72.

Photo by Joe Powelson, courtesy of Ernest M. Greenman

The breaking of a brake-chain of a passenger coach of the Denver, Boulder & Western railroad near Sunset this morning came near resulting fatally to a number of passengers in the coach. The mountain train, which leaves Boulder at 9:30 for Ward and Eldora, and arrives at Sunset, the division point on the road, at 10:45, stopped as usual at the water tank a thousand feet from the railroad station. The rear coach of the train was uncoupled with the intention of attaching it to the Ward stub at that point. After uncoupling the car the brakeman applied the brakes of the coach, but the chain broke and the car started down the slight grade at that point. The passengers jumped from the car at the warning given by the brakeman and all escaped without serious injury. The empty passenger coach jumped the track about half a mile down the canon, little the worse for the accident.—The Daily Camera, July 16, 1909.

201

Thursday, August 12th—Special Excursion from Northern Colorado Points to Ward.

Sunday, August 8th — Amalgamated Sheet and Metal Workers, Denver.

Sunday, August 15th—Red Men, Numerous Tribes, Denver.[48]

At the beginning of the tourist season the Stanley Hotel in Estes Park opened its doors, offering luxury and service comparable to the fine hotels in the Berkshire Hills and the White Mountains. It was built on an incomparable site by F. O. Stanley, one of the twin brothers who had been skyrocketed to fame with their Stanley Steamer.[49] The hotel and automobile were to loom large in the fate of the Switzerland Trail.

Bright promise filled the air. C. F. Lake began reducing tungsten ore in the Boulder County Mill at Cardinal.[50] The DB&W found itself with an unusual transporation job — the moving of 1,800 feet of steel pipe to Orodell for the new Boulder Canon power plant.[51] The pipe was of heavy steel, each section 30 feet long.[52] It took 30 flat carloads to do the job.

The demand for tungsten picked up. In September C. F. Lake started men clearing a site for a big mill at what was later called Lakewood.

Yes, life was good on the Denver, Boulder & Western during 1909. The railroad made a profit that year of $18,736.[53]

The happy prosperity carried over into 1910. Trains went out loaded with materials for the Barker Dam.[54] Trains pulled up to Orodell with machinery and equipment for the Boulder Canon power house. The price of tungsten was rising, more prospectors going into the field.[55] The new Primos tungsten mill at Lakewood began to operate.[56] The excursion business was good, and part of this was special trains to Barker Dam.[57] Smiling bookkeepers entered figures in black in the books.

On August 4th Mayor A. A. Greenman of Boulder, in a public ceremony at the Boulder Canon power house, threw a lever that started the big 12,000 horsepower turbine. Electricity flowed out over the lines to northern Colorado. The big project of the Barker Dam was finished.[58]

In October the DB&W received a welcome boon. Upon the recommendation of the commissioners of Boulder County the tax valuation was reduced from $233,000 to $114,975. ". . . on the grounds that it is a losing proposition and has hard work to keep from bankruptcy."[59]

The boys at the shops took a bow before the year ended. No. 33 broke the right front section of her frame at Glacier Lake and had to be carefully towed down to Boulder, where she was out of service for a couple of months. Then Master Mechanic J. C. Kennedy and Gus Knopf, Colorado & Southern welder, made the repair, welding the frame with the Thermit process.[60]

Auditor and Traffic Manager L. R. Ford smiled also. The railroad finished in the black with $27,142 for 1910.[61]

[48]*Boulder Tribune,* June 25, 1909.
[49]*Ibid.,* June 25, 1909.
[50]*Ibid.,* July 16, 1909.
[51]*Ibid.,* July 23, 1909.
[52]The pipe was 52 and 44 inches in diameter, *Boulder Daily Camera,* July 23, 1960.
[53]*Bulletin No. 65, Railway and Locomotive Historical Society.*
[54]*Boulder Tribune,* April 8, 1910.
[55]*Boulder Tribune,* April 8, 1910.
[56]*Ibid.,* June 17, 1910.
[57]*Ibid.,* June 24, 1910.
[58]*Ibid.,* August 5, 1910.
[59]*Ibid.,* October 7, 1910.
[60]*Ibid.,* December 9, 1910.
[61]*Bulletin No. 65, Railway and Locomotive Historical Society.*

Part II

Chapter VI

STANLEY STEAMERS AND THE BIG SNOW

In September, 1897, a sleek little buggy with wire wheels carrying two identical bearded men rolled down a street in Newton, Massachusetts. People stopped and stared— for no horse pulled it. It was running by itself, with the faint putt, putt of a steam engine's exhaust and trailed by a ribbon of spent steam.[1]

It was the first horseless carriage built by F. E. and F. O. Stanley, twin brothers, manufacturers of glass photographic plates.

The machine was an instant success, with buyers offering gold for it. The Stanleys began manufacturing automobiles, making improvements with each model.

In 1909 F. O. opened the Stanley Hotel in Estes Park.[2] He and his brother built 9 and 12-passenger Mountain Wagons that operated from Loveland, Lyons, and Longmont. They were powerful, fast machines.

C. G. Hickox, of the Hickox-Fields livery stable of Boulder, went up to Estes Park to see the new steam automobiles.[3] He was so impressed that he ordered two Mountain Wagons. When they arrived, he and his son George began carrying passengers for hire up the primitive wagon and stagecoach Boulder Canon road to Nederland and Eldora. They made trips to other points, including Estes Park.[4]

Others followed the lead. In June, 1911, a new Stanley Steamer ordered by R. C.

Heintz went into service between Boulder and Nederland.[5]

This improved transportation called for improved roads. F. O. Stanley spoke before the Boulder Commercial Association, outlining his fight to secure good roads for a Denver-Boulder-Estes Park trip. He had already spent $9,000 to improve the old wagon road between Lyons and Estes Park.[6]

By the end of July Stanley Steamers had transported 2,500 passengers from Loveland to the park.[7] Tourists in that day came out by train, put up at one of the park hotels for a few weeks, often all summer.

Near the end of August R. C. Heintz reported that he had averaged 10 passengers to the round-trip to Nederland and Eldora since May 29th. Part of the time he had made two trips a day.[8]

The Switzerland Trail ran its excursions as usual. On July 7th seven hundred passengers left Boulder in four trains to attend the picnic of the Knights and Ladies of Security at Glacier Lake.[9]

The freight business fell off sharply. The price of tungsten fell so low that most of the mines shut down. Ward was almost a dead camp.[10]

Nevertheless, the citizens of Ward complained to the Railroad Commission at Denver that the DB&W did not furnish their town frequent train service. The commission dis-

[1]*Historical Motor Car Scrapbook, Steam Car Edition,* by Floyd Clymer, published by Clymer Motors, Los Angeles, California, 1945.
[2]*Boulder Tribune,* June 25, 1909.
[3]*Boulder Daily Camera,* December 22, 1947.
[4]*Ibid.,* July 14, 1953.

[5]*Boulder Tribune,* June 16, 1911.
[6]*Ibid.,* June 23, 1911.
[7]*Ibid.,* July 28, 1911.
[8]*Ibid.,* August 25, 1911.
[9]*Ibid.,* July 7, 1911.
[10]*Ibid.,* July 21, 1911.

missed the complaint on the ground that there was not enough business at Ward to justify such service.[11]

With furrowed brow L. R. Ford looked at the figures in red ink. He kept seeing the Stanley Steamers rolling into Eldora and Ward. They could go anywhere a wagon and team could, and people were delighted with them. Ford was a realist: in time they could ruin the Switzerland Trail. Now if there were only some way to use them. . . .

That winter the DB&W had its old trouble with snow. On March 1st the crews were battling to open the cuts to Eldora. The Ward line had been closed for nearly two months.[12]

Over in China the Manchus had been toppled from their ancient throne by Dr. Sun Yat Sen.[13] Local people read with awe and pride that General Homer Lea, the little hunchback who had grown up in Boulder, had led the revolutionists to victory.[14]

With the coming of spring R. C. Heintz received a second Stanley Steamer for his Nederland-Eldora run.[15] Hickox & Fields also took delivery on a new Stanley Mountain Wagon.[16]

The boost in tungsten prices softened the news for the DB&W people.[17] The district around Nederland thrilled again to life, old mines opening and new ones reporting, the big mills at Lakewood and Nederland operating.

Reports came in of increased ore shipments ready at Ward, Puzzler camp showing activity, and a big tunnel project for the Ward mines.[18] General Manager Hayes hoped some of it was true.

In June a contract was awarded to construct a new highway between Estes Park and Ward, terminus of the Denver, Boulder & Western. This could be a valuable feeder to the Switzerland Trail.[19]

At the same time Hickox & Fields were meeting all trains at Boulder with their big Stanley Steamers and giving excellent service to Eldora, Nederland, and Estes Park.[20]

On the Fourth of July a special train made several trips to Orodell to accommodate people spending the day in Boulder Canon.[21] As they camped beside clear rushing Boulder Creek they saw the big Stanleys of Hickox and Fields whiz by, every seat filled with waving, laughing people.

At the end of the summer L. R. Ford reported that the Switzerland Trail had more excursions than for several years.[22] There had not been so many tourists, but the Trail had done all right for itself—despite the Stanley Steamers.

At the end of the year the freight business looked brighter. Mining was on the increase. The price of tungsten had taken a big jump.[23]

Boulder businessmen went out on a tour of good will to the tungsten camps — by Stanley Steamer.[24]

The next spring the railroad began rebuilding the track between Boulder and Eldora, in anticipation of heavy tonnage.[25] Down in the Boulder yards men were making extensive repairs on coaches and other rolling stock, preparing for a big excursion business.[26] The tungsten mines were going strong, taking up every idle man in the district.

L. R. Ford had his wish at last, with the Ward sky-line drive nearing completion. Tourists upon reaching Ward would be taken by J. E. Lee, a mining man who loved steam

[11]*Ibid.*, December 22, 1911.
[12]*Boulder Tribune*, March 1, 1912.
[13]*Ibid.*, February 2, 1912.
[14]*Ibid.*, March 1, 1912.
[15]*Ibid.*, April 26, 1912.
[16]*Ibid.*, May 3, 1912.
[17]*Ibid.*, May 3, 1912.
[18]*Ibid.*, May 10, 1912.

[19]*Boulder Tribune*, June 7, 1912.
[20]*Ibid.*, June 14, 1912.
[21]*Ibid.*, July 5, 1912.
[22]*Ibid.*, August 2, 1912.
[23]*Ibid.*, December 6, 1912.
[24]*Ibid.*, December 13, 1912.
[25]*Ibid.*, April 25, 1913.
[26]*Boulder Tribune*, May 2, 1913.

Photo courtesy of Reva Hickox Larson

C. G. Hickox and wife (at wheel) with friends in one of his new Stanley Steamers, flower-bedecked for the photographer.

Courtesy Mrs. Jack Gilman

Nederland-bound Stanley Steamer Mountain Wagon of Hickox & Fields, Boulder, in Boulder Canon a short distance below Boulder Falls. Driver has stopped on bridge to take water. Note hose at far right of bridge dropped down into water. Steam syphon is sucking it up into big tank beneath seat. Driver at left is the late Bob Burgener. Time: 1910.

One of the early Hickox & Fields Stanley Steamer 9-passenger Mountain Wagons stops in front of the Stanley Hotel in Estes Park with party of tourists from Boulder. Five-gallon can on running board has extra gasoline or kerosene.

Ives photo, from A. A. Paddock Collection

First auto stage in Boulder Canon stops at toll gate house, 1909. This is a 30-horsepower, nine-passenger Stanley Steamer Mountain Wagon. It has a folded down top but no windshield. There are no lights except the kerosene dash lamps. Boiler is in front under coffin-shaped hood. Burner, which operated on gasoline under pressure, is beneath boiler. Two-cylinder engine is in the rear.

Parting of the ways at Sunset. DB&W No. 1 is crossing the Eldora trestle. Brakeman stands at switch below trestles. Mixed train headed by one of the Consolidations (20 class) is descending grade from Ward. Eldora branch climbs

mountain to the right. On the short siding opposite water tank are spotted two gondolas, one filled with coal for emergency use. Station is in middle foreground.

power, in his 12-passenger Stanley to Estes Park. Connections would be made with all trains.[27]

Over in Boulder Canon 114 Boulder volunteers worked on the road. In one day they made a big improvement for the Stanley Steamers.[28] The DB&W officials looked on and frowned.

In June the Hickox-Fields Transportation Company filed articles of incorporation, with $25,000 capital stock. The company planned to have four steamers and several gas cars operating before the end of the season. It would engage in both passenger and freight business.[29]

On July 18th the Switzerland Trail handled its largest excursion to Glacier Lake: The Denver Grocerymen's Association. So great was the business that the DB&W had to borrow several Colorado & Southern locomotives and crews.[30]

The late R. D. Ward of Boulder, who was agent at Ward from 1905 until 1919, went over to Glacier Lake that day to act as agent. Ordinarily Glacier Lake had no agent. There was a telephone that trainmen used to call the dispatcher down in Boulder. R. D., as he was affectionately called by his many friends, had a heavy day's work handling train orders.[31]

Elbert Hubbard, who lives at Wall Street today, says there were 18 trains at Glacier Lake that day.

"I was brakeman on a C&S train that was pulled all the way through from Denver by two of their engines. Five coaches. I got on at Boulder.

"I was at the station waiting, and some of those trains went up before No. 35, which departed at 9:30. Trains kept pulling into Glacier Lake all that morning until about noon.

"Between Wall Street and Sunset— I think it was at Spruce Gulch—the 33 with five coaches caught up with us. I coupled her on, and she helped us all the way up to Sunset. She was a powerful engine.

"I think the firemen on those little C&S engines had trouble keeping up steam. When they got to Salina, they had burned all the good coal in the tenders. They ran into fine coal that had been in the (tender) tanks for a long time, and they couldn't make steam with that."

The climb from Sunset east along the south wall of Four Mile was always spectacular, but this morning it was unforgettable. Elbert could look down on miles of the main line twisting up the canon along the bright creek.

"It was quite a sight to see all those trains. This canon (Four Mile) was full of smoke. Some of those C&S engines sure had pretty whistles, and their engineers loved to blow them.

"Jap Reed was yardmaster at Glacier Lake that day. That was quite a job to get all those trains out of the way of No. 35 going to Eldora."[32]

Accident-free train operation on the Switzerland Trail with its heavy grades, sharp curves, many trestles, and rock cuts was considered by railroadmen as more than an achievement: it was next thing to a miracle. So far the little railroad had had an almost perfect record—in a day when serious wrecks the country over was the rule. Late in July this record was marred.

The Railroad Commissioner's report said: "Passenger train No. 36 on the Denver, Boulder & Western railroad was derailed at Sulphide station about 2:30 p.m., Sunday, July 27, 1913, which resulted in four coaches being overturned and about twenty-five passengers being more or less injured."

Eldora had no facilities for turning. En-

[27]*Ibid.*, May 9, 1913.
[28]*Ibid.*, May 20, 1913.
[29]*Ibid.*, June 13, 1913.
[30]*Ibid.*, July 15, 1913.
[31]*Boulder Daily Camera*, August 15, 1957.

[32]Interview with Elbert Hubbard, February 26, 1960.

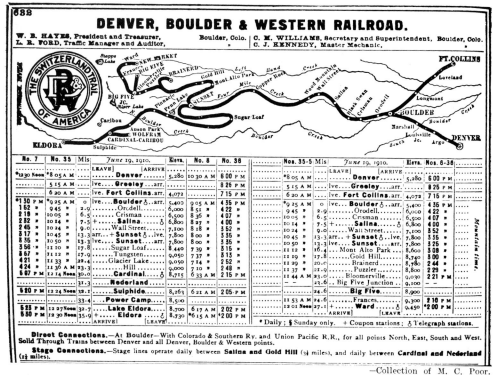

DENVER, BOULDER & WESTERN RAILROAD.

W. B. HAYES, President and Treasurer,   Boulder, Colo. | C. M. WILLIAMS, Secretary and Superintendent, Boulder, Colo.
L. R. FORD, Traffic Manager and Auditor, " | C. J. KENNEDY, Master Mechanic, "

No. 7	No. 35	Mls	*June 19, 1910.*	Eleva.	No. 8	No. 36			Nos. 35-5	Mls	*June 19, 1910.*	Eleva.	Nos. 6-36	
			LEAVE] [ARRIVE								LEAVE] [ARRIVE			
*12 30 Noon	*8 05 A M		....Denver......	5,280	10 30 A M	6 00 P M			*8 05 A M		....Denver......	5,280	6 00 P M	
	5 15 A M		lve...Greeley...arr.			8 25 P M			5 15 A M		lve...Greeley...arr.		8 25 P M	
	6 20 A M		lve. Fort Collins.arr.	4,072		7 15 P M			6 20 A M		lve. Fort Collins.arr.	4,072	7 15 P M	
*1 50 P M	*9 25 A M	0	lve....Boulder ẟ..arr.	5,400	9 05 A M	4 35 P M			*9 25 A M	0	lve....Boulder ẟ..arr.	5,400	4 35 P M	
1 52 "	9 45 "	2.9	......Orodell......	6,000	8 51 "	4 22 "			9 45 "	2.9	......Orodell......	6,000	4 22 "	
2 18 "	10 05 "	6.5	......Crisman......	6,500	8 36 "	4 07 "			10 05 "	6.5	......Crisman......	6,500	4 07 "	
2 32 "	10 14 "	7.5	+......Salina......ẟ	6,800	8 27 "	4 00 "			10 14 "	7.5	+......Salina......ẟ	6,800	4 00 "	
2 45 "	10 24 "	9.0	....Wall Street......	7,100	8 18 "	3 52 "			10 24 "	9.0	....Wall Street......	7,100	3 52 "	
3 17 "	10 45 "	13.3	arr. +Sunset ẟ..lve.	7,800	8 00 "	3 35 "			10 45 "	13.3	arr. +Sunset ẟ..lve.	7,800	3 35 "	
3 35 "	10 50 "	13.3	lve...Sunset...arr.	7,800	8 00 "	3 35 "			10 50 "	13.3	lve...Sunset...arr.	7,800	3 25 "	
3 56 "	11 10 "	17.8	....Sugar Loaf......	8,440	7 39 "	3 15 "			11 12 "	16.4	...Mont Alto Park......	8,600	3 08 "	
4 07 "	11 12 "	17.9	......Tungsten......	9,050	7 37 "	3 13 "			11 19 "	17.8	....Gold Hill......	8,740	3 00 "	
4 21 "	11 33 "	22.4	....Glacier Lake......	9,050	7 14 "	2 52 "			11 29 "	20.0	....Brainerd......	8,780	2 44 "	
4 24 "	11 36 A M	23.3	......Hill......	9,000	7 10 "	2 48 "			11 37 "	21.9	....Puzzler......	8,800	2 29 "	
5 07 P M	12 14 Noon	30.0	......Cardinal......ẟ	8,715	6 33 A M	2 15 P M			11 44 A M	23.0	....Bloomerville......	9,030	2 21 P M	
		31.3	......Nederland......						– –	23.6	Big Five Junction......	9,100	– –	
5 20 P M	12 24 Noon	32.1	......Sulphide......	8,263	6 21 A M	2 05 P M			24.6		......Big Five......	8,900		
		33.4	....Power Camp......	8,500					11 53 A M	24.6	......Frances......	9,300	2 10 P M	
5 25 P M	12 27 Noon	32.7	....Lake Eldora......	8,700	6 17 A M	2 02 P M			12 01 Noon	27.1	+......Ward......ẟ	9,450	*2 00 P M	
5 50 P M	12 30 Noon	35.9	+......Eldora......ẟ	8,730	*6 15 A M	*2 00 P M					ARRIVE] [LEAVE			
			ARRIVE] [LEAVE						*Daily ; § Sunday only. + Coupon stations ; ẟ Telegraph stations.					

Direct Connections.—At Boulder—With Colorado & Southern Ry. and Union Pacific R.R., for all points North, East, South and West. **Solid** Through Trains between Denver and all Denver, Boulder & Western points.

Stage Connections.—Stage lines operate daily between **Salina and Gold Hill** (3½ miles), and daily between **Cardinal and Nederland** (1½ miles).

—Collection of M. C. Poor.

July, 1910, time table of the Denver, Boulder & Western, taken from the 1910 Official Guide. The elevation of Fort Collins as given in the current Official Guide is 4,982 feet.

RESORTS AND FISHING GROUNDS

RED ROCK LAKE

Along

THE SWITZERLAND TRAIL OF AMERICA
(Denver, Boulder & Western R. R.)

Crossen Collection

Cover of booklet published by the Denver, Boulder & Western giving free publicity to resorts and fishing grounds, 1912.

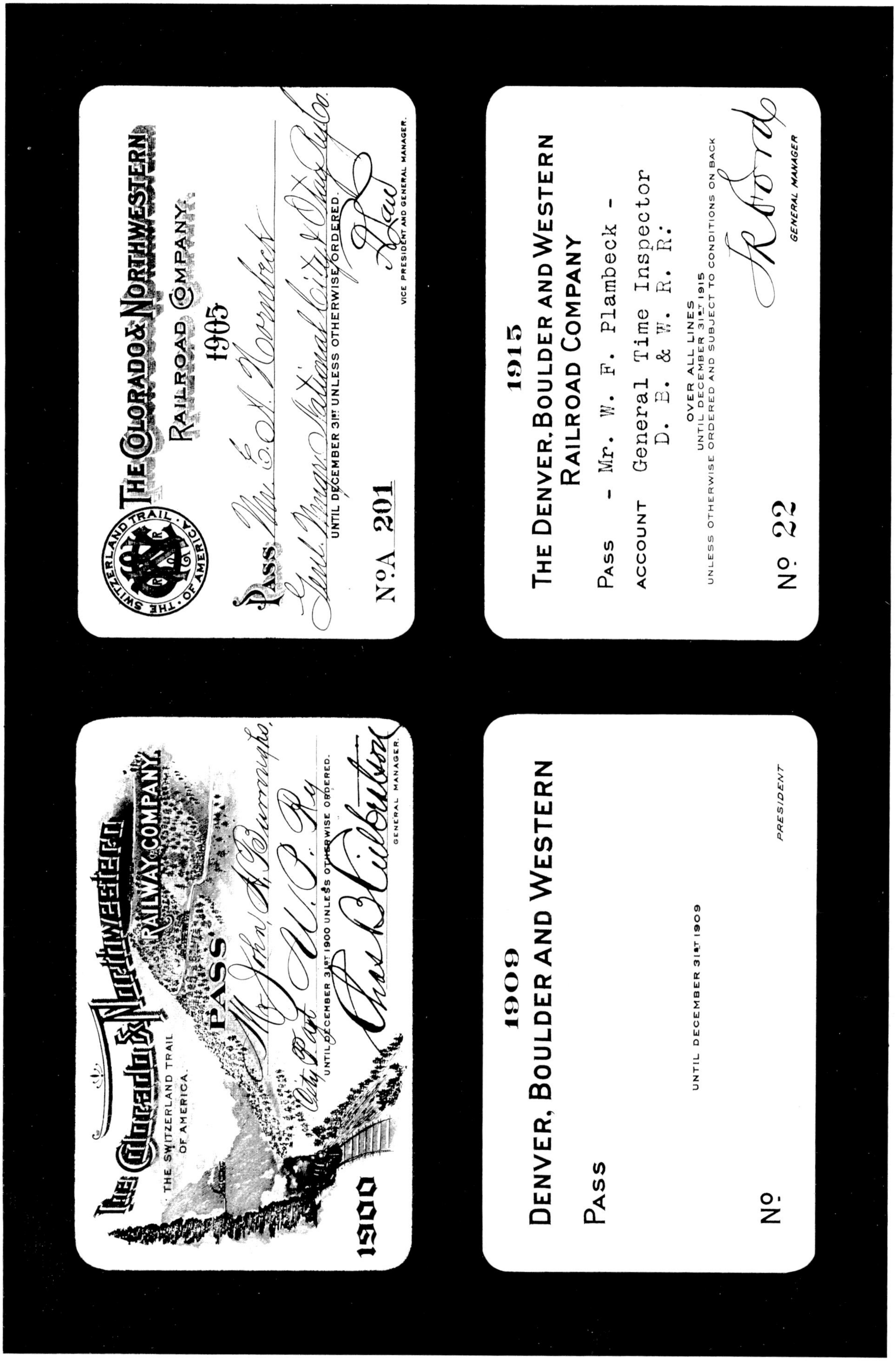

THE COLORADO & NORTHWESTERN RAILROAD COMPANY

THE SWITZERLAND TRAIL OF AMERICA.

1905

Pass Mr. E. A. Kornreich

Gen'l Manager National City & Nbx Ry Co.

UNTIL DECEMBER 31ST UNLESS OTHERWISE ORDERED.

VICE PRESIDENT AND GENERAL MANAGER.

No. A 201

1915

THE DENVER. BOULDER AND WESTERN
RAILROAD COMPANY

PASS   - Mr. W. F. Plambeck -

ACCOUNT   General Time Inspector
D. B. & W. R. R:

OVER ALL LINES
UNTIL DECEMBER 31ST 1915
UNLESS OTHERWISE ORDERED AND SUBJECT TO CONDITIONS ON BACK

No. 22

GENERAL MANAGER

THE Colorado & Northwestern
RAILWAY COMPANY.

THE SWITZERLAND TRAIL
OF AMERICA.

PASS

Mr. John A. Burroughs.

City Sept.   N. C. B. Ry.

UNTIL DECEMBER 31ST 1900 UNLESS OTHERWISE ORDERED.

GENERAL MANAGER.

1900

1909

DENVER, BOULDER AND WESTERN

PASS

UNTIL DECEMBER 31ST 1909

PRESIDENT

No.

Passes from Michael Koch Collection.

gineers had to back their trains down to the wye at Sulphide, 3.8 miles.

"Train No. 36 was in charge of Conductor R. J. Reed and Engineer C. W. Bent, two of the oldest and most efficient employees of the road. The train consisted of an engine and five cars; the last coach in the train was locked and unoccupied when the accident occurred. . . . The length of the train was 285 feet." — The *Boulder Tribune,* August 1, 1913.

Engineer Bent, evidently misjudging the length of the train, backed through the tie bumper on the stem of the wye. The rear pair of wheels of the rear truck of the last coach dropped off the end of the rails, stopping about two feet back.

Conductor Reed signalled Bent to go ahead, to pull the wheels back on the track. Ordinarily this procedure was sound, but one side of the track was pieced out with a section of rail about 4½ feet long. This piece broke loose and the rear end came up, catching the spring hanger and raising the coach, toppling it on its right side.

The couplings of the train held, all except the one on the head coach. The coaches toppled over to the crash of broken glass and screams of frightened people.

The train was full of excursionists, including most of a party of 75 University of Colorado professors and students who had climbed Arapaho Peak.

Word of the accident reached Boulder, and a crowd of about 1,500 was at the station when the train arrived. The injured were rushed to the University Hospital.

Everybody agreed that it was a freak accident. Bent and Reed were blamed, but it was labeled a "one in a thousand accident."

Summer swiftly passed and autumn with its bright blue weather and brief golden beauty of aspen and narrow leaf cottonwood slipped by. The first snow powdered the crests of the Continental Divide peaks. The officials and crews of the DB&W, lips tight, girded themselves for battle. Mercifully, they were not to know the terrible struggle that lay ahead—or its disastrous consequences to the railroad.

Early in December trouble came from the skies in soft white flakes. Oscar Bernsten always shook his head solemnly at mention of it.

"We went up to Eldora at 9:30 a.m. on the 3rd of December with No. 35. We had (engine) No. 32, Bill Tipps, engineer, myself as fireman. Jap Reed was the conductor and Harry Cluphf, brakeman. Mixed train. We had a few passengers, a car of hay, and a merchandise car.

"There was snow on the ground as we left Boulder. We looked up to the west and saw a horizontal cloud, so we hooked the plow on ahead. If it didn't blow, we didn't use the wedge plow; it weighed about 35 tons. We knew by that cloud that it was going to blow.

"There was snow in the cuts all the way to Glacier Lake and Cardinal. From Hill's Siding to Blue Bird the snow sloped off the mountain into the railroad. But we made it to Eldora.

"We left Eldora as quick as Cluphf took the mail sack over to the postoffice. We were always late getting in. This day we knew we didn't have a minute to lose.

"The weather was bright until we got back to Glacier Lake. It started to snow — and it really came.

"We got back to Sunset and were going to leave the plow there. Oscar Chambers, the agent, came out and said, 'no.' He handed us a message from Charley Williams to bring the plow on to Boulder. It had been snowing more down here.

"We got into Boulder about 5 o'clock. I imagine there was 10 inches or a foot of snow. Nice and warm. Snowing." Oscar laughed suddenly. "Holy mackinaw! It was coming down in gobs.

"The next morning, as usual, we were going up to Eldora. We started up and got

T. G. Black, Jr., photo. A. A. Paddock Collection

Officials of the National Hardware Association looking for a site for a big picnic during their forthcoming 1911 convention stop for a photograph in Boulder Canon. They have been taken to Eldora, are now coasting down to Boulder. Left to right: second man, Auditor and Traffic Manager L. R. Ford of the DB&W; fourth man, John W. Valentine, popular Boulder hardware merchant; last man, F. C. Moys, Boulder hardware dealer and secretary of the Mountain States Hardware Association.

West-bound train at Glacier Lake headed by No. 32.

The worst snowstorm in the history of the Switzerland Trail began in December, 1913. It soon blocked the railroad. On January 15, 1914, the DB&W management borrowed a rotary and crew from the Colorado & Southern to clear the Eldora branch. Here it is at Sulphide tank, pushed by Nos. 31, 32, and 30. Engines and plow took water here.

A. A. Paddock Collection

No. 33 charging upgrade over trestle at Sunset on her run to Eldora. Train at left, on the Ward branch, must wait until No. 33's train has cleared switch before returning to Boulder. The fireman has No. 33 hot, her safety valve blowing, so he can ride the seat box for a couple of minutes.

One-coach passenger train making a run for Boulder Canon on a summer day. The locomotive is probably No. 1. Ore dump gondolas are spotted on siding at right. On the left is scale siding with one boxcar. Present West Arapahoe Avenue section of Colorado Highway 119 is built on this grade.

216

just beyond Lover's Leap (in Boulder Canon). We couldn't push the snow.

"We came back and got another engine, the 31. Pat Dinley and Shag (W. C.) Bent were on it.

"So we started up and we hit it again up above Lover's Leap. We had a break and got up above the mouth of Four Mile. Wet snow. We could look ahead and see the snow moving, like a snake. Then we stalled."[33]

The crews settled down to bucking snow. By great effort they finally opened the road, as this story in the *Boulder Tribune* of December 12th shows:

Loaded to the limit with passengers, bread, meats and other provisions and with mail, the first DB&W train in a week left Boulder Wednesday (Dec. 10) nearly on schedule time for Eldora. The train consisted of but one engine, a freight car and a combination mail and passenger coach. Nearly 50 miners piled into the passenger coach. Some of them had come down on the train Tuesday, while the others had been stalled in Boulder for a week. A week's accumulation of mail matter was piled on the train.

Nearly every miner had a pair of skis or snowshoes.

All over Colorado people were battling the great snows. In Boulder 43 inches fell between December 4th and 11th. Boulder was a city of white silence, the only movement fingers of smoke rising straight from the chimneys. A Colorado & Southern train was stalled at Marshall, five miles south of Boulder, the passengers forced to spend all day Sunday in unheated coaches. Their relief came when a C&S rotary cut its way north from Denver. The rotary continued on through Boulder, relieving the congestion there.[34]

The DB&W had no rotary, but its crews performed a herculean job, as this story shows:

After bucking snow from noon Monday to 5:30 Tuesday morning, the DB&W Railroad company has finally succeeded in opening up its line, known as the Switzerland Trail, from Boulder to Eldora and on Wednesday began to operate its train on schedule time. Eldora, Cardinal, Glacier Lake and other points on the line have been without service since last Thursday and were beginning to run shy of provisions.

Drifts over 20 feet high were encountered by the train from Sugar Loaf station to Eldora. The average depth of the snow in cuts was 16 feet and on level places 4 feet. Although much lighter than that which fell here the snow was badly packed and frozen in many places, making the work of plowing extremely difficult. It took the train, consisting of three engines and a flanged plow, from 2 o'clock Monday to 5:30 Tuesday to buck from Sugar Loaf to Eldora. The line from Boulder to Sugar Loaf was opened Sunday after 19 hours' work by the same crew.[35]

The hard-won victory was short-lived. "As a result of the work of one of the worst blizzards that the mountain district of this county has experienced in many years," said the *Boulder Tribune* of January 2, 1914, "two engines and a snow plow of the DB&W railroad are stalled in a snow drift on the Giant's Ladder, two miles from Sunset, and a third engine sent out yesterday to assist them has been blockaded near Copper Rock by a snowslide which has badly covered the tracks for several hundred yards, shutting Boulder off from connection with Sunset and all points west.

"The line is completely tied up and it will be for several days, if not weeks, before traffic can be resumed to Eldora. The heavy wind that has been prevailing in the mountains was accompanied during the past 24 hours by a snowstorm, four inches falling at Sunset and a foot at Cardinal. The wind has filled to giant depths all the cuts on the railroad with snow. The double-header sent out from Boulder Wednesday morning was unable to get to Glacier Lake on account of the drifts, and in backing down to Sunset, over the line which it had opened up but a few

[33]Interview, September 12, 1955.
[34]*Boulder Daily Camera*, March 3, 1960.

[35]*Boulder Tribune*, December 12, 1913.

Denver Public Library Western Collection

L. C. McClure made this fine shot of the Denver, Boulder & Western operations on a spring day. Train at right is headed for Ward, train at left for Eldora.

Below in Four Mile Canon is the main line to Sunset, which is marked by three trestles.

Stanley Steamers and the Big Snow

It is little wonder that the Switzerland Trail delighted people. This grand view is the Eldora branch between Sugar Loaf and Glacier Lake. The track is here. At the left rises Arapahoe Peak and its glacier. This is the backbone of North America, the Continental Divide, its peaks sweeping the clouds at about 14,000 feet.

J. B. Schoolland Collection

No. 32 seems to be a big attraction of this Labor Day celebration at Glacier Lake. Engineer Bill Tipps, wearing white shirt and black bow tie, is at right in cab window. Oscar Bernsten, his favorite fireman, is at left. At the right is the pavilion which formerly stood at Mont Alto Park.

hours before, encountered a deep drift that completely stalled the train.

"After working for several hours in an effort to push a track through the drift the crew of the two engines gave up the helpless task and walked to Sunset, where they secured a push car on which they arrived in Boulder about 8 o'clock last night.

"Yesterday a force of twenty-five men with shovels and picks were endeavoring to clean the line from Sunset west, so that the stalled train can back into that camp.

"Traffic Manager Ford was hopeful yesterday of the double-header being released from its blockade. He was unable to make any predictions of how soon it would then be able to force its way through the snowslide."

One week later man's ancient enemy, Cold, still ruled:

W. B. Hayes, president of the Denver, Boulder & Western railroad, said Tuesday that further bucking of snow between Glacier Lake and Eldora was a fruitless undertaking. All day Sunday and Monday an engine crew bucked snow and made 300 feet in 16 hours. At that rate it would take two months to make Eldora. Mr. Hayes walked some distance and found there were some fills as deep as 25 feet for long distances over the rails. He has been negotiating for a rotary snow plow and now has the assurance from the operating department of the Colorado & Southern that they expect to be through bucking on the South Park branch and will place a rotary at his disposition early next week.

"It has cost us $3 a foot to buck snow with our facilities," said Mr. Hayes, "and you see where we are. We appreciate the people's handicap but it is idle for us to try further until we can get a rotary. We think we can clean the entire track in two or three days when we get one."[36]

The arrival of the Colorado & Southern rotary was a big event in Boulder, every person who could get free rushing down to the yards to see it. It arrived January 15th, shortly before noon.[37]

"I remember the day the rotary came up from Boulder," said Elbert Hubbard. "We were on No. 36, coming down from Glacier Lake. The road was blocked from there on. It was about 3 p.m. when we got to Sunset. They had the 31 and the 32 pushing the plow. They took our engine, the 30, to help.

"We put the passengers and the mail and express on two handcars and started down. Cold! You can't imagine how cold it was. There was snow on the rail from Sunset nearly to Wall Street. Charley Williams said we'd have dry rail from Wall Street on.

"On my handcar the brake was on one wheel only, which made it hard to control. There was a box of dry sand on the car, and one passenger dribbled handfuls of sand on the track to keep us from sliding. I was scared to death coming down.

"The rotary went on from Sunset. They were back in Boulder about noon the next day. They were out all night, for they got that rotary off the track west of Hill's Siding, and they had a terrible time getting it back on.

"The C&S crew was well fixed. They had a bridge and building boxcar outfit where they could eat and have hot coffee."[38]

The storm was to bring more trouble. Up in California Gulch near Ward the White Raven Mine was unable to ship a big tonnage of valuable silver-gold ore from Puzzler. Time and again its owners appealed to the DB&W officials to open the track and resume train service.[39]

The officials replied that they could not force their way through the deep cuts filled with hard-packed snow, some of which were thirty-five feet deep.

On April 24th the White Raven Company appeared before the Colorado Railroad Commission and petitioned to compel the DB&W to keep its line open and trains operating to Ward during the winter months. The mining company was being severely handicapped through lack of train service.[40]

The railroad officials replied that it was

[36]*Boulder Tribune,* January 9, 1914.
[37]*Ibid.,* January 16, 1914.
[38]Interview, April 6, 1960.
[39]*Boulder Tribune,* March 27, 1914.
[40]*Boulder Tribune,* April 24, 1914.

C&S rotary snowplow makes light work of snow on Sulphide Flats.

Rotary snowplow in action near Cardinal.

J. B. Schoolland Collection

Snow shovelers with rotary at Cardinal clear out spur switch by hand.

J. B. Schoolland Collection

Rotary and three locomotives, Nos. 31, 32, and 30 stop near Cardinal so snow shovelers can do final clearing. No. 30 is coupled ahead of bridge crew car.

impossible to keep the line open owing to the great snowfall on the south side of Left Hand Canon. If it were possible, the money required would be several times the income received at Ward.

On May 9th a train reached Puzzler — the first in more than four months. It brought up empty cars for White Raven ore, took down the loaded cars. Warm west winds and blazing sun, not court orders, had cleared the cuts.[41]

Once again the Switzerland Trail prepared for a big summer business. The first excursion of the year reached Ward in June.[42] From then on excursion after excursion train went out, the revenues swelling the bank balance. Gradually officials and crews forgot the terrible winter.

On June 29th an event occurred in an obscure city in Bosnia, Serajeveo, that was to change the face of the world. A student, maddened with the oppression of his Slavic people by the Hapsburgs of Austria-Hungary, killed the Austrian Crown Prince and his wife.[43]

It was a happy summer for the Switzerland Trail. The new service by train to Ward and from Ward to Estes Park by Stanley Steamer was a success. "No other route furnishes such a variety of scenic beauties," wrote Dr. J. C. Jower, state biologist of Missouri, to L. R. Ford.

In August the DB&W made a change that pleased its crews. A new state law required the installation of electric headlights, so atop the locomotive boilers went turbo-generators and into the headlights went carbon rods that made an intense arc light.[44]

Now engineers and firemen could see several hundred yards ahead of their swaying locomotives on the darkest nights.

President W. B. Hayes resigned in October to return to Pennsylvania to take charge of a big family-owned woodworking plant. He recommended retention of the office force and personnel of all departments.[45]

On November 20th at the annual meeting, Charles V. Martin of Oswego, New York, was elected President; Wm. Culbertson of Girard, Pa., Vice President; L. R. Ford, General Manager and Auditor; Charles M. Williams, Secretary-Treasurer and Superintendent.[46]

General Manager Ford predicted increased business for 1915 — the Panama Pacific Exposition year — because of heavy tourist and ore tonnage traffic. Retiring President Hayes laughed at a story in a local newspaper that the directors contemplated pulling up the tracks. "Nothing said about it," said Hayes, "—a pipe dream."

The portentous year drew to a close. The Germans had swiftly marched through Belgium, smashing the stout forts barring their way. The French had thrown them back at the Battle of the Marne and they were down now to bitter trench warfare in the mud and cold of northern France. The Panama Canal had been opened to ocean-going vessels. In Colorado a bitter coal mine strike raged, with men killed and wounded.

To cap it all for the Switzerland Trail of America, Hickox & Son received a luxurious new seven-passenger Stanley Steamer. They now had seven cars in service.[47]

[41]*Ibid.*, May 8, 1914.
[42]*Ibid.*, May 29, 1914.
[43]*Ibid.*, July 3, 1914.
[44]*Boulder Tribune*, August 7, 1914.

[45]*Ibid.*, October 30, 1914.
[46]*Ibid.*, November 20, 1914.
[47]*Boulder Tribune*, December 12, 1914.

Chapter VII

THE TUNGSTEN BOOM AND WORLD WAR I

Nineteen fifteen was fateful in the life of the Switzerland Trail of America. In February General Manager L. R. Ford, slender little dynamo of a man, always dressed in old-fashioned elegance with snowy stand-up wing collar, announced a new daily service by Stanley Steamer from Ward to Estes Park.[1]

During the tourist season the Estes Park Transportation Company, owned by F. O. Stanley, Hall, and Rockwell would operate on schedule with the DB&W trains. The new stage line would be known as The Rocky Mountain National Park Auto Route.

Mr. Ford also succeeded in making Boulder and Ward common passenger points, with stop-over privileges in Boulder, printing of tickets in the name of Boulder.

The Estes Park Transportation Co. had been operating nine and twelve-passenger Stanley Steamers for several years from Loveland to Estes Park. They also used several Stanley Mountain Wagons as baggage trucks.

The ink had little more than dried on the agreement when competition reared its head. The Boulder National Park Transportation Company filed articles of incorporation, bought out the Hickox Transportation Company, and ordered three new Stanley Steamers. They announced double daily service between Boulder and the Rocky Mountain National Park, also Nederland, Lakewood, and Eldora and special excursions to Rowena, Ward, Allen's Park, and Estes Park.[2]

Better roads were to aid the competition —at public expense. Up in Boulder Canon trusties—convicts—from the Colorado State Penitentiary were rebuilding the narrow wagon and stage road to a full two-way route.[3] Drivers of steam or gas cars could then gaily zip up and down the canon.

In March the eastern officials of the Denver, Boulder & Western came to Boulder to confer with leading shippers. They would either have to raise rates and fares or shut down the railroad. During the past year the Switzerland Trail had failed to earn its operating expenses. The officials asked for an increase of 20 percent.

The shippers generally agreed, realizing that the DB&W rates were below those of comparable mountain railroads. They were far lower than charges for hauling by slow freight wagon to Boulder and loading on standard gauge cars.[4]

In April the State Public Utilities Commission granted the 20 percent increase.[5]

At the same time the new Rocky Mountain Transportation Company met the competition of the MacKenzie Brothers of Nederland, who were operating Stanley Steamers between Boulder and the tungsten camps. They reduced the one-way fare from $1.50 to 50 cents, the round-trip from $2.75 to $1.00. People gaily rode the steamers.[6]

With the spring the war in Europe broke out in fresh fury. On May 7th the Cunard liner "Lusitania" was torpedoed by a German submarine with the loss of 114 Americans.[7]

The Switzerland Trail went ahead with its summer excursions. In June it issued two

[1]Boulder Tribune, February 19, 1915.
[2]Boulder Tribune, February 26, 1915.

[3]Ibid., February 19, 1915.
[4]Ibid., March 12, 1915.
[5]Ibid., April 23, 1915.
[6]Ibid., April 23, 1915.
[7]Boulder Tribune, May 14, 1915.

beautiful folders for free distribution.[8] One described the Estes Park trip via Ward, the other concentrated on the beauties of the Switzerland Trail.

The 5th of July (the 4th was on a Sunday) was a busy day on the Trail, with excursion trains rumbling up and down Four Mile Canon. Every available man was pressed into duty, including some new to the DB&W.[9]

Train No. 36 was on its regular trip from Eldora and had made its scheduled stop at Salina. Walter Flint of Denver was engineer, Earl Keith, eighteen years old, fireman of No. 30.

Conductor C. R. Phillips gave the highball, and Flint whistled off. The train rolled smartly down the short stretch of the heaviest grade on the railroad. Faster and faster it went, passengers clutching their seats in alarm. Then it happened . . .

On a curve (Black Swan) the tender suddenly derailed and turned over. The baggage coach ran ahead, tearing off the fireman's side of the cab, shearing steam lines. Instantly high-pressure steam enveloped the cab, billowed back into the baggage car. The mail messenger, George Shull, and the baggage messenger, Harry Cluphf, jumped. Flint was already on the ground.

From the fireman's side came agonizing screams. Flint leaped back into the cab, tried valiantly to find his fireman. The scalding steam drove him back.

The screaming stopped. A low agonizing moan went up. Then silence, terrible silence.

In the following coach, which turned over on its side, General Manager Ford and Conductor Phillips managed to apply first-aid to the five slightly injured passengers and calm the others.

The steam finally escaped from the boiler and a hushed silence fell. When the men reached Keith he was dead. Whether he died

from the crushing blow or scalding steam no one ever knew.

No man knows exactly why or how the accident happened.

In August a bright new star appeared in the west that gladdened every heart on the DB&W. Nederland was stirring mightily, new buildings going up. It was spoken of as the tungsten center of the world.[10]

Experienced miners, even boys and women were combing the hills for float—the tell-tale surface ore brought down by erosion from veins higher up. They found an eager market at local mills. Men began sorting over mine dumps for low-grade ore that in the old days would not pay milling charges.

In October tungsten miners' wages went up 20 percent. In November the price of tungsten advanced.[11] At the end of the year a new schedule of 60% ore ran $2.25 a pound, $45 a unit or $4,500 a ton.[12]

Nederland roared with a boom. So crowded was the street with freighters' teams and wagons, Stanley Steamers, and people that one had difficulty getting through. Drinking, gambling, gay women—everything went. Money from the black metal, so much in demand in manufacturing war material, flowed like Boulder Creek's waters.

Eighty percent of the tungsten produced in the United States was coming from Boulder County. The estimated value of the 1915 production was placed at $1,687,329.[13]

Freight poured into the Switzerland Trail's loading dock at the Boulder freight station. Trains went out heavily loaded to the hills, and crews began unloading at Tungsten station, one-half mile west of Sugar Loaf. They unloaded farther on at Lakewood station freight for Lakewood with its huge Primos Mill that ran night and day. Wolfram was another station. At Cardinal they set out

---

[8]*Ibid.*, June 4, 1915.
[9]*Ibid.*, July 9, 1915.

[10]*Boulder Tribune*, August 27, 1915.
[11]*Ibid.*, October 19, 1915.
[12]*Ibid.*, December 31, 1915.
[13]*Boulder Tribune*, December 31, 1915.

Sturtevant photo. R. H. Kindig Collection

Trestle over Coon Creek at Cardinal. Station is to the right of trestle. Beyond trestle is sprawling bulk of the Boulder County Mill. Its ore came from a tunnel that ran 6,000 feet into the mountain to right. Two miles up Coon Creek lay Caribou, once great silver mining camp, now all but dead.

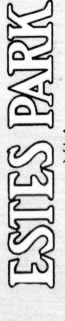

ESTES PARK

VIA

THE SWITZERLAND TRAIL OF AMERICA

DENVER BOULDER & WESTERN RR

AND AUTO FROM WARD, COLO

THE ROCKY MOUNTAIN
NATIONAL PARK ROUTE

ESTES PARK

VIA

THE SWITZERLAND TRAIL OF AMERICA

DENVER BOULDER & WESTERN RR

AND AUTO FROM WARD COLO

THE ROCKY MOUNTAIN
NATIONAL PARK ROUTE

Crossen Collection

Front and back cover of folder issued in 1915

ROUND TRIP FARES

VIA THE SWITZERLAND TRAIL—ROCKY MOUNTAIN NATIONAL PARK ROUTE

Tickets on Sale Daily July 1, 1915, to September 10, 1915

TO	FROM		
	DENVER Return Limit Oct. 31st (See Note)	BOULDER Return Limit Oct. 31st (See Note)	BOULDER Limit 30 Days
Estes Park	$9.60	$7.80	*$7.00
	Limit Sept. 10, 1915	Limit Sept. 10, 1915	One Way Rates from Boulder
Long's Peak Inn	$7.85	$6.25	$3.50
The Columbines	7.85	6.25	3.50
Hewes & Kirkwood Inn	7.85	6.25	3.50
Copeland Lake	7.10	5.50	3.00
Allen's Park	7.10	5.50	3.00
Peaceful Valley	5.60	4.00	2.25

One Way Rate BETWEEN Estes Park and Boulder, $4.00

*Applies also from Estes Park if routed both ways via the "Switzerland Trail." Note.—Return limit Sept. 10th if return trip is made via Ward.

HOTELS IN ESTES PARK

NAME	P. O. Address (Colorado)	Rates Per Week
Elkhorn Lodge	Estes Park	$16.00—$30.00
Hewes-Kirkwood Inn	Estes Park	12.00— 20.00
Horseshoe Inn	Estes Park	14.00— 25.00
Hupp Hotel	Estes Park	15.00— 24.00
Lester's Hotel	Estes Park	14.00— 20.00
Long's Peak Inn	Estes Park	15.00— 40.00
Moraine Lodge	Moraine Park	12.00— 21.00
Park Hotel	Estes Park	12.00— 18.00
Stanley Manor	Estes Park	5.00 day up
Stead's Ranch and Hotel	Estes Park	12.00— 17.00
The Hotel Stanley	Estes Park	5.00 day up
The Columbines	Estes Park	14.00— 20.00
The Brinwood	Estes Park	12.00—25.00
The Rockdale	Estes Park	On application
The Crags	Estes Park	13.00— 35.00

Crossen Collection

Travel and hotel rates in 1915 folder.

Copeland Lake and Copeland Mountain

TIME TABLE

Daily July 1 to Sept. 10, 1915
Subject to Change Without Notice

GOING	Miles		Elev.	RETURNING
Lv. {7 50 AM / 8 00 AM}	0	Denver	1 Mile	Ar. 6 05 PM
Lv. 9 15 AM	30	Boulder	5450	Ar. 4 40 PM
Ar. 12 05 PM	56	Ward	9450	Ar. 2 15 PM
(Lunch)		Stanley Steamer, D.B.&W.		(Lunch)
Lv. 1 00 PM	62	Peaceful Valley	8700	Ar. 12 30 Noon
Ar. 1 30 PM	70	Allen's Park	8500	Lv. 12 00 Noon
Ar. 2 15 PM	72	Copeland Lake	8500	Lv. 11 15 AM
Ar. 2 25 PM	76	Hewes-Kirkw'd Inn	9000	Lv. 11 00 AM
Ar. 2 55 PM	77	The Columbines	9000	Lv. 10 30 AM
Ar. 3 05 PM	78	Long's Peak Inn	9000	Lv. 10 20 AM
Ar. 3 45 PM	88	Estes Park	7500	Lv. 10 10 AM / Lv. 9 30 AM

L. R. FORD,
General Manager,
Boulder, Colo.

F. T. HARTMAN,
City Passenger Agent,
17th and California Sts.,
Denver, Colo.

CHAS. D. MARVIN,
President,
Boulder, Colo.

WM. M. CULBERTSON,
Vice-President,
Erie, Pa.

Denver Ticket Offices:
17th and California Sts. (Colo. & So. Ry.) and Union Station

Crossen Collection

Time table in 1915 folder.

229

Mrs. Berta A. Bailey photo. A. A. Paddock Collection

Wreck at Black Swan Curve in Four Mile Canon, July 5, 1915. After a wild runaway of 0.3-mile down the heaviest grade of the system, tender and combo car derailed with tragic results. Youthful fireman, Earl Keith, was killed. At left may be seen lower end of big Black Swan Mill.

Mrs. Berta A. Bailey photo. A. A. Paddock Collection

With horror in their eyes, passengers stand helplessly by as steam escapes from broken pipes of No. 30, unable to rescue entrapped fireman, Earl Keith. Wreck at Black Swan Curve, July 5, 1915. Train No. 36 was enroute to Boulder from Eldora.

cars for Nederland, to be unloaded by freighters and hauled down the road two miles to the big camp.

Even as the DB&W locomotives' exhausts sang their song of power the feeble automobile was growing stronger. Late in November a 30-horsepower auto truck made a trip from Boulder to Sugar Loaf with 4,000 pounds of coal, climbing the steep grade slowly but surely. This load tided the big U. S. Gold Corporation Mill over a delay in a carload shipment of coal on the Switzerland Trail.[14]

The DB&W proudly put into commission a new combination baggage and mail car which was built in its shops.[15] Its personnel, from president to section hand, threw back their shoulders. Let the tungsten boom roar! The railroad rounded out the year with only a trifling loss—$3,459.[16]

Nineteen sixteen began with a rush. *Mining In Boulder County, Colorado,* gives an excellent picture of what happened:

The Boulder County tungsten industry, which began in 1900 when a common 'black iron' ore was discovered to be of commercial value, developed by the close of 1918 into such proportions that there was a total of twenty-two mills, representing an aggregate investment of a million dollars, and hundreds of mines well equipped for operation. The tungsten belt of the county of which Nederland is the center reaches from Wolfram station on the west to Sugar Loaf on the east, and from Beaver Creek across the Middle and North Boulders to Glacier Lake. From this field production gradually increased from 46 tons in 1900 to some 953 tons in 1913. A better market during 1916, 1917 and 1918 stimulating a boom in tungsten mining which brought the county's yield up to an average of 2500 tons, 250,000 units per year for these past three years. Tungsten was called by some authorities the 'Key Mineral' of the war, being used for high-speed tool steel, valve steel, ordnance, armor-piercing steel, and various other purposes vital to the prosecution of the war. Fully 95% of local production was used in this manner.

The tungsten district was roughly 12 miles east and west, 9 miles north and south.

Before World War I began high-speed tool steel was worth about 70 cents a pound, tungsten about 60 cents a pound and tungsten ore about $6 a unit. In 1916 tool steel sold at $3 a pound, tungsten about $5 a pound, and tungsten ore about $50 a unit. Even with these high prices supplies were scarce.[17]

The DB&W profited in odd ways. Once a carload of tungsten ore from the Copeland Ranch on South Boulder Creek reached Lakewood for milling. It had been shipped on the Moffat Railroad to Denver, routed over the C&S to Boulder, where it was transferred to a narrow gauge car and taken to Cardinal for its final trip by wagon to the mill.[18]

Automobile travel to Nederland and the tungsten camps was increasing. The convicts kept steadily improving the Boulder Canon road, over which Stanley Steamers and improved gasoline cars rolled more easily. Even Model T Fords made the grades, their radiators spouting.[19]

On March 16th the tungsten price zoomed to $90 a unit for 60% ore.[20] The stampede set in in earnest, the flats and even the hills around Nederland sprouting tents and shacks. The boom roared even louder.

The newcomers protested the slow delivery of mail, which came up on the DB&W. They began circulating a petition to give the contract to one of the automobile transportation firms. The petition reached Boulder, and at once a protest arose against it. This would hurt the road, which had had such a hard time to exist.[21]

Suddenly dangerous c o m p e t i t i o n loomed. Between Nederland and the Gilpin County line to the south an estimated 2,000 men were combing the hills for tungsten leads. The Moffat Railroad began giving better service to nearby Rollinsville. If the

[14]*Ibid.,* November 26, 1915.
[15]*Ibid.,* October 1, 1915.
[16]*Bulletin No. 65, Railway and Locomotive Historical Society.*

[17]*Boulder Tribune,* January 14, 1916.
[18]*Ibid.,* January 21, 1916.
[19]*Ibid.,* February 18, 1916.
[20]*Ibid.,* March 17, 1916.
[21]*Boulder Tribune,* February 11, 1916.

Berta M. Bailey photo. Courtesy R. A. Curtis

Wreck of Train No. 36 at Black Swan Curve, July 5, 1915.

Berta M. Bailey photo. Courtesy R. A. Curtis

Wreck of Train No. 36 at Black Swan Curve, July 5, 1915.

Photo by Mrs. Berta M. Bailey. A. A. Paddock Collection

Derailed tender of No. 30 and combo coach in run-away wreck of July 5, 1915, at Black Swan Curve, 0.3 miles below Salina. Seventeen-year-old Fireman Earl Keith was killed. Steam is rising from broken pipes on his side of the cab. Conductor C. R. Phillips, atop tender, is trying to rescue Keith.

Denver Public Library Western Collection

No. 33 and tender undergoing repairs in the Boulder yards. Engine house is to left.

Early White gasoline-powered truck bus, probably a 1911 or 1912 model. ment of these machines cut deeply into the business of the Denver, Boulder

234

R. H. Kindig Collection

Passenger train heading west from the mouth of Boulder Canon. Wagon road at left. Goat Rock straight ahead, with line of Silver Lake Ditch along the mountain. On the skyline rises Sugar Loaf Mountain.

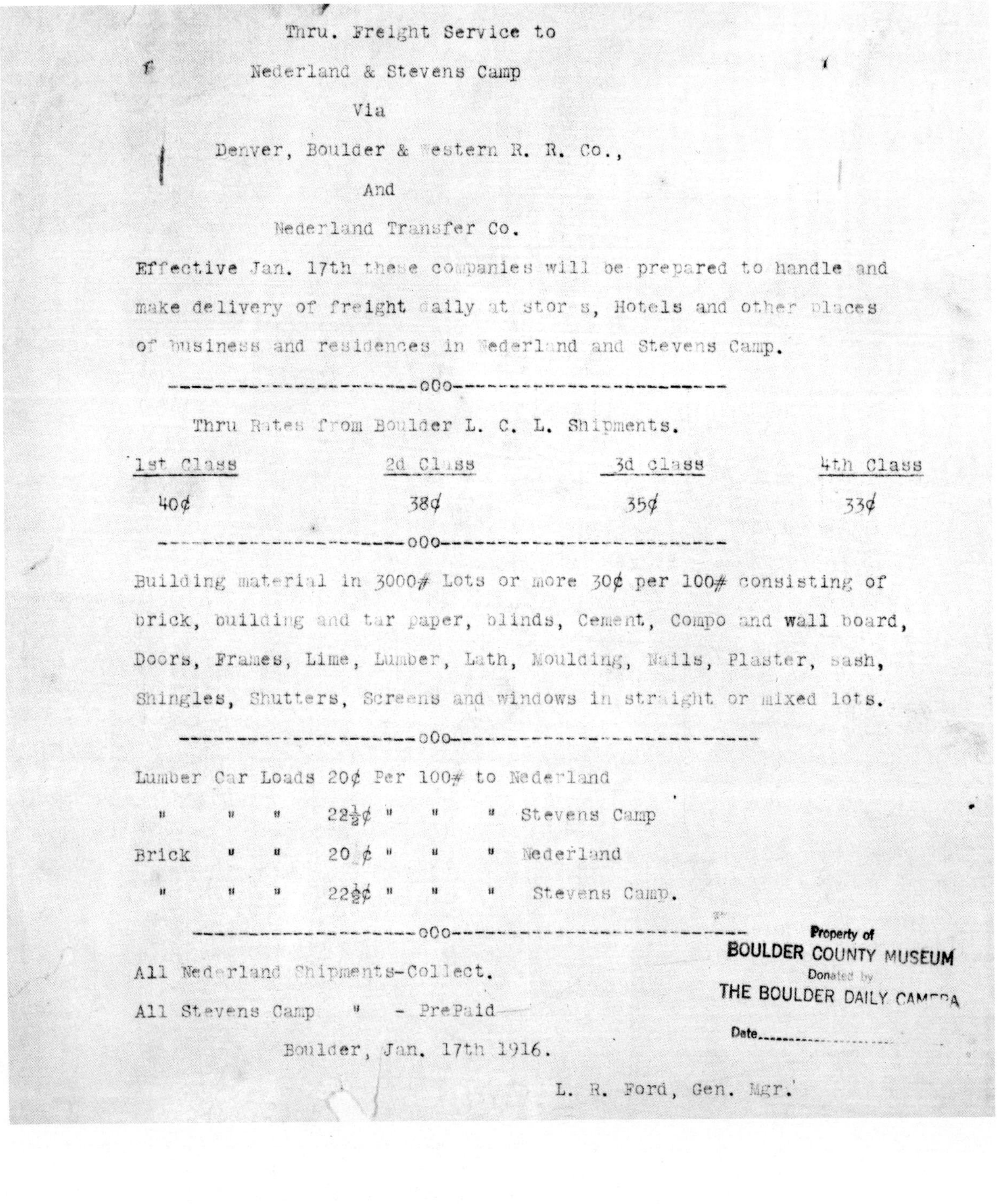

Thru. Freight Service to

Nederland & Stevens Camp

Via

Denver, Boulder & Western R. R. Co.,

And

Nederland Transfer Co.

Effective Jan. 17th these companies will be prepared to handle and
make delivery of freight daily at stores, Hotels and other places
of business and residences in Nederland and Stevens Camp.

-----------------------------oOo---------------------------------

Thru Rates from Boulder L. C. L. Shipments.

1st Class	2d Class	3d class	4th Class
40¢	38¢	35¢	33¢

-----------------------------oOo---------------------------------

Building material in 3000# Lots or more 30¢ per 100# consisting of
brick, building and tar paper, blinds, Cement, Compo and wall board,
Doors, Frames, Lime, Lumber, Lath, Moulding, Nails, Plaster, sash,
Shingles, Shutters, Screens and windows in straight or mixed lots.

-----------------------------oOo---------------------------------

Lumber Car Loads 20¢ Per 100# to Nederland

    "   "   " 22½¢ " " " Stevens Camp

Brick " " 20 ¢ " " " Nederland

    "   "   " 22½¢ " " " Stevens Camp.

-----------------------------oOo---------------------------------

All Nederland Shipments-Collect.

All Stevens Camp " - PrePaid

Boulder, Jan. 17th 1916.

L. R. Ford, Gen. Mgr.

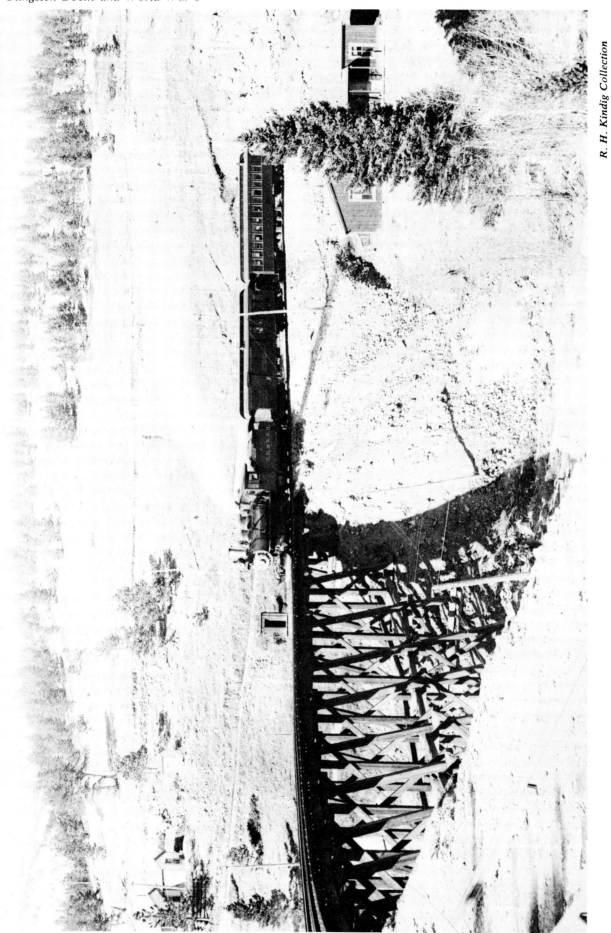

No. 32 about to start across trestle at Cardinal with her train for Eldora. Cardinal was the station for Nederland during the tungsten boom.

road to Nederland were improved, trucks and wagons could serve the big tungsten camp and get the business.[22]

By the end of April 1,500 people were receiving mail at the Nederland postoffice. It was estimated that 3,000 people were residing in the district around the camp. Some said this figure was far too low.[23]

In many places businessmen left their business, other men left their jobs, others their wives and hurried to Nederland. Some were destined to amass quick fortunes.

Increased business to Nederland was forcing the DB&W to run an extra train nearly every day, this in addition to the "Red Ball," which left Boulder early each morning. Fifteen men were handling freight at the Boulder station, the greater part of which was transferred for shipment to Cardinal and other tungsten district points. The Boulder station was doing its greatest volume of business.[24]

Conditions at the far end of the line were causing friction. The two-mile haul from Cardinal caused delay and expense. Nederland had the rugged pride of all boom towns; it wanted a railroad and an attractive station.

Prominent shippers, businessmen, bankers, and miners of Boulder and Nederland signed petitions recommending t h a t the DB&W be extended from Sulphide Flats to Nederland, a distance of 2 miles. The Boulder Commercial Association presented them to L. R. Ford, to be forwarded to the directors of the railroad.[25]

The real threat was that the tungsten business would go to Denver via the Moffat Railroad.

It was estimated that $15,000 would build the extension. It could use the grade over which construction trains had run during the Barker Dam building.

The directors answered this appeal,

President Charles D. Marvin and Vice President Wm. M. Culbertson arriving in Boulder in mid-May.[26] They carefully began going over the proposed extension, viewing the tungsten boom with cautious eyes.

They were spurred on by the Moffat Railroad, which was waging an active campaign to secure freight and passenger business. The Moffat put on a special tungsten train, arranged for an auto line to run between Nederland and Rollinsville. They even opened a depot in Nederland.

Marvin and Culbertson met with the Boulder Commercial Association and laid their cards on the table. If their stockholders would agree, they would stand half the expense of the extension. General Manager Ford gave a careful estimate for building the 2.3-mile line — b e t w e e n $14,000 and $15,000.

The people of Boulder were spurred on by the report of Secretary Eben Fine of the Commercial Association, who had accompanied the DB&W officials. He had counted 33 freight cars at Rollinsville loaded with merchandise for Nederland.

In Denver officials of the Moffat Railroad were talking with businessmen about improving the road between Rollinsville and Nederland.

A short time later, merchants and miners of Nederland, long demanding a better road to Rollinsville, had a promise of action. The commissioners of Boulder County ordered a survey for an improvement of the road.[27]

It seemed an easy task for determined men to raise donations of $7,000 to put in the Nederland extension. Then unforseeable fate struck again.

The price of tungsten slumped. One buyer on June 16th announced that he would pay $28 for 60% ore, $23 for 50%.[28] The mines and mills began to retrench. There was

[22]*Ibid.,* February 25, 1916.
[23]*Ibid.,* April 28, 1916.
[24]*Ibid.,* March 28, 1916.
[25]*Boulder Tribune,* April 28, 1916.

[26]*Ibid.,* May 19, 1916.
[27]*Boulder Tribune,* June 2, 1916.
[28]*Ibid.,* June 16, 1916.

L. C. McClure photo
Denver Public Library Western Collection

C&N No. 1 approaching Sunset tank with one-coach train. On the canon wall to the upper left may be seen the Ward branch. At the upper right is the grade made by the Greeley, Salt Lake & Pacific that eventually became the Eldora branch.

Two levels of track on the hard climb out of Four Mile Canon on the Ward branch. Top level is west of Mont Alto Park.

A. A. Paddock Collection

C&N No. 31 at Eldora before station was built. Ladies and gentleman are enjoying the singing beauty of Boulder Creek on a summer day.

COASTING ON CULBERTSON PASS, ON "THE SWITZERLAND TRAIL OF AMERICA,"
The Colorado & Northwestern Railroad, Denver to Eldora and Ward.

Postal card from A. A. Paddock Collection

One of the Big thrills remembered by favored passengers was riding up to Mont Alto Park or Glacier Lake on a train with a push car hooked behind. When they had enjoyed the resort, they made the return trip on the car.

The sun was high overhead on a summer day when Miss Helen Sherman took this shot of the Ward-bound mixed train from the Eldora line across Four Mile Canon.

gloom in the Nederland gambling houses and parlors of the gay girls.

Boulder County no longer had a monopoly on the production of tungsten. South Dakota, Utah, Arizona, New Mexico, Idaho, and. other parts of Colorado were mining it. Some was being imported from South America and Japan.[29]

The Estes Park business helped counteract this gloom. That summer an average of 25 passengers a day came into Ward and transferred to the big Stanley Mountain Wagons. One day 66 arrived, all laughing and gay as they set out on the new road winding through spruce and pine of unspoiled mountain land.[30]

R. D. Ward, agent at Ward then, said, "The buses from Estes Park were there at noon. The business got to be a big thing when they extended the road to Raymond's. They had been running up the South St. Vrain (from Lyons) to Estes Park for years. The road from Peaceful Valley to Raymond's was just an old wagon road. When they improved that road, I've seen a dozen big buses (Stanley Steamers), mostly red ones, there at Raymond's.

"I've seen old (F. O.) Stanley there in Ward more than once: One day Jane Adams of Hull House in Chicago came in on the train. I had the pleasure of meeting her."[31]

At Ward the automobile was helping the Switzerland Trail. Over in Boulder Canon it was taking business away. Near the end of August the convicts finished work in the "Narrows," that most difficult and steep part of the canon, and the road was opened to Nederland.[32] More and more Stanley Mountain Wagons rolled up there with every seat filled, every space filled with freight. More and more White gas trucks, offshoots of the fine steamers built by the White Sewing Ma-

chine Company, were grinding up the steep grades with freight, often going directly to the mines.

At the annual meeting in October the Switzerland Trail reported its greatest business volume since the construction of the Barker Dam.[33] That fiscal year it made a profit of $10,493.[34]

The DB&W planted 250,000 trout in streams and lakes along its right-of-way that year. L. R.Ford smilingly said that the railroad hoped to make Boulder County a fisherman's paradise.[35]

"We formed the Ward Improvement Association," said R. D. Ward, "and stocked the lakes to the west. When I went up to Ward in 1905, there weren't any fish in those upper lakes—Long, Isabell, Duck, Brainerd, and Mitchell. We put fingerlings in, and the next summer they were dandy fellows. The DB&W hauled the fish up for us free, and Boulder people who built cabins up there helped distribute them. Then they'd come up on the trains to fish."[36]

As 1917 began Boulder County was gradually recovering from its tungsten spree. People looked back on a record production of $5,357,732 for 1916, a price rise from $15 a unit for 60% ore to $90. Only for a little while had this dizzy figure held. In January, 1917, it was quoted at $15.[37]

The mines, however, still continued to operate, for the war in Europe ground on.

The people of Nederland had reason to think more kindly of the Switzerland Trail. The winter was severe and their favorite fuel —high-grade bituminous coal from Routt County—failed to come through Rollinsville on the Moffat Railroad. The DB&W brought up coal from Boulder County mines in its daily train and kept the camp from suffering.[38]

[29]*Ibid.*, July 21, 1916.
[30]*Boulder Tribune*, August 18, 1916.
[31]Interview with R. D. Ward, July 15, 1957.
[32]*Boulder Tribune*, August 25, 1916.

[33]*Ibid.*, October 6, 1916.
[34]*Bulletin No. 65, Railway and Locomotive Historical Society.*
[35]*Boulder Tribune*, October 27, 1916.
[36]Interview, July 15, 1957.
[37]*Boulder Tribune*, January 5, 1917.
[38]*Ibid.*, February 9, 1917.

Back in Boulder after a glorious day's sightseeing, these happy people are about to step down from DB&W observation coach No. 16. To left is water tank which stood directly east of the Boulder station. To the right is the third rail spur going into the McAllister Lumber Co. Refreshment stand to right did big business with the many trains, standard and narrow gauge. Time: 1916.

Courtesy Elbert Hubbard

Pretty girls greet crew of mixed train No. 8 coming down Four Mile Canon a short distance above Wall Street. House is summer residence of Charles O. Erbaugh, Denver attorney, who took this photo. No. 31 has cone screen spark arrester over smokestack, bespeaking dry condition of timber. Elbert "Jimmie" Hubbard, then a brakeman, atop boxcar. Time: 1916.

Party on push car pauses at Salina station on a fine summer afternoon.

Push car on the Eldora branch, with Continental Divide peaks in the background.

C. G. Hickox of Boulder was back in the transportation business. He began replacing his Stanley Steamers with improved gasoline machines.[39]

On April 6, 1917, drawn-faced men and women read the momentous news of the United States' declaration of war on Germany. The better informed ones knew that their world would never be the same again.

Many shook their heads as they read of the revolution in Russia, the deposing of the Czar, the return of the political exiles from Siberia and Lenin from Switzerland.

Meanwhile trains must be kept running, mines must be kept producing, people must earn their way in the world. On April 12th the Ward branch of the DB&W was opened as far as Puzzler, after having been closed for over a month by deep snowdrifts. Miners from the White Raven Mine, which wanted to make a shipment of ore, dug out the snow on contract for the railroad.[40]

June came with its exhilarating warm days and cool nights. The prosperity of the vastly increased war production reached nearly everyone. Tourists arrived, stepped aboard the trains of the Switzerland Trail to see the now widely advertised scenic wonders. The tungsten mines continued big production. The DB&W was a busy railroad.

That month a tragic accident occurred. "Switzerland Trail Push Car Gets Loose and Kills Boy Crossing Railroad Tracks" read a front-page headline of the *Boulder Tribune*.[41]

[39]*Boulder Tribune*, February 16, 1917.
[40]*Ibid.*, April 13, 1917.
[41]*Ibid.*, June 15, 1917.

That Sunday W. R. Keet, Master Mechanic of the DB&W, and two men had gone to Mile Post 12, 4 miles above Salina, to do some special work. They had gone up on a push car, which they had hitched to the regular Eldora train, No. 35. They uncoupled the push car and blocked the wheels.

Suddenly they looked around and saw the car moving down the heavy grade. They ran after it, only to see it pick up speed, tantalizingly keep out of their reach.

The agent at Salina saw the car go past. He telephoned Boulder, and the dispatcher immediately called the agent at Crisman to derail it. The agent ran out, just as the car whizzed by at terrific speed.

Down in the Boulder yards was the next derail. Men set it, anxiously settled down to watching the track.

A perverse fate led the boy, Donald Anderson, age 9, out on Bridge No. 2, just below the mouth of Boulder Canon. The car hit him, careened off into the creek. How it had stayed on the rails for 10 miles is still a mystery.

Push cars had been widely used. This was the first fatal accident.

The Switzerland Trail had been remarkably free of accidents. A handful of people had been killed, a few had been injured, but the record was envied by many railroads in gentle terrain. Had the revenue end been as perfect as its train operation, the Switzerland Trail would have had a far different ending.

Part II

Chapter VIII

THE END OF THE TRAIL

Ten thousand tourists traveled over the Switzerland Trail during the 1917 summer season.[1] This seemed to belie the insufficient business complaint of the Colorado & Southern that led to cancellation of the joint operating agreement in 1916 and removal of the third rail to Denver.

Despite this optimistic picture, the Switzerland Trail was in trouble. In September it applied to the Colorado State Public Utilities Commission for permission to raise freight rates, listing the following reasons:

A funded debt of $700,000 bearing 5% interest, outstanding capital stock of $300,000, no dividends ever declared or paid on its capital stock, operating expenses and taxes for the four and one-half years ending December 31, 1915, exceeding its gross operating revenue by $24,427.93. It was faced with increased cost of locomotive coal, of which it burned 4,000 tons a year. It had had to increase wages of all track men.

In mid-September it abandoned daily train service to Ward. It would run a mixed train once a week, with regular stage service between Sunset and Ward.[2]

Over at Nederland, Warden Tynan's convict road builders were building a good road around the north shore of Barker Reservoir—to benefit the DB&W's rival automobile stages and trucks.[3]

Employees, hill people, businessmen, and friends of the DB&W in Boulder drew back in shocked surprise at a story in the *Boulder Tribune* of November 9th.

---

[1]*Boulder Tribune,* September 7, 1917.
[2]*Ibid.,* September 21, 1917.
[3]*Ibid.,* October 19, 1917.

"You may say that we have decided to dismantle the road and discontinue business entirely," said Charles D. Marvin, president of the Denver, Boulder & Western road yesterday. . . ."

"We regret it, Mr. Marvin and I," said Mr. Culbertson. "We had hoped to 'carry through' as the English say, but we have borne the load for five years ourselves and what's the use? It isn't business and we can't do it any longer. . . ."

"Have you given orders to Mr. Ford when to discontinue service?" Mr. Marvin was asked.

"No. We will wind it up right away. We shall have to get the consent of the Public Utilities commission to junk it. We expect the order because it is only fair to us. There is now great demand for rolling stock and rails. They are needed for the service of the country here and abroad. Our five (six) locomotives are powerful and may play a prominent part for the country in Europe, who knows? Anyway we can dispose of our rolling stock and rails now and get back a few dollars of the great amount we have spent trying to operate the road without loss."

So spoke the retired banker of Oswego, New York.

Boulder people temporarily forgot the war, which had already taken some of their sons. The threatened Switzerland Trail was suddenly very dear to them. Anxiously they awaited the decision of the Public Utilities Commission.

On November 24th the commission issued the following order against the Denver, Boulder & Western:

"First not to sell or dispose of its property of any kind until further notice of the commission.

"Also, to continue to operate the railroad until further order of the commission, and to appear before the commission in the hearing room December 10th at 10 o'clock a.m. to show cause why it should not continue to operate its road."

The newspaper story continued, "The secretary of the commission was ordered to notify shippers and others interested through the public press of the warning.

"On October 13th, in hope that the road could be helped to a continuance of operations the commission allowed it an increase in rates, but the owners now say they can not operate the road at a profit. . . ."[4]

At the hearing officials of the railroad and protestants of the abandonment met head-on.

General Manager Ford showed that during the period, 1907-11, revenues of the railroad were gratifying. Since then they had gradually decreased.

E. E. Whitted, counsel for the railroad, testified that the net income was only $30,000 in 15 years and that at present the liabilities exceeded the assets.

(State) Senator H. O. Andrew of Boulder represented the White Raven Mining Company, one of the DB&W's heaviest shippers. He cross-examined Mr. Ford, bringing out that the railroad had recently offered the property for sale at $285,000, but that several years before it had asked $215,000.

"This is a scheme to junk the road," declared the senator, "instead of allowing its operation to continue. These owners are simply taking advantage of the advance in junk prices and are making the most of the opportunity. They have not given citizens of Boulder County an opportunity to take over the road at a reasonable figure in order to continue operations."

Senator Andrew had support from the United States Gold Corporation, the Up-to-Date Mining Company and the Allied Gold Mining Company, represented by attorney John R. Wolff of Boulder; the City of Boulder; Long Lake Lumber Company and committees representing the Boulder and Eldora commercial clubs.[5]

The decision to abandon or not to abandon was not long in coming.

"The Colorado Public Utilities commission today (Dec. 26th) rendered its opinion on the application of the Denver, Boulder & Western railroad to abandon its line. The commission decides it must continue to operate and the order forbids it to dispose of any of its property and orders it to continue to operate under the increased rates granted by the commission until further orders by the board.

". . . The DB&W failed to show this (that it cannot earn its operating expenses), the commission holds."

It found that for 10½ years the road earned $73,300 net and only in three of those years it failed to earn its operating expenses, also that operation under the new increased freight rates had not been tried out sufficiently.[6] It considered seriously the water works construction of the City of Boulder, to which continued railroad operation was vital. It took note of the fact that the owners had turned down the opportunity to construct the Nederland extension, thereby losing business to trucks and automobiles.

"The commission holds that when a railroad begins operations it gets advantages which other business does not get and because of these takes on burdens to serve the public adequately and, without consent of the state, it cannot quit unless it shows there is no demand for it and that it can not pay operating expenses.

---

[4]*Boulder Tribune*, November 30, 1917.

[5]*Boulder Tribune*, December 13, 1917.
[6]Table of outline of the railroad's financial operations gives a total for three profit years—1909, 1910, and 1916—of $56,371. From *Bulletin No. 65, Railway and Locomotive Historical Society.*

Lawrence Bass photo. A. A. Paddock Collection

C&N track rounds Goat Rock a short distance above the mouth of Boulder Canon. The wooden flume carries irrigation water from Boulder Creek through a break in the rock.

Trestle over Boulder Creek below Profile Rock and mouth of Four Mile Creek. Note fine Ashler stone masonry pier laid up for the Greeley, Salt Lake & Pacific in 1882.

Sturtevant photo. R. H. Kindig Collection

Freight wagon descending the high road to Salina above C&N track. This is Cobb's Pitch, one-half mile above Crisman.

University of Colorado Museum Collection

C&N main line along Four Mile Creek above Crisman. Mine dumps in the far background are of the Logan mines, No. 1, 2, 3, and 4 in Sunbeam Gulch.

"Paying interest on stocks and bonds is not considered in an application for a road to commit suicide. It must show that it can't live. The Denver, Boulder & Western in the commission's belief, can continue to live and serve the public. As long as earnings will move trains roads must continue to serve the public."—*Boulder Tribune*, Dec. 28, 1917.

In January, 1918, the superintendent of the Wolf Tongue tungsten mill and businessmen of Nederland sent a petition to the Colorado Public Utilities Commission. It asked that body to urge the DB&W to build the Nederland extension.[7]

The move was too late. The Nederland boom had collapsed. Business during the past year had decreased 50%.[8] Miners were still bringing out tungsten but the boom was over.

That spring the DB&W trains went out more lightly loaded than ever before. Boulder businessmen shook their heads solemnly. At a Commercial Association meeting they voted to do everything possible to aid the struggling railroad. They deemed it necessary to the mining and tourist business.[9]

In July the railroad had another streak of bad luck. A dam near the head of Left Hand Creek went out, and the resulting flood washed out the California Gulch bridge.[10] It came at the height of the tourist season, with passengers at Ward boarding the buses for Estes Park.

General Manager Ford quickly solved the problem. The railroad would operate to Puzzler, little station set amidst tall spruces of a grassy gulch running into Left Hand Canon. The Estes Park buses would pick up the passengers there.

Summer slipped past and autumn came again to the Rockies. Suddenly a rumor ran through the land, then a reality that made all hearts skip a beat, then swell wildly with joy.

World War I was over!

In the months that followed times were never harder on the Switzerland Trail. The tungsten mining stopped almost entirely. The railroad company laid off men, keeping only a skeleton crew of the oldest employees. Bill Tipps still went out at the throttle of his beloved No. 32, Pat Dinley firing for him. Pat was a fine engineer himself. Men scattered to other railroads, their experience in handling trains on the DB&W a good recommendation.

Somehow they struggled through the weary winter, which carried the added terror of the Spanish Influenza epidemic.

In March lights burned late in General Manager Ford's office. Solemn-faced men came and went. On March 28th the Denver, Boulder & Western Railroad Company sent a letter to the Public Utilities Commission of Colorado.

On May 1, 1919, it would permanently discontinue service, surrender its charter, take up its tracks, dismantle its property, remove and dispose of it. It would cancel and withdraw all tariffs. The corporation could not, under present conditions, be operated so as to pay its operating expenses and taxes.

For the press Mr. Ford said sadly: "I can no longer advise the company to try to operate the road. The closing of the tungsten industry made even me abandon hope that the road could some day be made to pay."[11]

The Public Utilities Commission ordered the DB&W to continue service until further notice. It would hold an investigation and hearing.[12]

Protests against abandonment had already been filed by the City of Boulder, residents of Ward, and heads of mining properties.

The Denver, Boulder & Western learned that abandoning a railroad is a long and trying business. The PUC notified the DB&W officials that before their request to abandon could be acted upon, the abandonment appli-

[7]*Boulder Tribune*, January 25, 1918.
[8]*Boulder Tribune*, February 22, 1918.
[9]*Ibid.*, May 3, 1918.
[10]*Ibid.*, July 26, 1918.

[11]*Boulder Tribune*, April 4, 1919.
[12]*Ibid.*, April 25, 1919.

A. A. Paddock Collection

Combo No. 51 coach train at the Eldora station.

Copy photo by Jack Thode. R. H. Kindig Collection

C&NW No. 32. In 1908 this engine was rebuilt at the Colorado & Southern Denver Shops at a cost of $4,000. Her cylinders were rebored, making them 16½ by 20 inches.

Switch for siding (right) that ran down to south shore of Glacier Lake.
This was part of the wye. Section house directly ahead.

George Hickox at the wheel of one of the early gasoline-powered Whites
that replaced the Stanley Steamers. Behind them is the stone garage
in Boulder that was formerly a livery stable.

No. 1 under steam in the Boulder yards. By this time her runs were occasional.

Photo by Clint O. Dumm

DB&W No. 1 in the Boulder yards. To right of her tender may be seen part of the steam-driven coal loader.

cation filed in November, 1917, would have to be acted upon. This had come about because of arguments by John R. Wolff, the attorney for the protestants.[13]

The railroad's attorneys at once filed application for reopening of the original application. The road was granted a hearing on June 16th.

The railroad continued operation. On June 4th it began operating a daily train, except Saturday, to Eldora. On Saturday the train would run to Ward. Summer rates were in effect.[14]

The stockholders held their annual meeting on June 4th, all wondering if they would ever meet again. The old officers were re-elected. L. R. Ford was re-appointed General Manager.[15]

The *Boulder Tribune* added a heartening note that is reminiscent of the old individualistic journalism of the frontier: "The Switzerland Trail of America is a valuable asset which it is hoped can be saved to Boulder. The owners are rich men and honorable men who will obey the law though first and last the road has cost them all and more than they invested in it.

"It will conduct a summer passenger schedule of trains to both Eldora and Ward and these will be popular rides for the great crowd of summer tourists here.

"Citizens who have not taken the trip should take it. Those who have not taken it recently will be delighted and surprised by the varied scenery it takes them through."

The June 16th hearing lasted two days. L. R. Ford, the railroad's sole witness, testified that it had steadily lost money during the last few years. The protestants declared that closing the railroad would jeopardize the mining industry in Boulder County. The City of Boulder added its protest.

L. W. Ewing of the White Raven Mining Company stated that the railroad officials

would never put a price on the road or for the junk value of rails and rolling stock. Mining interests had tried to get a price. He was ready to undertake raising money to purchase it within 90 days after an agreement was reached as to its value.[16]

On July 24, 1919, the Colorado PUC issued an order permitting the junking of the Denver, Boulder & Western on September 15th.[17]

The railroad had 46.2 miles of main lines, 4 miles of sidings, 6 locomotives, 65 freight cars, 15 passenger coaches, 35 employees. It had a roundhouse at 5th and Water Streets, 35 acres of land near the shops, 12 lots across Boulder Creek to the west, stations, etc.

Then Nature took a hand in the affairs of men. Creeks running through the mighty Rockies west of Boulder drain immense areas. Any run-off above normal cascades down the long slopes, gathering, until it spills into a gulch. Each gulch pours its flow into the creeks. The result can be terrible flood.

On July 31st such a flood roared down Four Mile and Boulder Creeks. It washed out 700 feet of DB&W tracks between Boulder and Crisman and damaged bridges 11 and 12. Most of the damage was in Four Mile Canon.

The DB&W owners ordered General Manager Ford to stop all train operations. Unless the PUC ordered it, the Switzerland

---

[13]*Boulder Tribune*, May 30, 1919.
[14]*Ibid.*, June 6, 1919.
[15]*Ibid.*, June 13, 1919.

[16]*Boulder Tribune*, June 30, 1919.
[17]*Ibid.*, July 25, 1919.

Opposite Page

Original painting by Howard Fogg

Passengers of the Colorado & Northwestern Ward-bound train are enjoying one of the unusual treats that the railroad offered — a stop to view Arapahoe Glacier and its guardian Arapahoe Peak. Site of this beautiful autumn picture is at the north end of the Culbertson Cut, .2 of a mile south of Gold Hill station.

Photo by Clint O. Dumm

DB&W No. 31 in Boulder Canon near Profile Rock.

T. C. Black, Jr., photo. Courtesy Jewell and Frank Black

Engineer's side of No. 32, showing reverse lever with many notches on quadrant for shortening stroke of engines.

T. G. Black, Jr., photo. Courtesy of J. B. Schoolland

Engineer's side of No. 32's cab. Injector at far right. Next to it is the throttle. To left of it is straight air brake valve for engine brakes and valve for train brakes. Farther to left are three try cocks to check water level in boiler. Beyond them is the flat glass water gauge. Hydrostatic lubricator to feed valve oil to cylinders is to left of steam and air gauges.

M. C. Poor Collection

DB&W No. 32 gleams with fresh paint in the Boulder yards.

Charles O. Erbaugh photo. J. B. Schoolland Collection

No. 32 heading up Four Mile Canon above Wall Street with an excursion train. Oscar Bernsten, fireman, Bill Tipps, engineer. It's a summer morning and all's well with the world. The dogs are barking at the locomotive but it's friendly barking.

Courtesy Mrs. Jack Gilman

Rock slide a short distance above Goat Rock in Boulder Canon tied up the railroad.

Courtesy Mrs. Jack Gilman

Work train which has backed to Blue Bird station from Glacier Lake waits beyond flood-damaged trestle over North Boulder Creek as section men begin repairs.

Trail would never again be operated as a commercial line. The reason was that an accident, such as a train wreck, might happen.[18]

The roadbed would have to be repaired before the lines could be junked, but the owners hoped to cast this expense upon the concern buying them.

John R. Wolff and several tungsten producers appeared before the PUC to protest against the immediate junking. Wolff expected to get an order tying up the junking for a year or two, unless the owners placed a price on the railroad. He intended to carry the question up to the Supreme Court if necessary.[19]

The railroad won. The PUC issued a decision August 21st permitting it to permanently cease activity and be scrapped. Estimates of expense of repairing roadbed ranged from $3,000 to $3,500 and two weeks' time. The commission held that it would be unfair to force the road to undergo the expense in order to operate from September 3rd to the 15th.[20]

Wolff filed for a rehearing with the PUC and threatened to take the matter to the Supreme Court.

The owners acted swiftly. They sold the road to Morse Brothers Machinery and Supply Company of Denver.

On September 18th George C. Morse came to Boulder and offered to sell the DB&W for a price considerably lower than its salvage value. He did not want to see the road junked.[21]

A mass meeting was to be called to present the proposition to the people of Boulder. The outcome could be organization of a local company—through popular subscription—to buy and operate the railroad.

John R. Wolff secured a writ of review of the decision of the PUC permitting the junking. The decision would be carried to the

Supreme Court. However, if the Boulder men interested in buying the road could raise the purchase price, the case would probably be dismissed before the Supreme Court could act on it.[22]

Evidently the money was not raised, for Morse Brothers began boldly to junk the lines. During the last week of October four carloads of rails were brought down to Boulder. The wires to the telegraph office at Ward were taken down. The switch and siding of the Big Five Junction and the switch to the Newmarket Mine at Ward were torn up.[23]

Attorney Wolff fumed but admitted that the protestants had not asked for the writ of review because of the large bond required.

In February, 1920, the Morse Brothers' crews began tearing up the track at Eldora, moving steadily eastward. A big snowstorm on April 17th delayed them, but by May 1st they were at Bluebird station west of Glacier Lake.[24]

The right-of-way reverted to the former owners of the land. **Boulder County** began seeking portions of it. Its commissioners especially wanted Bridge No. 2 at the mouth of Boulder Canon, planning to widen it for a new automobile road.

The pavilion at Glacier Lake, lunch room, section house, and other buildings were sold to Fred Fair and associates, who planned to convert them to summer tourist homes.[25]

Late in May the crews battled through deep snowdrifts on the Ward line and began once more tearing up the track.[26] The autumn before they had taken out one mile. The people of Ward looked on solemnly. When the last locomotive disappeared around the bend, its smoke drifting away, they knew that a part of them had gone. Never again would they hear the hauntingly beautiful whistles

---

[18]*Boulder Tribune*, August 8, 1919.
[19]*Ibid.*, August 15, 1919.
[20]*Ibid.*, August 22, 1919.
[21]*Boulder Tribune*, September 19, 1919.

---

[22]*Ibid.*, October 17, 1919.
[23]*Ibid.*, October 31, 1919.
[24]*Daily Camera*, February 11,1920.
[25]*Daily Camera*, May 21, 1920.
[26]*Ibid.*, May 25, 1920.

267

Courtesy Otto C. Perry

No. 30 was the only Consolidation with flat valves. Her running boards have been raised from their original position, making her a more shapely engine.

She now has a turbogenerator and an electric headlight. At right of her smoke-box may be seen the steam-powered coal loader.

No. 1 was a shapely little engine but her 44-inch drivers were too high for the heavy grades of the Switzerland Trail. Her steam pressure of 150 pounds was too low. In later years she was idle much of the time.

The Switzerland Trail always had its motive power and rolling stock in Class A condition. Here No. 32 is being overhauled outside Boulder shops. This was veteran Bill Tipps' assigned engine. His love for her is shown in her shining boiler jacket, deer antlers atop headlight, and chime whistle.

Photo by Otto C. Perry

The Switzerland Trail of America

270

Courtesy Otto C. Perry

Fireman's side of No. 25 in the Boulder yards.

echo back from the hills, never again would they feel the excitement of arrival and departure of trains.

Morse Brothers converted the DB&W yards into a factory. Here men unloaded the rails and sorted them. Those needing it were run through a straightener. A sawmill ripped bridge timbers into lumber. A machine straightened rail spikes. All equipment went out in first-class shape, much of it nearly as good as new.

A ready market awaited the excellent 56-pound rails. One contract called for shipment of 5,000 tons to Kobe, Japan. A sawmill in California purchased rails for seven miles of track. Several carloads went up to the Saratoga-Encampment Railroad in Wyoming, owned by the Morse Brothers.

No. 32 and No. 25 had been shipped to Denver. At the Morse Brothers yard they were repaired and painted, made ready for sale.

Morse Brothers shipped one locomotive to Alaska (evidently No. 1). When it arrived in Seattle, the tender was missing. Section men along the line of transit were instructed to look for it but never a trace did they ever find. It was presumed to have fallen off a bridge into some river enroute.

In late June the wrecking crews on the Eldora line reached Sunset. Here they stopped at the comfortable camp and added their force to the crews on the Ward branch.

Down in Boulder the rolling stock was disappearing. No. 33 had been shipped out to a lumber company in Louisiana.[27]

Thirty men were at work in the Boulder yards. The rails, which had originally come from the Carnegie and Lackawana Mills, were being shipped out as fast as processed.

On July 6th Boulder people read a startling headline, "Can't Junk the Switzerland Trail Is The Order of The Supreme Court After Much of It Was Junked."

"The Colorado Supreme Court set aside an order issued by the state utilities commission one year ago permitting the dismantling of the Denver, Boulder & Western Railroad.

"The supreme court decision of today held 'There is no direct evidence that the road under normal conditions might not earn enough money to justify its continued operation.'

"John R. Wolff, who conducted the fight for himself and other mining men, said today that the victory is sweeping and the junking must cease under penalty of $1000 a day for every day the road is not operated. The case will be appealed to the supreme court of the United States."[28]

General Manager Ford commented that the court order made him weary. Now in business for himself, selling stocks and bonds, he had no intention of trying to operate a railroad with only one locomotive, four freight cars, and no passenger cars.[29]

The junking went swiftly ahead. The wrecking crews on the Ward line were nearly to Sunset by July 10th. Seven-tenths of the rails had been taken up, the most of them were far away.[30]

John R. Wolff, acting for the Up-to-Date Mining Company, filed a petition with the Colorado Supreme Court to stop the junking.[31]

The Morse Brothers went steadily ahead. On July 29th their crews were at Sunset, ready for the final dismantling of the main line.[32]

On September 9th the wrecking crew steamed out of Four Mile and into Boulder Canon. They eased down toward Boulder, taking up a half-mile of track a day.[33]

Boulder County purchased Bridge No. 2 and Bridge No. 7, the latter near Four Mile Canon mouth. They were excellent steel bridges. Today automobiles roll over them.

[27]*Daily Camera*, June 24, 1920.

[28]*Daily Camera*, July 6, 1920.
[29]*Ibid.*, July 7, 1920.
[30]*Ibid.*, July 10, 1920.
[31]*Ibid.*, July 20, 1920.
[32]*Ibid.*, July 29, 1920.
[33]*Ibid.*, September 9, 1920.

No. 25 looks forlorn and forgotten at the west end of the enginehouse in Boulder yards. Although dependable and a heavy lugger, she was considered too slow for ordinary use. Her original cost was $6,805.23.

Photo by Otto C. Perry

No. 31 still has her extended piston rods in this photo, although she now sports an electric headlight and automatic couplers.

Courtesy Otto C. Perry

This rare photo shows No. 1 being coaled up in the Boulder yards. This mechanical loader, driven by a vertical steam engine and mounted on a four-wheel car, was far easier than shoveling up to tender by hand. The railroad never had a coal chute, piled coal on ground.

On September 28th the crews dismantled the water tank near the mouth of Boulder Canon. They took up the scale track immediately above Bridge No. 1. Then:

"The Switzerland Trail is no more," read the *Daily Camera* story of October 1, 1920. "This railroad, which played a prominent part in Boulder county's history, passed away at 4:30 last night when the last rails except those in the immediate vicinity of the round house, were torn up. The wye and switches of the Denver, Boulder & Western, in the local yards, were dismantled yesterday. . . ."

The last locomotive (either the 30 or the 31) stood ready with steam up for loading onto a standard gauge flatcar. Bill Tipps climbed into the cab, eased the throttle back. Gallantly she took the heavy short grade, her exhausts full-throated. Bill pushed the throttle shut, set the air. The last locomotive on the Switzerland Trail of America stopped with a little shudder.

Along Boulder Creek the cottonwood leaves flashed golden in the sunlight. The great foothills, so near at hand, were soft with the blue haze of Indian Summer.

Bill stepped down from the cab and started home, holding himself firmly erect. He saw none of the beauty of the glorious day, felt none of its tingling life. The familiar path he had trod so long swam hazily before him. He had gone out on one of the first trains in 1898 and all the years since he and his beloved 32 with the deer antlers above the headlight had been part of the Switzerland Trail. Now the rails were gone from the canons and the mountainsides; the hills were as empty as his heart.

Courtesy Mrs. Jack Gilman

Floods caused by cloudbursts played havoc with mountain railroads. This damage to trestle at Blue Bird in the summer of 1911 or 1912 was done by ordinarily pleasant North Boulder Creek.

Chapter IX

THE LURE OF THE TRAIL

Romance has all but vanished from railroading. Not so once, not so when curving, climbing rails threaded the Rockies to remote mining camps and summer resorts with names that quickened hearts. People were lured west by word of mouth and exciting words in advertising folders and pamphlets. They were looking for romance and adventure and many found them.

The writers of the Switzerland Trail's advertising material were often spendthrifts with words, but I cannot find it in my heart to censure them. Rather, I find it easy to slip back into that rosy expectation and throat-tightening pleasure of the summer boy and girl stepping gaily aboard the trains. Some people so treasured these memories of youth that they carefully preserved the printed words.

In September, 1898, the railroad issued a booklet entitled "Colorado and Northwestern, the Switzerland Trail of America." On the cover an artist sketched terrific mountains rising from the cathedral-spire Red Rocks at Boulder's western edge. In the foreground steams No. 31 with coaches of the C&N, headed for Sunset, where a freight train waits. The track winds, crossing a long trestle, which has another train rumbling over it. Then on, the track climbing in great curves to Mont Alto Park and on to Ward, somewhere among the cloud-swept peaks. It was at once romantic and alluring.

"Modern skill in railway engineering has accomplished for Colorado a n d Boulder County what no other agency could have wrought," the story begins. "Lying beneath the surface of these wild, rugged and weird regions of apparent mountain waste, are to be found millions untold in wealth. . . .

"The richness of the ore here found and the frequency of the veins have tempted the mining engineer and prospector into these hills. Their hopes by day and their dreams by night have been . . . for a railroad to connect these untold millions of treasured wealth with the mills and markets. That hope and dream is now a reality. . . .

"At the Union Depot in Boulder (referred to as 'The Athens of Colorado') the traveler finds the comfortable train of the Colorado & Northwestern Railway, and is soon off for a whirl among scenes not surpassed in the Alps—where the music of the tumbling water and the breath of the mountain pine and spruce is as a tonic to the body and rest to the wearied mind. . . .

"At Four Mile Canon the road leaves Boulder Creek and follows one of its branches through a similar canon for about ten miles 'till at the end Sunset is reached. . . .

"Like a chased deer the train now stands at bay at the head of Four Mile Canon and to escape must take to the mountain side; so around a sharp curve it starts and almost bounds away along the walls of Four Mile Canon running parallel with its track in the bottom of the canon hundreds of feet below. . . . At last the Ox Bow bend is reached, around which the train turns and soon pulls up at Mont Alto Park.

". . . here is a grassy oasis in the midst of this wild desert of rocky waste, 'like a little corner of paradise in the midst of Nature's awful chaos'. . . . Look to the west and you behold the great towering heights; to the east, between the almost perpendicular walls of the canon and where the foaming Boulder Creek dashes from its confines like an antelope, is nestled the charming city of Beautiful Boulder. . . . It is no wonder that tourists tarry here among the mountain pines and trembling aspens. . . .

"Ward is the present terminus of this meandering route. . . . Up to Mont Alto the view has been amazingly grand; from here on, it will be found sublime and bewildering. . . .

"Our train has crossed one divide at Gold Hill Pass and looking ahead it seems we must descend into Left Hand, but not so. . . . Rounding Klondike Point comes into view Camp Talcott. . . . We are entering a locality known in the early history of the State, yet in the past rendered almost wholly secluded from development by man. Shafts now multiply on every hill side. Across the canon from our train stands the old 'Miser's Dream' — the Ward mine — the first discovery in this district and from which this locality took its name. . . . Across the canon, rounding dizzy Alpine Point, is seen one of the C&N trains coming down from Ward. . . .

"Another point is passed and Camp Frances comes into view, while down near the bottom several hundred feet below are seen the immense ore dumps and machinery buildings of the Big Five properties, better known as the Adit-Dew Drop tunnel. . . . Here starts a tunnel driving under the hills for nearly a mile along a drift of glistening ore. . . .

"On we go and rounding another intervening hill the old camp of Ward comes into view. . . . Behind us lies the most wonderful scenic route in the world. . . ."

The 30-page booklet is well illustrated with good photographs. The frontispiece is a view of Boulder taken from Lover's (Sunset) Hill, with the small State University and the great wooded foothills in the background. There's a fine shot of No. 1 and a two-coach train at the Union Depot. There are pictures

along the way: Profile Rock in Boulder Canon, Saw Mill Hill and Puzzler, Bloomerville Loop, Sunset, Mont Alto Park, Glimpse of the Arapahoes from the Ox Bow, a magnificent panorama from Four Mile Canon to Mont Alto Park, Klondike Point and Camp Talcott, Bald Mountain and Alpine Point, California Gulch, Ward, and the Reduction Works of the Pennsylvania Mining and Milling Company of Culbertson.

Some years later tourists drinking in the exhilarating air of Colorado for the first time were lured to Boulder by a free booklet entitled "A Trip To Cloudland via The Switzerland Trail of America." No date is given, but there is evidence that it was either 1909 or 1910.

It measures about 8 by 8 inches, is folded over once, so that front and back covers present one scene. It is in color, taken at the beginning of a curve on the Eldora branch, ahead the great snow-patched peaks of the Continental Divide: Arapaho with its huge glacier, Kiowa, and Navajo Peaks.

On the front is the eye-catching circular emblem of the railroad. The center is yellow, with D and B in bold red intertwined with a black W, a smaller & in white. In the outer band, in black, is The Switzerland Trail of America.

"No visit to Colorado is complete unless one indulges in a trip to Cloudland and experiences the sensation of careening around the extinct craters of the volcanic age, on the crest of the continent. After one trip over the Famous Switzerland Trail of America (The Denver, Boulder and Western Railroad), the traveler will want to repeat the enjoyment and have all his friends share the same pleasure.

"The Switzerland Trail of America operates a continuous line from Denver to Eldora in northwestern Colorado, with a line from Sunset (thirteen miles west of Boulder) to Ward.

"At Sunset the line diverges; the road to Eldora turning abruptly to the east and pur-

Cover of booklet issued by the Colorado & Northwestern Railway Company in September, 1898.

Officers of C. & N. R'y Co.

W. C. CULBERTSON, President,
Girard, Pa.

CHAS. W. MACKEY, Vice President,
253 Broadway, N. Y.

CHAS. B. CULBERTSON, Secretary,
Girard, Pa.

THOS. R. MANN, Treasurer,
Boulder, Colo.

J. T. BLAIR, General Manager,
Boulder, Colo.

Climate

IN Colorado the three great physicians—sunshine, altitude and dry air—have gone into partnership and are building up the brain, body, blood and bone. The genial warmth of the sun renders outdoor life a joy at all seasons of the year. Its glow takes the sting from the wintry winds and its heat is moderated by the snow-clad peaks in summer, which renders its climate a boon to the health-seeker.

Boulder

THIRTY-TWO years ago, the celebrated Bayard Taylor, tourist and author, found himself on the elevated mesa, now the site of the City Park. Glancing into the valley where now lies Boulder, as the lovely vision burst upon him, in a transport of ecstacy he exclaimed: "This is the loveliest spot my eye has ever rested upon." Now the site of the great Chautauqua pavilion.

Published by Representative Printing Co., Boulder.
Engravings by Williamson-Haffner Co., Denver.

Copied from "The Switzerland Trail of America"
Courtesy H. B. Rosenkrans

Proud in her shining newness, C&N No. 1 stands with full steam pressure up before the Union Station, Boulder, to take her train to Ward. It is a pleasant morning of that exciting first summer for the new railroad.

Copied from "The Switzerland Trail of America"
Courtesy H. B. Rosenkrans

View across Left Hand Canon of Sawmill Hill (left), showing present steep road crossing railroad track. To the right is the little mining camp of Puzzler, with freight cars spotted on its siding.

The old Miser's Dream Mine on mountainside to left. Train is headed east toward Klondike Point.

Alpine Point on Grassy Mountain east of Camp Frances. Below is one of the headwater streams of Left Hand Cre
Bloomerville lies to the west, the railroad making a complete loop.

The Lure of the Trail

Chance for Energy and Grit. from this vein during the past thirty-eight years, while yet the deepest shaft has only reached a depth of eight hundred feet below the surface.

For the treatment of the ores of the district, ample mills and smelters are being erected. The largest is situated at Culbertson, a suburb of Boulder. This mill can treat the lowest grade ore with profit to the miner, while the untold millions of tons of $40 to $100 ore are yielding fortunes to the holders of these numerous fissure veins. The arrival of the Colorado & Northwestern has brought a transformation to Boulder County. Opportunities that have been locked in a granite vise for all these ages past are now at the bidding of enterprise, capital and grit, while to the health-seeker and the annual tourist, no spot under heaven's blue dome can offer such surpassing attractions as those now found in Boulder County.

Dr. Charles E. Bessey OF LINCOLN, Nebr., wrote the *State Journal:* "Have you ever been over the 'Loop' near Georgetown? You wondered at that and told the story over and over to your admiring neighbors. Don't boast about that little bit of engineering any longer. Go over the 'Golden Whiplash,' climb the 'Golden Stairway' which connects Boulder with Ward, and you will begin to realize what crooks and curves an engineer must use when climbing the 'Golden Mountains' of Colorado. * * Any more? Yes; but there is not space left for it. Go to Boulder and see for yourself. Go and cool off. Go and climb and scramble for strength. Go away up two miles above the sea level and breath the thin, pure air of the golden mountains. If you go once you'll go again."

The Editor of Chicago Sentinel SAYS: "It has been my fortune to travel over the most famous railroad routes of this continent,—over the Alleghanies and Cumberland mountains of the East, and the Rockies, the Sierras and the coast mountains of the West, but I can say without hesitation, that the route of the COLORADO & NORTHWESTERN between Sunset and Ward surpasses them all in scenic beauty, in magnitude of undertaking and in skill required in construction."

The last page of the booklet, "Colorado and Northwestern — The Switzerland Trail of America" shows the sky-high optimism aroused by the building of the railroad and appreciation of its scenic beauties.

Copied from "The Switzerland Trail of America"
Courtesy H. B. Rosenkrans

East-bound train from Ward approaching Bloomerville after rounding Alpine Point of Grassy Mountain.

283

"THE SWITZI

FROM BOU

FOUR MILE CANON   SUNSET   THE ARAPAHOES   MOUNT AUDOBON

Scenic Grandeur
The English language and cold type are inadequate to do justice to the scenery from Sunset on. To one unaccustomed to it, the ride up the mountains, and over them, borders on the thrilling. A glance up the mountain side would here and there reveal the track 400 to 500 feet above us, only to be there a few moments later.—*Editor Oklahoma Champion.*

Picturesque and Enchanting
Marvelou beautiful yonddescri is the landscape revealed from the more elevated points of the where may be seen valleys and mountains blending in grand mony of exquisite colorings. Silver streams are dancing and sl mering in the sunlight; lakes, like mirrors, nestling in the fo form a panorama of awful grandeur and beauty.—*Prof. Rule.*

Copied from "The Switzerland Trail, Summer Season, 1900."

RLAND TRAIL"

ER TO WARD

GOLD HILL PASS   MT. ALTO   LONG'S PEAK

d Hill Pass You see the mighty Giant's Ladder by which the train has ascended from Four Mile Canon, nearly 2,000 feet be- By a bewildering series of turns and cuts and curves, forming and bridging chasms, has this road risen at a rate of over 200 the mile of track, and here you stand, where with a good bow row, it would seem you could land a shaft over the fifth track in the dim shadows of the canon below.

Among the Clouds To "Climb a mile on the Sky-High Line" is the invitation the Colorado & Northwestern extends to Coloradoans and Tourists. You cannot truthfully say "all scenery looks alike to me," after you have seen the "scenes shifted on this new road. It is a panorama furnished by nature in no other portion of this glorious country.

Folder courtesy A. A. Paddock

Gold Hill Pass was later renamed Culbertson Pass.

285

suing a tortuous course to Sugar Loaf Mountain, thence swinging west on a sharp curve towards Eldora, passing enroute Beautiful Glacier Lake, Anson Park, a beautiful verdant valley called The Meadows, Cardinal, the gateway of the famous Caribou Mining District and also the railroad station for Nederland, located in the heart of the wonderful Tungsten Field and within which time bringing into full view famous mountain peaks as Long's, James', Gray's, Saw Tooth, Mount Audubon, and the Arapahoes.

"To the south and east of the line between Sugar Loaf and Cardinal stations are a number of concentrating mills operating constantly in reducing Tungsten ore. Statistics show that seventy-five per cent of the output in America of this rare and newly discovered ore is produced in the territory contiguous to the Denver, Boulder and Western Railroad. . . ."

Facing a map of the railroad is a color reproduction of the Columbine, the state flower. Scattered throughout are color cuts of the Anemone, Gilia, Scotch Thistle, Prickly Poppy, Cactus, Yellow Prickly Pear, Primrose, Sand Lily, Mariposa Lily, and Indian Pink (Paintbrush), all beautifully and accurately done, all flowers growing along the railroad.

The full-page black and white shots are intriguing: Lover's Leap in Beautiful Boulder Canyon, On The Summit Of Sugar Loaf Mountain, Birdseye View of Four Mile Canon And The Ward Line, Long's Peak From Near Sugar Loaf, Panorama of the Great Snowy Range (with five trains on the Ward and Four Mile lines), The Arapahoes and Mount Audubon from Glacier Lake, Beautiful Glacier Lake (with boating parties, the pavilion, and a long train), North Boulder Falls near Blue Bird Station, The Arapahoe Glacier, reached from Eldora and Silver Lake Stations, and a few more.

The Switzerland Trail's officials in their quest for business gave local resort keepers much free publicity. In 1912 the railroad issued a booklet, "Resorts And Fishing Grounds Along The Switzerland Trail of America." The cover photo is forest-surrounded Red Rock Lake with a fisherman in a boat, the great Continental Divide peaks in the background.

Sportsmen were attracted by low round-trip rates from Denver and Boulder to Anson Park, Hill, Glacier Lake, Lake Eldora, Orodell, etc. They were guided by condensed game laws of Colorado, detailed information about resorts, fishing, camping sites, etc.

The one-page photograph of Lake Eldora, Colorado, and caption is typical. Here we see an intent fisherman in a boat out on the waters. "Lake Eldora, Colorado—(Elevation 9,280 feet; 63 miles from Denver; 33 miles from Boulder). Among the pines. Within the shadow of James's Peak. Healthful spring water. Wonderful mountain scenery. Beautiful Lake stocked with millions of mountain trout. Boating, fishing, baths, telephone, free to guests of Pine Log Inn. P. E. Chamberlain, Proprietor. Capacity of hotel and cottages seventy-five. Rates $13.00 to $14.50 per week. Cuisine the best."

In 1913 the Switzerland Trail of America issued a folder advertising a Wonderful One-Day Trip. "The trains which make possible this wonderful trip leave Denver Union Depot daily, and without change of cars, convey the traveler to the Crest of the Continent, in less than three hours, traversing a distance of 50 miles and unfolding a volume of panoramic beauty and grandeur unequaled in the world."

Front and back covers are a photograph of the awesome Arapahoe Peaks, far above timberline.

The booklet advises one to "Ask About The New Ward-Estes Park Auto Route—The Skyline to the Park."

The illustrations are alternate color reproductions of flowers and black and white scenes along the route. The latter include

Beautiful Glacier Lake, The Parting of The Ways (Sunset, with train in Four Mile Canon, another on the Ward branch, a third on the Eldora line), Four Rounds of the Giant's Ladder (Ward branch), etc.

In 1915 the railroad issued two folders. One's cover showed the new auto road approaching Meeker Park (present Peak-to-Peak Highway). It is entitled "Estes Park via The Switzerland Trail of America, Denver, Boulder & Western RR, And Auto From Ward, Colo. The Rocky Mountain National Park Route."

It describes amply the trip, detailing the transfer at Ward to Stanley Steamers and the new route to Estes Park. Its time table shows leaving Denver at 8 a.m. and arriving in Estes Park at 3:45 p.m. It lists resorts enroute to the park and hotels in Estes Park. The

illustrations are very good; particularly interesting are the Stanley Steamers on the one-way roads.

The round-trip fare from Denver was $9.60, from Boulder, $7.80.

The other folder was "The Switzerland Trail of America—The Denver, Boulder and Western RR—A Wonderful One-Day Scenic Trip From Denver." Its illustrations show one of particular interest: No. 25, the Shay, in snow level with her boiler top, a party of excursionists posing. This was taken near Ward in June.

The Switzerland Trail had much newspaper advertising, as has been told elsewhere. It received much free coverage from Boulder papers. Its big pull, however, came by word of mouth from people who had been thrilled by its trips, who felt its lure.

Copied from "The Switzerland Trail of America"
Courtesy H. B. Rosenkrans

East-bound train approaching trestle over headwater stream at Left Hand Creek. This was known as California Gulch. The Big Five's Adit-Dewdrop Tunnel lies below, to right of gulch. Frances is still farther to right.

Goat Rock, in Boulder Canon.   **A Run for the Range, near Bloomerville.**

Copied from "The Switzerland Trail of America"
Courtesy H. B. Rosenkrans

Klondike Point and Camp Talcott, also called Camp Brainerd, in Left Hand Canon below.

Ward, terminus of the Colorado & Northwestern.

THE ...
One Day
TRIP

The trip over the "Switzerland Trail" from Denver or Boulder is the shortest and cleanest one day trip into the mountains. ☙ It will show you the snowy range ✿ ✿ and more high mountain peaks than any other one day trip.

Leave Denver, 8:20 a. m., leave Boulder, 9:40 a. m., arrive Boulder, 4:10 p. m., and arrive Denver, 5:45 p. m.

CHAS. B. CULBERTSON, General Manager, Boulder, Colorado

For further information, excursion rates, etc., call on or address
H. G. GARWOOD, City Passenger and Ticket Agent.
1025 Seventeenth Street, DENVER, COLO.

CARSON-HARPER PRINTING AND ENGRAVING, DENVER
Photos by Smith-Hassell Photo Co.

A. A. Paddock Collection

At the beginning of the summer tourist season in 1900, the Colorado & Northwestern issued this attractive folder. Front and back cover.

Standard Time, 105th Meridian.

East Bound Trains FIRST CLASS		Distance from Ward	Stations and Passing Places Via Colorado Southern Ry.	Altitude	West Bound Trains FIRST CLASS	
9 Daily A.M.	3 Daily P.M.				2 Daily A.M.	10 Daily P.M.
9 32	5 45	55 6	Ar. Denver Lv.	5147	8 20	5 15
8 10	4 10	26 1	d Boulder	5400	9 40	5 50
f 7 50	f 3 59	23 2	Orodell		f 9 52	f 6 05
s 7 36	3 45	19 9	Crisman	6300	s10 07	s 6 23
s 7 28	3 38	18 6	d Salina	6800	s10 14	6 33
s 7 18	3 31	17 1	d Wall Street	7100	s10 21	s 6 45
f 6 58	3 18	14 5	Copper Rock	7550	f10 33	f 6 58
s 6 48	3 05	12 8	d Sunset	7800	s10 45	s 7 10
f 6 28	2 51	9 7	Mt. Alto Park	8600	s11 00	f 7 25
f 6 21	2 45	8 3	GoldHill	8750	s11 06	s 7 31
s 6 11	2 27	4 2	Puzzler	9000	s11 22	s 7 50
f 6 05	2 22	3 1	Bloomerville		f11 28	f 7 56
s 5 57	2 16	1 5	d Frances	9300	s11 34	s 8 03
5 50	2 10	0	Lv. d Ward Ar.	9450	11 40	8 10

READ UP

READ DOWN

Camp Talcott, in Left Hand Cañon.

Sunday Excursion Rates

Denver to Ward and return $2.25

Denver to Mt. Alto Park and return 2.00

Boulder to Ward and return $1.75

Boulder to Mt. Alto Park and return 1.00

Secure tickets of the Colorado Southern R. R. Office, 17th and Curtis Streets, or at Union Depot Denver. ✍ ✍

Mont Alto Park

Mont Alto Park is a most delightful resort for picnic parties and excursionists. A new pavilion and a lunch room have recently been added, and the management will spare no effort to please everybody. There is an abundance of pure mountain water, fresh from the snowy range, cold as ice, and clear as crystal. Plenty of shade trees, and every convenience that goes to make an enjoyable day's outing will be found at Mont Alto Park.

Officers of Colorado & Northwestern Railway Co.

W. C. CULBERTSON, President
Girard, Pa.

J. T. BLAIR, Vice-President
Greenville, Pa.

CHAS. B. CULBERTSON, General Manager,
Boulder, Colo.

Returning you reach Denver in ample time for dinner at the hotels, and make connections with all fast lines East and West. ✍ ✍ THIS IS THE SHORTEST AND CLEANEST ONE-DAY TRIP OUT OF DENVER.

A. A. Paddock Collection

Time-table published in the 1900 Summer Season Colorado & Northwestern folder.

*Copied from Summer Season, 1900, C&N folder
Courtesy A. A. Paddock*

The Colorado & Northwestern was enterprising in pushing its Sunday excursions.

290

The Colorado & Northwestern Railroad
"THE SWITZERLAND TRAIL OF AMERICA"

TIME TABLE
IN EFFECT JUNE 18, 1905

No. 27-7 Daily p.m.	No. 35-1-5 Daily a.m.	Altitude	STATIONS	Miles from Denver	No. 36-2-6 Daily p.m.	No. 8-22 Daily a.m.
1.00	8.00	5280	Lv. Denver — Ar.		5.45	9.15
1.30	8.38		" Louisville Jct. — Lv.	16	5.05	-----
1.37	8.48		" Louisville — "	19	4.55	-----
2.00	9.17		Ar. Boulder — Lv.	29	4.25	8.10
5.00	9.25	5400	Lv. Boulder — Ar.	29	4.15	8.05
5.38	9.57	6300	" Crisman — Lv.	35	3.48	7.30
5.48	10.05	6800	" Salina — "	37	3.40	7.20
5.58	10.15	7100	" Wall Street — "	38	3.32	7.12
6.25	10.45	7800	" Sunset — "	42	3.15	7.00
	11.12	8600	Lv. Mont Alto — Lv.	45	2.45	-----
	11.20	8800	" Gold Hill — "	47	2.40	-----
	11.30	8950	" Brainerd — "	49	2.30	-----
	11.52	9300	" Frances — "	54	2.08	-----
	12.01	9450	Ar. Ward — Lv.	55	2.00	-----
6.50	11.06	8430	Lv. Sugar Loaf — Lv.	46	2.54	6.34
6.55	11.09	8500	" Tungsten — "	47	2.50	6.30
7.20	11.30	9050	" Glacier Lake — "	51	2.30	6.11
7.27	11.37	9000	" Silver Lake — "	53	2.24	6.05
7.52	11.57	8595	" Anson Park — "	56	2.02	5.38
8.10	12.14	8710	" Card'l-Caribou — "	59	1.48	5.22
8.24	12.24	8530	" Sulphide — "	61	1.36	5.06
8.30	12.30	8730	Ar. Eldora — Lv.	62	1.30	5.00
p.m. Daily	p.m. Daily				p.m. Daily	a.m. Daily

L. R. FORD
General Passenger Agent
BOULDER

O. J. WATROUS
General Agent
BOULDER

E. A. COOPER
City Passenger and Ticket Agent
SEVENTEENTH AND CURTIS STREETS, DENVER

R. LAW
Vice-President and Gen'l Mgr.
BOULDER

Courtesy of A. A. Paddock

Copied from "A Trip to Cloudland via the Colorado & Northwestern Railroad."

Round Trip Rates

MAY FIFTEENTH
TO OCTOBER THIRTY-FIRST

SATURDAYS and SUNDAYS

Denver to Ward or Eldora $2.00

SUNDAYS

Denver to Glacier Lake or Mt. Alto Park . . . $1.75
Denver to Sugar Loaf Mountain 1.50

Special low rates on other days.

All Round Trip Tickets from Denver to Ward or Eldora will be good for passage to either of those points.

STAGE LINES OPERATE AS FOLLOWS:

Between Salina and town of Gold Hill, three and one-half miles daily:

Lv. Salina . . . 10.10 a.m. Arr. Gold Hill 12.00 m.
" " . . . 5.50 p.m. " " 7.10 p.m.
" Gold Hill . . 6.30 a.m. " Salina . . . 7.15 a.m.
" " . . 2.25 p.m. " " 3.25 p.m.

Connection is also made daily at Ward for Stapps Lake, 8 miles; and Allen's Park, 14 miles; and at Cardinal-Caribou for Nederland, 1½ miles; and the town of Caribou, 2 miles.

THE WILLIAMSON-HAFFNER CO., DENVER

Courtesy of A. A. Paddock

Copied from "A Trip to Cloudland via the Colorado & Northwestern Railroad."

Crossen Collection

Cover of Booklet issued in 1909 or 1910.

Courtesy A. A. Paddock

Front cover of folder issued by the **Colorado & Northwestern** in 1905.

The Denver, Boulder and Western Railroad
"THE SWITZERLAND TRAIL of AMERICA"

TIME TABLE
SUBJECT TO CHANGE WITHOUT NOTICE

No. 35-5 Daily a. m.	Altitude	STATIONS	Miles from Denver	No, 36-6 Daily p. m.
8.00	5280	Lv._____Denver_____Ar.	_____	6.00
8.47	5300	" _____Louisville_____ "	19	5.05
9.15	5400	Ar._____ Boulder _____Lv.	29	4.40
9.25	5400	Lv,_____ Boulder _____Ar.	29	4.35
9.45	5900	" _____ Orodell _____Lv.	32	4.22
10.05	6300	" _____ Crisman _____ "	35	4.07
10.14	6800	" _____ Salina _____ "	37	4.00
10.24	7100	" _____Wall Street_____ "	38	3.52
10.45	7800	" _____ Sunset _____ "	42	3.35
11.12	8600	Lv._____ Mt. Alto _____Lv.	45	3.09
11.20	8800	" _____Gold Hill_____ "	47	3.00
11.30	8950	" _____Brained_____ "	49	2.44
11.52	9300	" _____Frances_____ '	54	2.10
12.01	9450	Ar._____Ward_____Lv.	55	2.00
11.11	8430	Lv _____Sugar Loaf_____Lv.	46	3.13
11.33	9050	" _____Glacier Lake_____ "	51	2.52
11.36	9000	" _____Hill_____ "	52	2.48
11.37	9000	" _____Silver Lake_____ "	53	2.47
11.57	8595	" _____ Anson Park _____ "	56	2.25
12.14	8710	" _____ Cardinal _____ "	59	2.15
12.24	8530	" _____ Sulphide Park _____ "	61	2.05
12.27	8700	" _____Lake Eldora_____ '	61	2.02
12.30	8730	Ar._____ Eldora _____Lv.	62	2.00
p. m. Daily		Note:—Cardinal is the railroad station for Nederland.		p. m. Daily

L. R. FORD, *Traffic Mgr.*   W. B. HAYES, *President*
Boulder, Colo.   Boulder, Colo.

E. A. COOPER
City Passenger and Ticket Agent
1000 Seventeenth Street
CORNER SEVENTEENTH AND CURTIS, DENVER, COLO.

Crossen Collection

The date of this timetable is either 1909 or 1910.

Map of

The Denver Boulder & Western Railroad

"The Switzerland Trail of America"

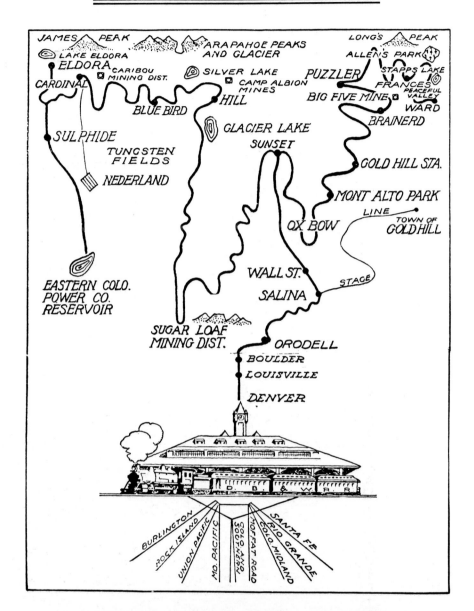

SOLID THROUGH TRAINS FROM DENVER UNION DEPOT

THE ROUTE TO NEDERLAND

The Famous Tungsten Mining District, in the center of which
is Nederland, is cut in twain by The Denver Boulder &
Western Railroad. ::: Passengers for Nederland
should ask for tickets to Cardinal.

Crossen Collection

Published in "A Trip to Cloudland," in 1909 or 1910.

Crossen Collection

Crossen Collection

Front covers of folders issued by the DB&W. The one on the left in 1913, the one on the right, 1915.

THE SWITZERLAND TRAIL OF AMERICA

ROUND TRIP RATES

*Ordinarily in effect May 15th to October 31st,
but not guaranteed beyond October 31st, 1913*

SATURDAYS *and* SUNDAYS

LIMIT—DAY OF SALE

Denver to Eldora or Ward . . .	$2.00
Boulder to Eldora or Ward . . .	1.50
Boulder to Glacier Lake . . .	1.00
Boulder to Sugar Loaf Mountain . .	.75

SUNDAYS

LIMIT—DAY OF SALE

Denver to Glacier Lake . . .	$1.75
Denver to Sugar Loaf Mountain . .	1.50

OTHER DAYS

Denver to Eldora or Ward . . .	$3.00
Boulder to Eldora or Ward . . .	1.75

ON SALE SATURDAYS *and* SUNDAYS

LIMIT—FOLLOWING MONDAY

Denver to Eldora or Ward . . .	$2.50
Denver to Glacier Lake . . .	2.10
Boulder to Eldora or Ward . . .	1.75
Boulder to Glacier Lake . . .	1.25

All Round Trip Tickets from Denver to Eldora or Ward
are good for passage to either of those points

ASK ABOUT THE
NEW WARD-ESTES PARK
AUTO ROUTE
"THE SKYLINE TO THE PARK"

A WONDERFUL ONE-DAY TRIP

Crossen Collection

Copied from 1913 folder advertising The Switzerland Trail of America.

THE SWITZERLAND TRAIL OF AMERICA

CIRCLING THE CRATER on
the CREST *of the* CONTINENT

To experience the sensation of careering
around the extinct craters of the volcanic age
on the Crest *of* the Continent is to indulge in
a trip to *cloudland* over the

FAMOUS SWITZERLAND TRAIL
OF AMERICA

(THE DENVER, BOULDER & WESTERN RAILROAD)
FROM DENVER TO ELDORA OR WARD

The trains which make possible this wonderful trip leave the Denver Union Depot
daily, and without change of cars, convey the
traveler to the *Crest of the Continent*, in less
than three hours, traversing a distance of 50
miles and unfolding a volume of panoramic
beauty *and* grandeur unequaled in the world.

TIME TABLE

SUBJECT TO CHANGE WITHOUT NOTICE

Going			Returning
Leave	8:05 a. m.	DENVER	Arrive 6:00 p. m.
"	9:25 "	BOULDER	" 4:40 "
"	11:10 "	SUGAR LOAF	" 3:23 "
"	11:33 "	GLACIER LAKE	" 3:02 "
"	12:14 p. m.	CARDINAL	" 2:30 "
Arr.	12:15 "	WARD	Leave 2:15 "
"	12:30 "	ELDORA	" 2:15 "

L. R. FORD
Traffic Manager, Boulder, Colo.

W. B HAYES
President, Boulder, Colo.

DENVER TICKET OFFICES
Corner 17th and California Sts. (Colorado & Southern Ry.) and Union Depot

A WONDERFUL ONE-DAY TRIP

Crossen Collection

Copied from 1913 folder advertising The Switzerland Trail of America.

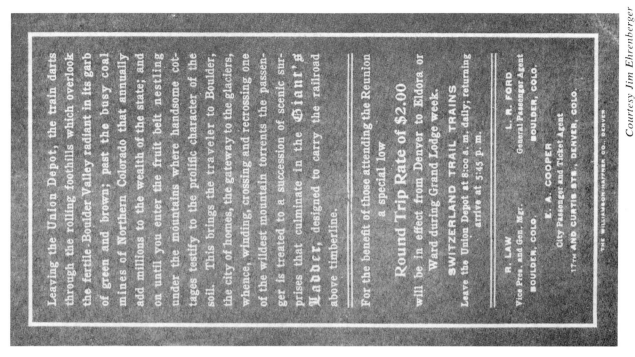

Courtesy Jim Ehrenberger

The flowery language of this special booklet attracted many an Elk attending the Grand Session at Denver, and we'll bet that most of them agreed after taking the trips.

Courtesy Jim Ehrenberger

The officials of the Colorado & Northwestern passed no opportunity to secure business for their railroad, as shown by this special folder issued for the Annual Session of the Grand Lodge, B.P.O.E., at Denver, July 16-20, 1906.

Copy of cover of elaborate 8½ by 11½-inch 30-page picture booklet issued by the C&N about 1900.

Boulder, Colorado

Known as "Beautiful Boulder,"—"The Place to Live,"—Right at the Foot of the Rocky Mountains—at the Mouth of Boulder Canon.

Seat of

THE UNIVERSITY OF COLORADO

Home of

THE COLORADO CHAUTAUQUA

Altitude, 5,400

Population, 15,000

29 Miles N. W. of Denver

Unexcelled Climate. Purest of Water.

Hourly service by the Denver & Interurban Electric Railway.

5 Daily Trains Each Way via. Colorado & Southern Railway.

4 Daily Trains Each Way via. Union Pacific R. R.

Courtesy of Richard Lind

Advertising bill issued shortly after the 1909 reorganization.

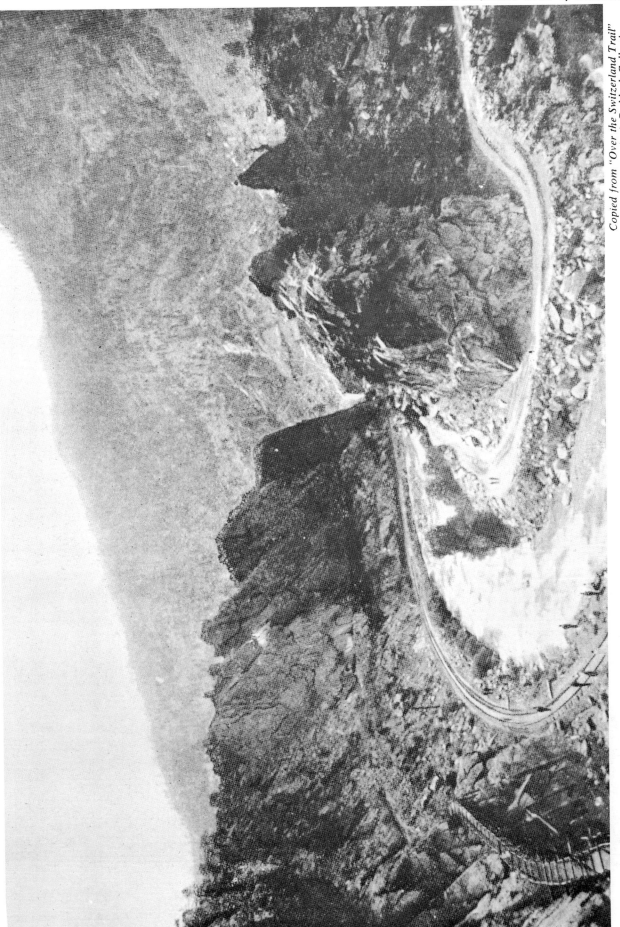

Many a young heart thrilled to the story of the beautiful Indian girl leaping to her death for love of her white lover as the Switzerland Trail trains grandly rounded Lover's Leap in Boulder Canon.

CLIMBING GIANT'S LADDER

Copied from "Over the Switzerland Trail" booklet
A. A. Paddock Collection

"The Giant's Ladder" was the hard climb out of Sunset to and beyond Mont Alto Park.

Copied from "Over the Switzerland Trail"
A. A. Paddock Collection

Two levels of track on the way to Mont Alto Park. The locomotive of train in foreground is No. 30.

Part II

Chapter X

STATIONS

Nearly all the station sites on the Switzerland Trail Of America can be reached today by automobile. Three of the station buildings—Ward, Eldora, and Lake Eldora—remain, but of these only one (Eldora) is in its original location.

The stations were substantially built, in keeping with the policy of the railroad's builders of using only the best. They were painted red and were kept in first-class condition. The mountain people had reason to be proud of them, for the management would tolerate no shoddy housekeeping.

The information of yard lay-outs, facilities, elevations, mileages, etc., has come from study of employees' timetables. Much has been gleaned from interviews with former employees. The elevations were taken from employees' timetables and may differ from U. S. Geological Survey figures. Some elevations not listed on timetables were taken from U. S. G. S. topographical maps.

BOULDER

Milepost 0.0, Elevation 5,351.[1]

Directly in front of the handsome grey sandstone union station at 14th and Water Streets the Old Main Line standard gauge track ran west. At about 8th Street it became a third rail, continuing up to near the east end of Bridge No. 1 over Boulder Creek.

South of the Old Main Line ran the parallel narrow gauge main line, a third rail from 15th Street nearly to 12th Street (Broadway). Near 13th Street a third rail spur ran southeast into the McAllister Lumber and Supply Company's yard. The main line continued west, crossing Boulder Creek on Bridge No. 1.[2]

At 10th Street a short wye ran to the south, the stem ending on the bank of Boulder Creek. At 9th Street stood a switch for the cross-over track to the Old Main Line.[3]

Here the narrow gauge yards began. From the cross-over track three sidings ran west, connecting with the narrow gauge main line at about 6th Street. The first of these sidings on the north, parallel to the main line, was the coach track. Next was a track for freight cars. Last was the transfer track for standard gauge cars. On these two last named tracks all transferring of coal, machinery, and general freight was done by a special crew.

Cars with narrow gauge locomotive coal were switched west of 6th Street and unloaded on the ground. At first men probably shoveled it by hand into the locomotive tenders. Later the company had a conveyor loader run by a steam engine mounted on a little four-wheel car.

At about 7th Street a third rail spur ran north to an ore sampling works at 8th and Pearl Streets. A third rail siding ran east from 8th Street to the north side of the freight house at 12th (Broadway) and Water Streets.

At 6th Street a third rail ran off the Old Main Line west to the Boulder Farmers' Milling and Elevator flour mill and ore mills on the north side of Boulder Creek.

From the third rail spur immediately west of 6th Street, three narrow gauge spurs ran into the engine house and shops located at 5th Street.

---

[1]The Denver, Boulder & Western Railroad Company Employees' Time Table No. 10, June 29, 1913.

[2]Interview with Elbert Hubbard, April 6, 1960.
[3]*Boulder Daily Camera*, September 4, 1952.

The engine house and shops were one long frame structure with vertical board siding and pitched roofs. The engine house, two locomotives wide with work pits for each, had doors opening to the east. Adjoining it on the north was the shop where the carpenters repaired and rebuilt passenger coaches. In the spring they had them finished like new, varnish gleaming. Atop the engine house were two sheet iron smokestacks topped with raised caps. The shop was in the west end.

The narrow gauge main line joined the Old Main Line immediately east of Bridge No. 1. A small sandhouse stood north of the transfer track near its junction with the narrow gauge main line.

No. 1 Bridge was a curved structure over Boulder Creek. The red rock base of the west abutment may still be seen. At its west end a scale track some 300 to 400 feet long took off. Here the crews weighed all ore, timber, lumber, etc., they brought down from the mountains.

Beyond the scale track was the first water tank, supplied by Boulder city pressure. All locomotives filled here as they came down from the hills. Engines in the shop were supplied by a 2-inch fire hose on a city line.

The water tank and nearby section house occupied land that the railroad is said to have intended originally for its yards.

The track ran up what is now West Arapahoe Avenue and crossed Boulder Creek again on Bridge No. 2. About one-fourth mile west was the 2-car Powder Spur, entered from the west. If a merchandise car had even one box of powder (dynamite) aboard, the car had to be left here. After the disastrous explosion of 1907, the City of Boulder forbade any cars containing explosives to be left in the yards overnight.

ORODELL

Milepost 2.9, Elevation 5,800.

This little camp, located about one-half mile above the mouth of Four Mile Creek, originally was called Orodelphan.[4] The 1893 timetable of the Boulder Canon Branch of the Union Pacific (Greeley, Salt Lake & Pacific) names it Oredel.[5] The 1910 timetable of the Denver, Boulder & Western Railroad lists it as Orodell. There was no station, only a sidetrack 355 feet long.

In 1865 J. P. Maxwell and Captain C. M. Tyler came down from Central City and built a sawmill at the junction of Four Mile and Boulder Creeks. They put a timber dam across Boulder Creek, using the mill pond to catch logs floated down during high water time. From their steam-powered sawmill lumber went out by wagon to help build Boulder and Cheyenne.[6]

At low water time one can see the once vertical timbers of this old dam, placed there nearly a century ago.

Maxwell and Tyler abandoned their sawmill in 1870. Shortly afterward Hunt and Barber built a smelter on the site. The Greeley, Salt Lake & Pacific ran between the smelter and the north wall of the canon. Water from the dam furnished part of the smelter power.[7]

Above the mouth of Four Mile Creek Chinese washed placer gold as late as 1900.

Miners working in the nearby Poorman Hill lived here for years. Men thought nothing of walking two or three miles to work.

During the construction of the hydroelectric plant in Boulder Canon, 1907-10, all materials were unloaded at Orodell. The railroad ran two spurs off to the west, crossing Four Mile Creek, for a switching yard.

OLD ORODELL

Milepost 3.5.

It had a spur connected at the west end 200 feet long.

---

[4]*Boulder Daily Camera*, October 23, 1954.
[5]*Bulletin No. 65, Railway and Locomotive Historical Society.*
[6]*Boulder By-Ways* by Forest Crossen, published by Boulder Savings and Loan Association, 1959.
[7]*Boulder Daily Camera*, October 23, 1954.

1453 DEPOT, BOULDER, COLO.

Post card, courtesy of Stuart Anderson

A morning train pulls into the Boulder station. Covered section of waiting room (to left) was added after station was built. Engine is a standard gauge on Old Main Line. Third rail track to right.

Elbert Hubbard Collection

New rolling stock of the Colorado & Northwestern at Wall Street about 1899. Four Mile Creek in foreground was scene earlier of extensive placer mining by Chinese.

Photo by Otto C. Perry

This fine shot shows No. 32 being overhauled outside the Boulder shops of the DB&W. At her right is No. 33. The shops had two pits for engine work.

At the right is the one-stall carpenters' shop for rebuilding passenger coaches and freight cars.

Canon Park, Boulder, Colorado, today. Up the gravel road to the right ran the main lines of the Greeley, Salt Lake & Pacific and the C&N-DB&W. The Powder Spur was located near the last house. Bridge in foreground crosses Boulder Creek on the improved Colorado Highway 119.

Sturtevant photo. R. H. Kindig Collection

C&N No. 1 returning from Ward with her two-coach train stops in rock cut 1.3 miles above mouth of Four Mile Creek, near Old Orodell. Bill Tipps, who started as a fireman on the C&N and who served to the end as a regular engineer, at left. Conductor Jap Reed standing on pilot. The well-dressed engineer may be Jim Marsh.

LANGDELL

This was not listed on the timetables and there was no siding, only a platform for quick handling of freight. It stood opposite the foot of Poorman Hill, which was dotted with mines that hoisted telluride and rusty gold, free gold and silver ores.[8]

TWO BROTHERS

Milepost 5.9.

It had a spur 184 feet long connected at the east end.

CRISMAN

Milepost 6.2, Elevation 6,300.

Strung out along Four Mile Creek, this camp began as a general store and postoffice in 1875. G. A. Kelley, postmaster and storekeeper, named it for Obed or Abed Crisman, who had built an ore concentrating mill nearby in the early 1870's.[9]

Crisman's prosperity came largely from two mines at the head of nearby Sunbeam Gulch. On one side lay the Yellow Pine with its silver-lead-copper ore, opposite clung the Logans with high-grade free gold and telluride ore. Miners living in Crisman walked to and from work.[10]

When the Greeley, Salt Lake & Pacific came through, Crisman was an important station. The Union Pacific erected a water tank, using gravity flow water from Sunbeam Gulch. The Colorado & Northwestern had a tank, and it may have been the same one.

The station was in Farnsworth's general store, a two-story frame building. Welcome Farnsworth acted as agent. Every two or three days the agent at Salina would coast down on a little track tricycle and check up on the business.[11]

Crisman had a siding 569 feet long and a telegraph box.

BLACK SWAN

Milepost 7.2.

The Black Swan Mill rated a spur 300 feet long, connected at the west end. Black Swan was not a regular stop. If anyone wished to board a train, he had only to flag it down.

SALINA

Milepost 7.5, Elevation 6,571.

In 1873 a colony from Salina, Kansas, settled here, naming the camp for their old home.[12] It was a prosperous place, with rich strikes of tellurium ore in the Emancipation, Richmond, and Ingram Mines furnishing much employment.

The most famous mine was the Melvina. In 1875 Henry Augustus Meyring, a German sailor, came to Salina and worked as a carpenter during construction of an ore mill. When the job was finished, he bought a pick and shovel and went prospecting, though he knew nothing of this specialized craft. Some wags told him to dig on top of a nearby high hill. The day was hot, so he sought the shade of a big pine for his work. Presently along came an honest miner who gasped at the ore Meyring was throwing away. He agreed to help develop the mine for an interest. It proved to be a bonanza.[13]

During the Greeley, Salt Lake & Pacific days the station was named Gold Hill. Stagecoaches and freighters operated to the important camp of the same name a few miles away and 1,726 feet higher.[14]

The Colorado & Northwestern station stood below the junction of Gold Run and Four Mile, on the right bank (looking downstream). It was a frame building with a waiting room and freight room and a platform all the way around. It measured about

[8]Interview with Oscar Bernsten, May 2, 1955.
[9]*Boulder Daily Camera*, May 28, 1956.
[10]*Mining In Boulder County,* published by Boulder County Metal Mining Association, 1910.
[11]Interview with R. D. Ward, August 27, 1957.

[12]*Boulder Daily Camera,* May 28, 1956.
[13]*Boulder Daily Camera,* January 20, 1953.
[14]*Bulletin No. 65, Railway and Locomotive Historical Society.*

West-bound train with combo car No. 51 stops at the Salina station. Note heavy drop in grade to the east.

THE DENVER, BOULDER & WESTERN R. R. CO.

NOT GOOD FOR PASSAGE.

Conductors will preserve this half of all Duplex Tickets issued, and after making their report from them at end of the trip, send them to the Auditor with their Ticket collections.

L. R. FORD, General Manager.

No. 59314

Form C. F.

HALF FARE	CLERGY
O	O
FARE	FARE

Boulder	Hill
Orodell	Blue Bird
Langdell	Anson Park
Crisman	Lakewood
Salina	Cardinal
Wall Street	Sulphide
Freese	Lake Eldora
Copper Rock	Eldora
Sunset	Mont Alto
Sugar Loaf	Gold Hill
Tungsten	Brainerd
Glacier Lake	Puzzler
	Bloomerville
	Frances
	Ward
	Nederland

Ticket form used in the latter days of the Denver, Boulder & Western.

Crossen Collection

Link and pin coupler of Colorado Central boxcar at Sunset. Car was once used on the Greeley, Salt Lake & Pacific.

Sunset, summer of 1898. Both trestles are in and station is finished.

312

Stations

Sturtevant photo. R. H. Kindig Collection

C&N No. 1 at Sunset with a two-coach train. From the unfinished look of Columbine Hotel, beyond locomotive, and station at rear of train this photo was probably taken in early summer of 1898.

Elbert "Jimmie" Hubbard, former fireman and brakeman on the DB&W, right, and Ray Friese on site of Sunset station. To the left is a Denver, South Park & Pacific boxcar of Greeley, Salt Lake & Pacific days.

Crossen photo

Remaining back wall of portal house of the Big Five Company's tunnel at Sunset. In the middle is the portal of the tunnel which was to be driven over three miles in under the Dew Drop vein at Frances and the Columbia Lode at Ward.

20 by 30 feet. The station had local and long distance telephones.[15]

The track ran between the station and the cliff. This was at the steepest grade on the railroad—some said 7%, the locating engineer, J. L. Frankeberger, giving it as 5%. Passenger trains headed west pulled by to easier grade so they could start.[16]

Salina had a siding 1,254 feet long. Heavy tonnages of ore were loaded here; much freight and coal were unloaded.

TAMBOURINE

Milepost 8.5.

Its spur, 400 feet long, connected at the east end, served the nearby Tambourine and other mines.

WALL STREET

Milepost 9.0, Elevation 6,825.

It was originally called Sugar Loaf, for the high wooded mountain to the southward.

In 1866 Gardner P. Wood, a Civil War veteran, located the Wood Mountain Mine one-half mile west. The ore was high-grade tellurium, metallic gold, and silver. Mr. Wood was the first postmaster at Sugar Loaf.[17]

About 1901 the Wood Mountain and the Franklin Mines of Gardner P. Wood were sold to a Wall Street, New York, syndicate. Its officials changed the name to Wall Street.[18]

There was a 545-foot siding and a small frame building about 20 by 20 feet.[19] This was across the canon from the huge stone and frame mill of the Wall Street Gold Extraction Company. This mill was a failure, and long after its abandonment the machinery was moved to a mill site near Sugar Loaf station. Today the weathered stone foundations jutting out from the north wall of the canon make one think of some robber baron's stronghold of the Middle Ages.

Wall Street today is a pleasant summer place. Some people live there the year 'round, commuting to Boulder and other points to work.

WOOD MOUNTAIN

Unlisted flag stop for passengers. Up and down Four Mile Creek Chinese placer miners worked over the gravel already worked by white men and made good cleanups of gold. They had a camp nearby.[20]

FREESE

Unlisted flag stop a short distance west of Wood Mountain. Piles of gravel from placer mining today mark the spot.[21]

COPPER ROCK

Milepost 11.6, Elevation 7,375.

Gold discovered nearby in 1891 set off a flash boom, and a tent and shack camp sprang up overnight on the Greeley, Salt Lake & Pacific.[22] The Orphan Boy Mine, high on the mountainside to the south, continued to produce for years. The camp drew its name from greenish copper stains on a cliff that prospectors pierced with tunnels.

A small frame station stood at the lower end of the camp. There was a siding 585 feet long. Copper Rock was a flag stop.

SHELTON

Unlisted spur that ran into a mine.[23]

SHALE

Milepost 12.5.

Opposite a talus slide ran a siding 440 feet long where the City of Boulder loaded the loose rock onto gondolas. At Boulder the rock went through a crusher and was used for street paving.[24]

[15]Interview with R. D. Ward, August 27, 1957.
[16]*Frankeberger Autobiography.*
[17]*Boulder Daily Camera*, February 26, 1957.
[18]*Ibid.*, October 10, 1956.
[19]Interview with Elbert Hubbard, May 12, 1960.

[20]*Boulder Daily Camera*, February 26, 1957.
[21]*Ibid.*, December 22, 1954.
[22]*Ibid.*, May 28, 1956.
[23]*Ibid.*, December 22, 1959.
[24]*Boulder Daily Camera*, December 22, 1954.

These steel rods in concrete in the portal house of the Big Five Company tunnel at Sunset once held a steam-powered air compressor. It was to furnish air to drillers driving the three-mile-plus tunnel.

Photo by T. C. Black, Jr. A. A. Paddock Collection

Bill Tipps and fireman and two pretty girls in cab of No. 31 at Mont Alto Park.

SUNSET

Milepost 13.3, Elevation 7,750.

When the Greeley, Salt Lake & Pacific in 1883 reached this beautiful wide spot at the junction of Four Mile Creek and Pennsylvania Gulch, the officials named it Pennsylvania Gulch, later shortening it to Penn Gulch.[25] Still later it became Sunset.

The Colorado & Northwestern reached Sunset February 21, 1898, and proceeded with all speed toward Ward. The track crossed Four Mile Creek on a curved trestle and started boldly east up along the north wall of the canon.

The C&N built a wye, which the GSL&P had lacked. This necessitated building a long straight trestle parallel to the curved one.[26] At the lower end the track had to make a sharp bend to swing onto the trestle, and many an engineer cursed it. Once across, the rails ran up and connected with a long east-west wye leg which tied into the Ward line.

When construction of the Eldora branch began in 1904, trains crossed on the straight trestle, continued west, crossing Four Mile Creek on a long curved trestle before starting east up along the south wall of the canon. East of the twin trestles were two switches some 10 feet apart. The main line switch was always left lined up on the Eldora track.

Still farther east on the main line, hard against the mountainside on the south, was a water tank. It was fed by gravity flow from a pipeline running down from an intake box up the creek. Cinders where firemen cleaned their fires may still be seen here.

North of the tank ran a siding, where a carload of coal was spotted for emergency use. Often during snow-bucking locomotives would have to make a run for Sunset to coal up.

The length of siding or sidings at Sunset is given at 1,065 feet.

The attractive frame station, rectangular in shape, stood west of the Ward line. It had a large waiting room and a freight room, measured about 20 by 30 feet. Crews unloaded freight off the cars on the east-west leg of the wye. The station had a day telegraph office and a composite telephone. All train crews had to sign the register.

The C&N pulled some old Colorado Central and Denver, South Park & Pacific boxcars up to Sunset during construction days and set them off their trucks. They were used for storage, etc. One with "Sunset" on its side stood west of the station site, the other farther west. The "Sunset" boxcar, DSP&P No. 24268, was torn down in 1961 to make room for a real estate development.

Charles M. Williams was agent at Sunset during the early days of the C&N. He came down to Boulder as train dispatcher and later was promoted to Secretary and Superintendent. C. H. Chambers was agent at Sunset for many years.[27]

The business section of Sunset was a row of buildings running west of the station and north of the track. There was a saloon, general store, one hotel, etc.

The Columbine Hotel, operated by Alfred Perkins and his family, was an excellent place to stay. Room and board was five dollars a week.[28] Its four long tables were nearly always full, for who could resist mountain-raised beef, vegetables, fruits prepared by wonderful cooks? Tourists came up during the summers and some stayed all season, roaming the hills. Health seekers came, some so weak they could scarcely walk from the station. Plenty of good food, rest, and walks, as their strength increased, put them back on their feet.

At the west end of Sunset stood a landmark, a stone powder house built by the Big Five Company. It too was torn down in 1961 to make way for a real estate development. Trainmen unloaded dynamite here for use in

[25]*Boulder News & Courier,* April 6, 1883.
[26]*Boulder Daily Camera,* December 22, 1954.

[27]Interview, R. D. Ward, August 27, 1957.
[28]*Boulder Daily Camera,* July 15, 1957.

Sturtevant photo. R. H. Kindig Collection

C&N No. 1 on Sawmill Hill, west of Brainerd, with her regular train. Train is standing near crossing of wagon road at left. Later C. W. Strong, mine and mill owner, made this stop the unofficial station "Dawn."

Louis Meile photo

Siding, trestle, and station at Puzzler, mining camp built up around the Puzzler Mine, which was developed by Robert Duncan. Station is the small building to extreme left. Note effective derail of a tie wedged across rail.

C&N boxcar on siding at Puzzler above the Puzzler Mine. Car has link and pin coupler. At upper left the main line continues on up Left Hand Canon to

Bloomerville. At top of mountain to left of center is line beginning its big curve before the final swing into Ward.

driving the tunnel that was to cut in under the fabulous Columbia vein at Ward, some three miles away.[29] The tunnel driving began with a grand flourish but it was abandoned a short distance inside its fine stone portal. Its ruins today mark another vain hope in the history of the Switzerland Trail.[30]

A short spur ran into the tunnel portal. The railroad often stored the snowplow here.[31]

The section men were Old Country Italians and they lived in a log house east of the station. Phillip Gonneley was the boss, a shrewd man who often carried 500-dollar rolls of bills in the pockets of his coat. He later was promoted to Roadmaster.[32]

All west-bound engines took water at Sunset. Before the Eldora branch was built, stagecoaches took train passengers on to the booming camp via the steep road up Pennsylvania Gulch. After 1910 the railroad abandoned daily passenger service to Ward from November until spring. Thereafter a stage line operated daily, meeting morning and afternoon trains at Sunset.

MONT ALTO PARK

Milepost 16.4, Elevation 8,600.

This beautiful resort site, developed by the Colorado & Northwestern, was opened July 15, 1898.[33] It was at once popular for all-day picnics, evening dances, and moonlight excursions. Excursion trains pulled out of Boulder in sections for Mont Alto, one baggage car usually filled with beer on ice. Many were the good times under the big Ponderosa pines. Many were the love troths plighted here under the influence of moonlight and strong lager.

Mont Alto was largely abandoned after the completion of the Eldora branch. The

pavilion was taken down and transported in sections to Glacier Lake on flatcars before the opening of the tourist season of 1905. Sightseers still made the trip there but it was never the same.

Today the U. S. Forest Service maintains Mont Alto as a picnic ground. The stone ruins of the fountain remain, the work of vandals making the heart sad. The tall, grey stone fireplace chimney is a landmark on the site of the pavilion. One can easily reach Mont Alto from Sunset via the grade of the Switzerland Trail. It is a place of haunting memories and inspiring scenic beauty.

There was originally a siding at Mont Alto, but it was pulled up in later days. The crews went on to Ward with the trains, turned on the wye there and returned in time to pick up the excursionists.[34]

GOLD HILL

Milepost 17.8, Elevation 8,740.

A small frame station, about 12 by 12 feet, stood east of the track and south of the intersection of the grade and the road running west from Gold Hill to the Peak-to-Peak Highway.[35] There was a spur 330 feet long with a switch at the west end. Many carloads of coal for Gold Hill and nearby mines were unloaded here.

Two-tenths of a mile south, at the north end of the Culbertson Pass cut, excursion trains would stop. The passengers "oh'd" and "ah'd" at the magnificent view of the Arapahoe Glacier and its attending peak standing out against the western sky.

HOLTVILLE

This was no station or even a siding. It was named for a brakeman, Holt, who owned some mines in the gulch below.[36] He met his

[29]Interview with Ralph Duncan, Colorado Springs, Colorado, July 11, 1959.
[30]Interview, R. D. Ward, July 16, 1957.
[31]*Boulder Daily Camera*, December 22, 1954.
[32]Interview with R. D. Ward, June 30, 1957
[33]*Daily Camera*, July 15, 1898.
[34]Interview with Elbert Hubbard, October 11, 1956.
[35]*Boulder Daily Camera*, October 11, 1956.
[36]*Boulder Daily Camera*, October 11, 1956.

death here one black night, falling under a train. This was one of the worst points for snowdrifts on the Ward line.[37]

BRAINERD

Milepost 20.0, Elevation 8,780.

The railroad, running north, made an abrupt turn to the west through a cut in the shoulder of a mountain above Left Hand Canon. This was called Klondike Point.

Down in the canon lay a small camp named Talcott, more often Camp Brainerd, after Colonel Wesley Brainerd, who developed mines nearby.[38]

At the west end of the cut stood a small frame station covered with sheet iron. A wagon road led down to the camp.

PUZZLER

Milepost 21.9, Elevation 8,800.

About 1890 Robert Duncan discovered and began developing a mine which he named the Puzzler in this beautiful little side gulch running into Left Hand Canon. There was nothing puzzling about the high-grade gold ore that he took out in one month—$39,000 worth. He later built a mill to handle the low-grade ore.[39]

The railroad had a siding 430 feet long below the trestle that crossed the gulch. The track made a complete loop before starting up Left Hand Canon. The station was a small frame building with a loading platform and composite telephone near the upper switch east of the trestle.

This was an important shipping point for silver ore from the nearby White Raven Mine. The low-grade went into gondolas, the sacked high-grade into sealed boxcars. Machinery, coal, and supplies came up in quantity.

In July, 1918, a dam near the head of Left Hand Creek burst and a wall of water ripped out the bridge over California Gulch (North Left Hand branch). Trains ran only as far as Puzzler.

Mrs. M. F. Thompson was operating the boarding house then, and tourists stopped for excellent meals before going on to Ward and Estes Park in Stanley Steamers. The train waited here two hours, giving the crews time for leisurely strolls up the beautiful grassy gulch set with tall spruces.

BLOOMERVILLE

Milepost 23.0, Elevation 9,030.

Bill Bloomer, an early-day miner, drove a tunnel into the mountain here and did considerable mining. The railroad made a complete loop, crossing the wide gulch and starting east up along the slope of Grassy Mountain. A short distance beyond stood a gravity-fed water tank on the north side of the track.[40]

Up west of Bloomerville, in the face of Bald Mountain, lay a big snowdrift that would last most of the summer. The railroad ran Snowball Specials, stopping at Bloomerville. The passengers hiked up to the snow and pelted each other with snowballs, returning wet but hilarious with laughter.[41]

BIG FIVE JUNCTION

Milepost 23.6, Elevation 9,100.

Immediately beyond Alpine Point, the east shoulder of Grassy Mountain, a spur line 0.7 of a mile long ran down to the portal of the Adit-Dew Drop Tunnel of the Big Five Company.

BIG FIVE

Milepost 24.3, Elevation 8,900.

The Big Five was a combination of five mining companies, formed in 1897. Robert and John Duncan worked out the plan to tunnel in under the big ore deposits at Ward, at one stroke providing an annual gold produc-

[37]Interview with R. D. Ward, August 23, 1958.
[38]*Boulder Daily Camera*, October 11, 1956.
[39]Interview with Ralph Duncan, July 11, 1959.
[40]Interview with R. D. Ward, August 23, 1958.
[41]Interview with R. D. Ward, July 16, 1957.

Stations

Crossen Collection

The C&N and the mining camp were new when Louis Meile of Boulder made this photo at Frances, Colorado. The log building at left is postoffice. The long frame building in center foreground under construction was later a general store. The road curving up the hill to the right leads to Ward. The camp straggles down the gentle gulch to the Big Five Mining operations.

325

Crossen photo

Present-day Ward. The big white building at lower left is the Columbia Hotel. The building immediately above and slightly to the right is the Ward Union Congregational Church. Still farther up and to the right is the C&N Hotel. The station which has been turned around and located on the opposite side of the former yards, is at upper right. The mines running up the hill are on the Columbia Lode, with the famous Niwot at the top.

Wye at Ward, located beyond station on spur to New Market. It was large enough to turn locomotive and baggage car. Mont Alto excursion trains, after their passengers alighted, ran on to Ward to turn.

327

A. A. Paddock Collection

Locomotive type boiler, ore bucket, water bailer, mine ore car, steam hoist, smokestack, and pipe for Meade Mine at Ward. Barney & Smith of Dayton, Ohio, were builders of this 40,000-pound capacity flatcar, which is spotted on New Market Extension north of Ward station.

tion of $5,000,000. Unfortunately, it never materialized; neither did the big tonnage promised the Culbertson Mill. This was one of the causes for the failure of the Switzerland Trail.

At the height of activity an estimated 200 men worked in the Big Five and the mill opposite the mouth of the tunnel.[42] Now it's a place of ghosts, the only sound in summer the sigh of occasional winds and the gurgle of water running from the tunnel portal.

The Big Five rated a siding 218 feet long connected at the east end.

FRANCES

Milepost 24.6, Elevation 9,300.

Originally it was Dew Drop, named about 1894 after the Dew Drop Mine.[43] Later the name was changed to Frances, in honor of Frances Daniels, daughter of the president of the Big Five.[44]

It was one of the most peaceful and attractive sites in the mountains, a grassy, gentle vale that sloped down to the north to the Adit-Dew Drop Tunnel. Cabins lined the street, and people cultivated little fenced gardens in the rich soil. At the head of the vale, below the loop the railroad made, stood a log post-office and a frame general store. There were two hotels and a schoolhouse. A small frame station with platform stood beside the track. An estimated 35 families lived in Frances at the peak of its prosperity.

WARD

Milepost 26.1, Elevation 9,450.

This camp had an exciting and promising start. In 1859 one of the prospectors fanning out from Gold Hill struck the lead that developed into the rich Niwot Mine. In 1860 Calvin Ward discovered the Miser's Dream and his name stuck to the camp that mushroomed up along the great Columbia Lode.[45]

Slow expensive transportation by freight wagons retarded Ward's progress. The arrival of the Colorado & Northwestern in 1898 brought wild excitement and sky-high hopes of mass ore shipments.

The ore tonnage failed to materialize, and this caused the beginning of the end for the little railroad.

Tourists found Ward a delightful place. They could stay at the C&N or the Columbia Hotels, take hikes to Red Rock, Duck, and Brainard Lakes, go down in mines, and go fishing. The musical steam whistles of the mines awakened them for golden days, which were followed by the peace and beauty of the mountain nights. They had the exciting Switzerland Trail trains to ride back and forth on. Life was very good.

The big frame station stood east of the tracks. On the south was the waiting room and agent's office. The north end was the freight house, its raised floor and platform at car level. All train crews registered here.

After the railroad's abandonment, in 1920, former agent R. D. Ward bought the station. He converted it to a store, after turning it around and setting it on the west side of the roadway.

Ward had a short wye, where a locomotive and one car or the snowplow could turn. Passenger train crews turned locomotives and baggage cars.

NEW MARKET

Milepost 26.6.

A loading platform built of timber cribbing stood near the New Market Mine and Mill. Hundreds of cars were loaded with lumber, coal mine props, and railroad ties here. There was a siding 430 feet long connected at the east end.

A grade had been built around to the Utica Mine but no track was ever laid on it.

The Colorado & Northwestern had grandiose plans for extending the railroad beyond

[42]*Boulder Daily Camera*, December 4, 1941.
[43]*Boulder Daily Camera*, June 17, 1960.
[44]Interview with Mrs. Nellie Van Patten, July 8, 1959.
[45]*Mining In Boulder County*, published by The Boulder County Metal Mining Association, 1910.

Crossen photo

On the Eldora branch of the Switzerland Trail of America. Ahead is the Arapahoe Glacier and Arapahoe Peak of the Continental Divide. It is now possible to travel by automobile from Sunset to Glacier Lake and from Sunset beyond Mont Alto Park on the old grade.

Ward, even over Buchanan Pass to Middle Park. The loading dock at New Market was its end of steel.

SUGAR LOAF

Milepost 17.3, Elevation 8,475.

From Sunset the Eldora branch climbed steadily along the south wall of Four Mile to the hogback at the foot of Sugar Loaf Mountain. Here it made a complete loop and headed west. On the south side of this loop stood Sugar Loaf station, a little frame building with a loading platform.[46]

At first trains did not use this stop. Locomotives slid off the track in starting, for the grade had not settled correctly. So trains let their passengers off at Tungsten station. Finally one day Jap Reed, veteran conductor, stopped at Sugar Loaf station. The train started normally; the grade had settled.

The station was at once moved from Tungsten to Sugar Loaf, saving people enroute to the mining camp of that name about a one-half mile walk.

On the north side before the curve began there was a siding 368 feet long. Here crews set out cars of coal and mining supplies. They also used it as a passing track. One may still see cinders and pieces of coal here.

Much equipment for the big U. S. Gold Corporation at Sugar Loaf was unloaded at the station. Teams and wagons were used for freighting at first, then trucks.

TUNGSTEN

Milepost 17.9, Elevation 9,050.

It had a 342-foot siding where cars of freight were set out during the tungsten boom of World War I. Ore and concentrates were also loaded here.[47]

GLACIER LAKE

Milepost 22.4, Elevation 9,050.

A small natural lake lay here amongst

the pines called Pennsylvania Lake. After completion of the Eldora branch in 1904, the railroad changed its name to Glacier Lake and began building it up as its big picnic resort. They set up the Mont Alto pavilion here and greatly enlarged the lake by throwing a dam across its lower end.

Through the summers Glacier Lake was the scene of big picnics of lodges, unions, associations, etc. The largest was the Denver Grocerymens' Association, with 18 trains required to bring up the crowd from Boulder.

The view of the Continental Divide peaks from Glacier Lake was grand and the trip up there was of startling, always-changing beauty. Little wonder that the trip became famous.

In an effort to create winter business, the railroad officials formed a company to cut ice on the lake. They did this for years, shipping most of it to Denver.

Glacier Lake had a wye, a small station with a composite telephone, telegraph box, and local and long distance telephone, and a water tank. There was a house for the section men who vainly tried to keep the road open during the winters. There was a lunch room, open in the summers. The length of siding is given as 1,928 feet.

PINNACLE

(Not listed on official 1913 Employees' Timetable).

This was the highest point on the Eldora branch, located where the present Peak-to-Peak Highway crosses the grade west of Glacier Lake. From here on the hard-working fireman could get up on the left-hand seat and watch the scenery go by.

HILL

Milepost 23.3, Elevation 9,000.

E. B. Hill of Boulder had a sawmill nearby, and many carloads of lumber went out from here. This was also an important point when the City of Boulder was building a dam

[46]*Boulder Daily Camera,* January 5, 1955.
[47]*Ibid.,* January 5, 1955.

331

Here locomotives once rambled easily. On the Eldora branch west of Glacier Lake.

Crossen photo

332

T. C. Black, Jr., photo
Courtesy Jewell and Frank Black

Two trains at Eldora on a summer afternoon. Photo taken before erection of station, probably in 1905. Near lead locomotive is site of the Monte Carlo Dance Hall, a lively spot during the boom of 1898-1900. Many business and professional men flocked here, far from home, for a wild fling with the wine, the girls, and the song.

at Albion Lake. There was a small frame station at the south side of the track, at the east end of the cut. Elbert Hubbard said there were two sidings, one on the right (as one faced west) called Hill, the other on the left for the City of Boulder. The length of siding was 639 feet.

SILVER LAKE SIDING

(Not listed in 1913 Employees' Timetable).

Heavy freight shipments were unloaded here by the City of Boulder for construction of the dam at Silver Lake and for Camp Albion, at one time a promising mining camp.

BLUE BIRD

Milepost 26.7.

This was a flag stop station for the nearby Blue Bird Mine. There was no building, only a platform for freight handling.

Excursion trains came here in the summers, people hiking up to nearby North Boulder Falls.

ANSON

Milepost 27.3, Elevation 8,595.

It had a passing track 584 feet long and a water tank. The water came from a spring on the hill to the right. The downgrade ended here, and the firemen had to get off their seats. The grade, however, was gentle.

LAKEWOOD

Milepost 28.5.

This station and the camp of the same name on North Boulder Creek, one and one-half miles away by wagon road, were named for C. F. Lake, manager of the Primos Mining & Milling Company. During the tungsten boom this flag stop in the pines was a busy place. Crews set out cars of coal and supplies for the big Primos Mill at Lakewood and the mines operated by the Primos Company. Car-

load after carload of tungsten concentrates were shipped from here. Its spur, 639 feet long, was connected at the west end.

WOLFRAM

Milepost 29.4.

Coal and supplies for the Conger Mine, said to be the world's largest tungsten mine at that time, one mile away, were unloaded here. It had a spur 375 feet long connected at the west end.

CARDINAL

Milepost 30.0, Elevation 8,710.

This was the station for Nederland and for Caribou. The latter camp, however, furnished little business to the Switzerland Trail, for its greatness passed with the demonitization of silver in 1893. The business for Nederland was very heavy during the tungsten boom. Local business from the Boulder County Tunnel and other nearby mines helped swell the revenues of the railroad.

The station stood west of the track at the north end of the trestle crossing Coon Creek. It had an agent.

After the railroad crossed the curving trestle, it continued east through the spruces, then made a right-hand curve to the south. A spur ran west from the south end of the trestle to the Boulder County Tunnel.

One can still see a boxcar which stood almost under the short trestle east of the main trestle, on the present road to Caribou. It was one of the old Colorado Central cars used by section men. It is now a summer cabin, its sides covered with shingles.

SULPHIDE

Milepost 32.1, Elevation 8,530.

During the construction of the Barker Dam east of Nederland, 1907-10, this was an important stop. A spur line belonging to the construction company ran down to the dam. Trainloads of cement, materials, and supplies were delivered here to crews of the construction company to take down to the dam site with their saddle tank locomotives.

Sulphide had a wye. Trains had to back down from Eldora to turn here. Siding length is listed as 953 feet.

A water tank stood at the west side of the open valley north of the trestle crossing Middle Boulder Creek and west of the track.

LAKE ELDORA

Milepost 32.7, Elevation 8,600.

A steep road led from the flag stop up to Lake Eldora, popular summer resort when the Switzerland Trail operated. It was an important point for shipment of timber cut on the higher slopes. There was a west-end connected spur 258 feet long. Today the place is commonly called Marysville.

There was a small square frame waiting room, enclosed on three sides, here. It contained one long bench and was unheated. After abandonment of the railroad, it was moved to Eldora and now stands directly west of the station building.

ELDORA

Milepost 33.4, Elevation 8,730.

Set in a wide valley between Spencer Mountain (south) and Eldorado Mountain, Eldora is one of the most beautiful places in Boulder County. It is now a quiet summer resort, with many cabins along the banks of clear rushing Middle Boulder Creek.

Eldora has not always been quiet. In 1875 C. C. Alvord discovered the Fourth of July Mine to the northwest. In 1891 John H. Kemp of Central City and seven partners located the Happy Valley Placer. They called the little camp Happy Valley.[48]

Prospectors discovered gold on Spencer Mountain in 1892. The camp grew, taking the name of Eldorado. A town of the same name

in California caused mix-ups in mail, so the U. S. Postal Department changed the name to Eldora.

More gold discoveries and lavish promotion in the spring of 1897 started a boom. It roared through 1898, one of the last of the old wild-day stampedes. Eldora had four stage lines into it, several dance halls, nine saloons, 1,000 people.

The Colorado & Northwestern built the Eldora branch on the lure of vast tonnages promised by the Mogul Tunnel and other mines. None materialized. The rails reached the camp at the end of 1904.

The railroad strove valiantly to maintain daily service to Eldora. Many times in windy winter weather the locomotive cut off the train at Glacier Lake and made the run with passengers, mail, etc., in the cab. The menace of snow drifting in behind the engine often stopped the crew at Sulphide Flats. Then it was up to the brakeman to hike to the camp with the mail.

The station was an attractive frame building south of Boulder Creek. It was a day telegraph office, and all train crews registered here. It had a west end connected spur 608 feet long. The rails ran between the station and Spencer Mountain, ending in a barrier. Today the station is a summer cottage. One may still see cinders nearby from cleaning fires at the end of this run.

DAWN

The character of the Switzerland Trail and the affection held by the mountain people for the little railroad were never better expressed than in the station "Dawn." Located at the junction of the Sawmill Hill Road and the railroad, it was totally unofficial. It was, however, a recognized stop by train crews and officials alike.

C. W. Strong, mine and mill owner who lived a short distance below, in Left Hand Canon, chose this as a convenient spot to

---

[48] *Stampede To Timberline* by Muriel Sibell Wolle, sponsored by University of Colorado, published by Artcraft Press, Denver, Colorado, 1949.

board the trains and alight from them. One day he erected a sign that looked official with the neat lettering "Dawn." Why he chose this name no one knew or cared. The name had a good sound, reflecting the bright promise of new day, so there it remained . . .

Now the stations of the Switzerland

Trail have disappeared or been converted to other uses. They have not, however, been forgotten. Around their sites there still hangs the aura of that warm, throbbing day when trains arrived and departed and strong, happy people filled with hope rode the curving rails of the Switzerland Trail of America.

Photo courtesy of Mary E. Strong

Sign of unofficial station "Dawn" erected by C. W. Strong, mine and mill owner, at junction of Sawmill Hill wagon road and the Colorado & Northwestern. Mr. Strong was owner of the Boston Mill, which may be seen in far middle background below in Left Hand Canon. The big grey building at left between signposts is the Ward Pyritic Smelter, then shut down.

336

Part II

Chapter XI

STORIES OF THE TRAIL

People still tell stories of the Switzerland Trail, though few remain who rode it and lived along its curving rails, still fewer the men who operated its trains. Fortunately, we have some stories from those no longer with us.

C. O. "Ode" JONES[1]

C. O. "Ode" Jones lived up in the west end of Boulder, almost under the foothills, the part least changed from the old days. Ode was a tall, slender man with white hair and blue eyes, a ready smile and laugh. He had been a steam hoisting engineer at the hard-rock mines and he had gone to Sunset shortly after the Switzerland Trail was built.

"Sunset was pretty lively then. Two hotels, two grocery stores, one meat market, and one saloon. There was plenty of work in the mines and the railroad had a pretty good payroll there.

"There were some characters around . . .

"There used to be an old Dutchman down there at Copper Rock. It used to be a lively little place. It had a store, postoffice, and saloon. Now look at it. Nothing there except the cliff and one building.

"Well, this old Dutchman went away for a long time. When he came back, the railroad had come up through there. They'd moved his cabin back off the right-of-way. He was a hot-headed old devil, so he flew mad.

"The boys told him if he'd go down and see the Superintendent, maybe he'd give him a hundred dollars for his trouble. 'But don't lose your temper,' they warned him. " 'All right,' he said. 'I won't.'

So he came down to Boulder on the train and went up to the railroad's offices in the National State Bank Building. J. T. Blair, the Superintendent, was sitting there in his office reading a newspaper.

" 'Good morning, Mr. Blair,' said the old Dutchman, as polite as could be.

"Blair didn't look up, he just nodded.

"That started the old Dutchman up. 'Good morning, you son ....!'

"Blair got up and threw him down the stairs!"

When Ode quit laughing, he looked up brightly. "That time we had the big snow up there—in December, 1913—the narrow gauge was blocked. They had to get a rotary snowplow from the C&S to open up the railroad.

"They got up there to Glacier Lake and stopped. The railroad had all its section men out there helping. They were Old-Country Italians.

"A shovel fell off the engine and landed down underneath. Williams (C.M.), the Superintendent, was there. 'Mike,' he said to one of the Italians, 'get down there and get that shovel.'

"Mike took a look at the engines with steam up and the big rotary, its smokestack boiling out black smoke, and shook his head. 'They can make more shovel. They can't make another Mike!' "

DORA JONES[2]

Mrs. (Dora) Jones, a brisk little woman big in spirit and kindliness, was listening in. She handed me a faded photograph.

---

[1]*Boulder Daily Camera*, June 7, 1957.

[2]*Boulder Daily Camera*, July 15, 1957.

"This is a picture of the Columbine Hotel at Sunset, taken in the spring of 1898. My father, Alfred Perkins, built it. It had 14 rooms and we served meals to a lot of boarders who didn't live at the hotel.

"The people up there were the finest I ever knew. They had their differences but they forgot them when there was a social gathering. And people helped each other, let me tell you. Yes, I've always been glad I lived in the mountains.

"We sure had good times up there. We used to dance all night long, start in about 8 o'clock.

"In the wintertime most of our boarders and roomers were miners. In the summertime we had tourists. Sunset was a great tourist camp. They'd come up on the trains and some would stay all summer.

"I used to get out in the summers with the tourists and climb mountains. We used to walk half way to Sugar Loaf (Mountain), picking raspberries, pin cherries, and chokecherries." She smiled. "In those days we wore long dresses, so climbing wasn't so easy. It would have been a real insult if a woman had come out in a pair of overalls . . ."

ERNEST GREENMAN[3]

Ernest Greenman of Boulder, a tall, very active man who climbed mountains almost until the day of his death, had a warm spot in his heart for the Switzerland Trail.[3] He joined the survey gang headed by Daniel S. Hooker three weeks before Thanksgiving, 1897, retracing the old right-of-way of the Union Pacific (Greeley, Salt Lake & Pacific) from Sunset to Glacier Lake.

In the early 1880's the Union Pacific had made the grade, put in bridges, but had not laid any track. The Colorado & Northwestern tied the line into the Government section lines so that rights-of-way could be filed.

Late in the fall of 1898 Ernest had charge of grading and building a spur line

from the point of Grassy Mountain (Alpine Point) on the Ward line to the Adit Tunnel of the Big Five Group.

Section gangs and all the extra men available were put to laying track. Winter, however, swooped down and stopped them. They had to wait until the next spring to complete the work.

"The drifts on Grassy Mountain piled up until they were 40 feet deep in places. The railroad company had been awarded the mail contract to Ward, so it had to deliver it. The officials had as high as 270 men shoveling snow to keep the track open. And even then they couldn't do it."

The railroad had to abandon service from Puzzler on, a messenger taking the light mail on a saddle horse. Then the weather became so severe that service had to be abandoned beyond Sunset. The heavy mail did not go through until spring.

"I worked on the gang clearing snow," Ernest said. "We would leave the (Boulder) yards at 5 o'clock on those bitter cold mornings and go as far as possible. We usually started back early, always fearful that the snow would pile in behind us. We had to shovel out by hand what the wedge plow ahead of the engine could not push to one side."

Ernest knew the early train crews. Jim Marsh was one of the first engineers, and Bill Tipps was his fireman. Bill Hannan was another engineer. Johnny Milner came out from Pennsylvania to fire an engine. His eyes were so weak that he had to wear thick-lens spectacles, and this defect kept him from getting an engine. Jasper "Jap" Reed and Fred Conrad were conductors. Dan O'Brien, an old Irish railroader from Pennsylvania, was the first Roadmaster.

FRANK TIPPS[4]

Frank Tipps of Boulder was a son of Bill Tipps, the best known of all Switzerland Trail engineers.

[3]*Boulder Daily Camera*, April 7, 1938.

[4]*Boulder Daily Camera*, February 27, 1953.

Sturtevant photo, from Mary Elizabeth Wirtz Collection

Everything is raw and new at Sunset when C&N No. 1 arrives with her short train. Bridge over little side stream in foreground lacks outside flooring. To the right above Four Mile Creek, is the ditch dug for the pipeline to run water from a headgate farther upstream to the unfinished water tank. In later days a short siding was built below trestles opposite tank. It held a gondola or two of coal for emergency fueling. Columbine Hotel is two-story building at left. Time: Spring of 1898.

"I guess everybody in the mountains knew my father," he began. "He came here from Nebraska and was up on the narrow gauge at least 21 years. So that puts him back at the start of the railroad, in 1898.

"We lived at 4th and Pearl. The railroad shops were over at 5th and Water, so I spent a lot of time as a boy there. One of my proudest recollections is Father taking me in the cab with him with a trainload of ore out to the Culbertson Mill."

Frank mentioned that Pat Dinley was fireman for Bill Tipps in those first days.

"I fired for him (Pat) in later years," Frank continued. "Pat would have a cigar in his mouth when we'd leave Boulder but never light it. I'd look over the boiler at him and the cigar would be getting shorter and shorter. He never took it out of his mouth and he never spit.

"Father had a steady job as engineer the year 'round. The other engineers were cut back to firemen but he always had the passenger run. He was assigned to No. 32 and he was very proud of her.

"They put straight air brakes on the 32, a novel thing at that time. Father understood the system and he had to make the repairs himself until the Master Mechanic learned how to handle it.

"The 33 was the largest narrow gauge engine in the world at the time she was delivered here in Boulder. She had a 200-pound pop valve. They later cut it back to 180 pounds.

"One time up at Mont Alto Park they had a grocerymans' picnic and had to lease C&S engines and coaches to handle the big crowd. Our engines would take up four coaches; it took two of theirs to handle them. They looked like toys . . . I've known my dad to take three coaches and two observation cars up to Mont Alto."

Frank was proud of his own rating as a fireman.[5]

_____
[5]*Boulder Daily Camera,* March 23, 1953.

"I started working when I was fourteen —but the management didn't know I was that young," he said, a twinkle in his eye. "I used to stop on the way to and from school and pump the bellows for Charley Harvey, the blacksmith.

"I quit school when I was 16 and started to work. My first job was wiping engines. I must have done a good job shining them up, for after three days the Master Mechanic put me to helping anyone who needed help. I helped the carpenter, car whacker, boiler maker, machinist, blacksmith, the painter— and I shoveled coal and cinders. My pay was $1.50 a day. I don't remember whether it was 9 or 10 hours. This was in 1907.

"Then I got on nights helping the hostler and eventually got to be a hostler. And that brings me to an experience one night when I had a new helper, name of Charley Humphrey.

"We had three engines to coal. We coaled engine 30 and ran it over on the main track that ran from the trestle (over Boulder Creek) to 9th Street, blocked the engine, and filled the boiler with water. Then we coaled the 31 and put it to bed in front of the 30. Last came the 32. All engines were headed west for their runs up into the mountains.

"As the 32 had straight air, I cracked the valve on the pump just enough to start it and was running the engine over to put it to bed in front of the others.

"I called to my helper to watch and not let me bump them. He, being new, didn't stop me in time and let me bump the 31, knocking

_____

Opposite Page

Original painting by Richard Ward
Courtesy of Michael Koch

Proud and powerful in her shining newness, Colorado & Northwestern No. 30 charges through the deep Adit Cut with the Ward train during the first winter's operations on the new railroad, 1898-99. The cut, rammed and hand shoveled through the great snowdrift near Frances, has caused enough trouble and expense to merit a name.

WARD.—'62.

it off the block and it in turn knocked the 30 off. From there down to the main part of Boulder there is a considerable grade.

"I slammed the air brake on the 32, jumped off and ran as fast as I could—to find both the 31 and the 30 moving off down the track in front of the still moving 32, making all three engines moving at the same time.

"I ran almost to 6th Street before I could catch the 30. It being full of water, I had to open the cylinder cocks and use the reverse lever to slow the engine down. As I did so the 31 would bump me and we would go a little farther down the track. We bumped along almost to 9th Street.

"Finally I got both engines stopped and ran them back toward the roundhouse. Here I found my helper too scared to talk, but we finally got all three engines put away for the night."

Frank paused a moment, reflecting. Then he nodded at a memory."I was called to make my first trip firing on passenger with John Wilson on the one spot (No. 1) before I was 17. There were a lot of us young fellows working on the railroad because our dads were railroad men.

"I recall one trip during the construction of the Barker Dam. We went out on a double-header hauling cement with the oldest one of our crew the conductor. He was 23. The engineer I was firing for, Fred Wilson, was 21. Fred and I were assigned to the 25, the Shay engine, or 'Coffee Grinder' as we called it.

"We used to have fun on those big Sunday excursions. My dad would take the first section out to Mont Alto Park. The rest of us would go out about five minutes apart — John Wilson, Henry Gormley, and Pat Dinley. We'd hurry and try to catch up to Dad and push him."

Frank grinned. "I'll tell you about a Negro excursion from Denver that I went out on.

"We were going up the (Boulder) Canon. I started to put in a fire when I hap-

pened to look up and see a big black fellow come down over the coal in the tender. He wore good clothes and had big diamonds.

"He wanted to put in the coal. 'I used to be a fireman,' he said. He was about half drunk. All of them back in the coaches had been drinking.

"I talked him out of it but he wanted to go out on the running board. I told him he'd get all dirty but he said he was going anyway. So he crawled out through the front window of the cab on my side.

"No sooner had he got out there than some others back on the platform of the head coach began shooting at him. You can bet your life I ducked! Fortunately, they didn't hit him."

OSCAR BERNSTEN[6]

Oscar Bernsten began railroading on the Colorado & Northwestern in 1907, when he was 17. In August, 1909, he became a fireman and in 1916 was promoted to engineer. He worked for the DB&W until 1918.

"The water all along the line was good," Oscar once told me. "It wouldn't foam and give you trouble. When they washed out the boilers they'd get only a little scale. No mud. They never used any compound, never knew what it was."

He spoke of the tank at Crisman, where every engine going up filled its (tender) tank.

"We needed it all right. It was a hard pull up Four Mile, the hardest pulling on the railroad. We used so much water that we were always worried whether we'd make it up to Sunset tank.

"We used to hang up at Walters' place, above Wall Street and the Wood Mountain Mine. There was a curve there and mighty steep. Right down below was a nice stretch of straight track. We'd get up all the speed we could but going around that hook lots of times we'd hang up.

---

[6]*Boulder Daily Camera*, March 16, 1957.

Borrowed Denver & Rio Grande diamond-stack No. 41 lies over the bank of Four Mile Creek. This was the first wreck of the C&N, occurring in 1898 or 1899. Fred Conrad, who had hired out as a conductor, was given the job of rerailing her. From then on he was in charge of wrecking operations until the end of his service.

Boxcar loaded with lumber wrecked in Four Mile Creek behind borrowed D&RG No. 41.

One of the Consolidations lies upside down in Four Mile Creek. Note the blind (flangeless) drivers and the double eccentric big ends of the Stephenson valve gear.

"We'd uncouple, take a couple cars up to Copper Rock, the only place you could set 'em on a siding. Then we'd double back for the rest of the train.

"Before that, lots of times we'd have to double at Salina. We'd hang up on that curve just below the depot—on the steepest grade on the railroad. We'd uncouple, pull up two cars to one or the other of the sidetracks above, set 'em out, and go back for the others.

"That used up the water. More than once we'd get to Sunset with only six inches of water in the rear of the tank. Sometimes the injectors would start breaking before we could reach Sunset."

Prompted a little, Oscar told about firing for Bill Tipps.[7] "Going up the (Boulder) Canon Bill would have his injector on all the time. He pinched the water valve down so that only a little went into the boiler, but that went in hot. Then when we'd stop he'd open the water valve up, fill the boiler. And you had to keep the water high. If you let it and the steam get down you were finished.

"Comin' down I'd generally work my injector. On that Eldora run going up with two coaches and two observation cars a fireman had all he could do from here to Sunset to keep her hot. Every time you stopped that blower went on.

"After you left Sunset you had a breather. You could get by on 150 pounds of steam, but going up you had to have the pop valve singing."

Oscar would talk of the locomotives almost as if they were human.[8] "The Shay would pull 110 tons. She would pull her tonnage from Glacier Lake to Nederland Dam alone. We couldn't get much speed out of her, only 15 miles an hour. The reason was that she was a rigid engine—engine and tender together—and she would jump the track if we pushed her too hard.

"I'll never forget the first time I fired her up the canon. I happened to look ahead as we were going around a curve. The pony wheels at the head end were eight or 10 inches off the track! I thought sure she was going to turn over, but as soon as we straightened up she climbed back on the track."

It took good coal and plenty of it to pull the tonnage to Ward and Eldora. "When I first went to work they were getting coal from the Green River field in Wyoming. Then later they got coal from the Trinidad field. That Wyoming coal was much the best. It wouldn't clinker and it'd burn like pop corn. It really made steam."[9]

Oscar would shake his head solemnly when the talk swung around to winter operations.[10]

"We used to have an awful time buckin' snow. Winters used to be harder then. When the White Raven Mine was producin' big, we kept the road open to Puzzler. It was tough goin', for those cuts would drift full of snow.

"We'd pick up the big blade snowplow at Sunset and couple it on ahead of the engine. It weighed 30 tons and we'd ram it through those drifts. The DB&W never owned a rotary.

"We'd back up about a quarter of a mile from the cuts and take a run at them, getting up to 25 or 30 miles an hour. I had to have the boiler full of water and a heavy fire on the grates. My place was at the engineer's side.

"We'd hit the drifts with terrific force but not always did we get through. The engine would start slowin' down to a stop. That was one thing we couldn't let happen!

"Without shuttin' off the throttle, the engineer and I would grab the Johnson Bar and yank it back to reverse position. The way those drivers would spin! The engine would back out of the drift, so we could take a new run at it.

"If the engineer had shut off his throttle,

---

[7]*Boulder Daily Camera*, December 13, 1956.
[8]*Ibid.*, February 25, 1938.

[9]*Boulder Daily Camera*, September 14, 1952.
[10]*Ibid.*, January 18, 1957.

we would have had to be shoveled out. The engine couldn't have backed out from a dead stop.

"That was railroadin'. The next spring we'd find places in the rails that the drivers had burned into 'em as they spun.

"Again and again we'd buck into the drifts, until finally we would force our way through.

"By that time we'd be almost out of water and we'd have to back down to Sunset, nine miles or more away, to fill up."

Oscar paused, his lips tightening to a thin grim line. "I remember the time Pat Dinley and I got to Bloomerville water tank with the 30 and there wasn't any water in the (tender) tank and mighty little in the boiler! And the gooseneck on the water tank was froze up!

"We'd cleaned out the snow to Puzzler and decided to go on up to the tank at Bloomerville. It wasn't very far. Only that day it was too far. We were out of water in the tank.

"We'd have made it all right, but just this side of the Bloomerville tank was a long shallow cut full of snow. It must have been a hundred feet long.

" 'We've got one more spurt,' said Pat. 'If we don't make it, you grab the shaker bar and dump the fire out of her.' "

This was the last resort, for it meant draining the boiler and all the pipes, the latter by uncoupling the unions. Then a long walk to the nearest telephone and wait until a locomotive from Boulder could arrive to take them and the dead engine back to town.

" 'All right,' I told him. It was colder than the devil, the wind blowin', snow flyin'.

"I got her hot. There was only about an inch of water in the glass.

"Pat took a run. We hit that snow with a thud. The 30 commenced to slow down. My heart was 'way up here in my throat; I was sure she'd stop. But she kept on, slower and slower. Finally we broke through.

"Pat stopped under the water tank and

I ran up the coal in the tender to the manhole on the tank. Then I really got scared. The gooseneck on that old wooden water tank was froze up!

" 'What are we goin' to do now?' I yelled to Pat. 'She's froze up.'

" 'We'll have to back up and thaw it out,' he yelled back.

"That really scared me. I knew there couldn't be any water in that glass; ramming through that drift had used it up. And I had a heavy fire. 'Shall I shake the fire out of her?' I yelled.

" 'No. I get a flutter out of this lowest try cock.'

"He backed up and I started to thaw out that gooseneck with the steam hose. I was out on the running board along the boiler where the blower pipe came out. We carried the steam hose wrapped around the sand dome—in case we had to use it quick.

"Pat was rocking the engine back and forth. I knew what he was doin'—sloshin' water over the crownsheet to keep her from blowin' up.

"Finally I got it thawed out and the water broke through with a rush. Pat had to pull ahead about 12 feet, so I could get the spout in the tank manhole. We had about 175 pounds of steam. It gave me a funny feelin'—it's all right to sit here talkin' about it now—but there was no water over the crownsheet. And there was a heavy fire. At any moment she might collapse and blow up.

"Water ran down into the tank, enough so that the injector would take. Pat never stopped shaking the engine. Then—

"When I heard that old injector go on and take, I thought, 'Goodbye, Pat.' And, of course, for me. You turn water in on a red hot crownsheet, and you'll blow a boiler all to ....!

"But he was still there. Little by little the water in the glass went up."

Oscar let out a long sigh. "That was the

C&N No. 25, the Shay, has jumped the track and fallen over the bank of Four Mile Creek. Crew is about ready to pull her out, as attached chain would indicate. This happened near Crisman.

No. 25, the Shay, lies over the bank of Four Mile Creek. Silhouetted workmen face hard task rerailing her, for the C&N-DB&W never owned a wrecker.

Robert J. "Jap" Reed, popular veteran conductor at left. Beside him is Engineer Pat Dinley. J. L. Lloyd, a miner, is at right with flag. Brakeman unknown.

Facsimile of pass forms issued by the Colorado & Northwestern Railroad Company in 1907.

closest call I ever had. The level track there at the Bloomerville tank was the only thing that saved us."

FRED HEATON[11]

"Most interesting of all were the characters who worked on the Switzerland Trail, who kept the trains running," said Fred Heaton, who returned to Boulder in 1957 for a visit after many years in Los Angeles.

"There was Pat Dinley, engineer. He was a Rock Island engineer when I first knew him, back in Goodland, Kansas, when I was a small boy. Pat was buckin' the extra board then. This was about 1895.

"He came here to Boulder shortly after that and started firing. This must have been not long after the road started. He was on the extra board as an engineer and he also worked as a hostler.

"Pat was a wiry little fellow, with a typical Irish button nose. He was never married that I know of and he was full of fun. He used to drink quite a bit, like a lot of men did then."

Fred's half grin exploded into a laugh. "One time when Pat was hostling at night he was getting up steam on the 30. The 30 had a peculiarity. When the steam would go down, the weight of the rod that pulled the whistle valve would make the valve stick open.

"Pat had been on one of his periodicals but he was working right along. He got a fire going, and the steam commenced coming up. The whistle commenced blowing, low at first. Then it got louder, for the 30 was a good steamer.

"Dick Williams, the Master Mechanic at that time, heard that whistle going and down he came to the roundhouse. He hurried up to the 30 and climbed up into the cab.

"He took one look and reached up on the engineer's side and shoved the whistle valve shut. There was Pat on the fireman's seat, sound asleep.

"No, nothing happened. Williams had to laugh, for he was a drinker too."

I laughed, then silently urged Fred to tell more.

"Dick Williams had the third and fourth fingers of one hand off. When he was drinking in the saloons, he'd emphasize his points by jabbing you with his two remaining fingers. It felt like being punched with a baseball bat!

"Williams was an able man. He was of medium build, don't think he'd weigh over 160. Sharp features, hair a little grey. Quick spoken. Never had to grope for words.

"Henry Gormley was a boomer engineer. He'd worked around on several railroads. He worked summers here and he was here some of the winters too.

"He was always called High Water Gormley. He carried it up almost against the dome. If it got down to the second try cock, he'd raise the devil. If the fireman didn't keep it up, he'd throw his injector open and put in some more.

"None of the firemen liked to fire for him. On these heavy drags, like from here to Sunset, he'd work the devil out of them. It's hard to keep up steam with so much water.

"He'd probably had some bad experience with low water on some road before coming here." Fred grinned widely. "He never lost a crownsheet when he was working here. He always had 'em buried deep."

FRED CONRAD[12]

I used to see him walking slowly about the streets of Boulder, a slender, fine-looking old man in a carefully pressed blue serge suit.

"There are so many things in a man's life that change everything for him," he said to me one day. "When I left New York I was headed for California, to go to work on the Santa Fe."

He stopped off to see a boyhood friend in Denver. This man urged him to stay in

---

[11]*Boulder Daily Camera*, July 22, 1957.

[12]*Boulder Daily Camera*, April 9, 1938.

Colorado, for the railroads here wanted good men. Fred agreed, speedily found a job with the Colorado & Southern.

"Then, before I finished learning the railroad," he continued, "I heard that the Colorado & Northwestern wanted trainmen. I found that I could go to work as a conductor right away. And so I came to Boulder in the fall of 1898."

Not long after that an engineer derailed a borrowed Denver & Rio Grande engine, Number 41. The engineer barely escaped with his life when she went off the track in Four Mile Canon and landed on her side about 12 feet away, down in the creek.

The railroad officials called all the men into the office and asked if any had had any experience in wrecking service.

In the days of his youth on the Lehigh Valley Railroad Fred had worked with an Irishman who was the champion wrecker of that part of the country. He seemed to have a genius for getting locomotives back on the rails. Fred had earned his praise by attention to duty and aptness in learning this ticklish business.

"If you'll give me the equipment and men I want," he spoke up, "I'll put that locomotive back on the track."

"All right," the Superintendent agreed.

Fred asked for a big pulley and cable, but there was no derrick. Very well, he would do the job without it.

First he planted a timber 18 inches square and several feet long in the ground to serve as anchor for the big pulley. Then he cut the rails and curved them down the creek bank over the boulders to the side of the overturned locomotive. The next step was to hook the cable to an engine with full steam up on the track.

Three days later he had the locomotive back on the track. Thereafter he was given all wrecking jobs. His biggest and hardest job was rerailing the two locomotives swept down

by an avalanche on Grassy Mountain when bucking snow April 18, 1901.

"I never had a wreck on the road," he said proudly. "But I had an experience at Salina one Saturday night that came near turning my hair white.

"Every Saturday night I would pull out of Boulder with my train at six o'clock for Ward. This summer night I had two passenger coaches loaded with about fifty people, a merchandise boxcar, and a car of coal. In addition, Charles Culbertson, the General Manager and one of the owners, and William Allison and their wives were riding a little push car roped on behind. They were going to Mont Alto Park for a picnic. With the push car they could coast down to Boulder whenever they pleased."

At Salina they broke the train apart to set out the car of coal. Fred had a brakeman named Albert Stockin, a new man.

"Always set the brakes by hand when we stop, Al," he had told him. "Never trust the air brakes; the air might leak out and release them."

The engine had just spotted the car of coal on a sidetrack when Fred looked back toward the train. It was moving ever so slightly! It was on the steepest grade of the railroad.

He ran like a person possessed to the merchandise car, skinned up the iron ladder and grabbed the hand-brake wheel. He twisted it down with all his strength, then raced down to set the brakes on the two passenger coaches.

The train stopped before it had gained much momentum.

"I don't think any of the passengers realized what had happened," he said, smiling, "but I never forgot it."

F. R. DUNGAN[13]

In the summer of 1897 F. R. Dungan began working as a surveyor under Chief

[13]*Boulder Daily Camera*, July 2, 1938.

RECEIPT FOR FREIGHT DELIVERED

Form 9

....Station,....................................191........

Received of the **DENVER, BOULDER & WESTERN RAILROAD CO.,**

FREIGHT BILL No.

....

Following Articles from...

Date of Way-Bill	ARTICLES	WEIGHT	RATE	FREIGHT	ADVANCES	PREPAID
No. of Way-Bill						
Car No.						
Initials						
Consignor, Connecting Line Reference, Original Car No., Way-Bill No. and Point of Origin.						

$..................... TOTAL TO COLLECT

Deliver freight only to Consignee or on his written order. Receipt of person to whom freight is delivered must be taken on this form, which must be carefully filed in numerical order at station.

.... **Consignee**

Date.......................................191......

FREIGHT BILL

Form 9—50M—8-16—C

....Station,....................................191........

To the **DENVER, BOULDER & WESTERN RAILROAD CO., Dr.**

FREIGHT BILL No.

For Charges on Articles from...

Date of Way-Bill	ARTICLES	WEIGHT	RATE	FREIGHT	ADVANCES	PREPAID
No. of Way-Bill						
Car No.						
Initials						
Consignor, Connecting Line Reference, Original Car No., Way-Bill No. and Point of Origin.						

Total to Collect $.....................................

Received Payment...191......

.... **Agent**

CLAIMS FOR OVERCHARGE OR LOSS AND DAMAGE SHOULD BE SENT TO AUDITOR WITH FREIGHT BILL AND ORIGINAL BILL OF LADING ATTACHED.

Courtesy Richard Lind

Freight receipt form used by the Denver, Boulder & Western.

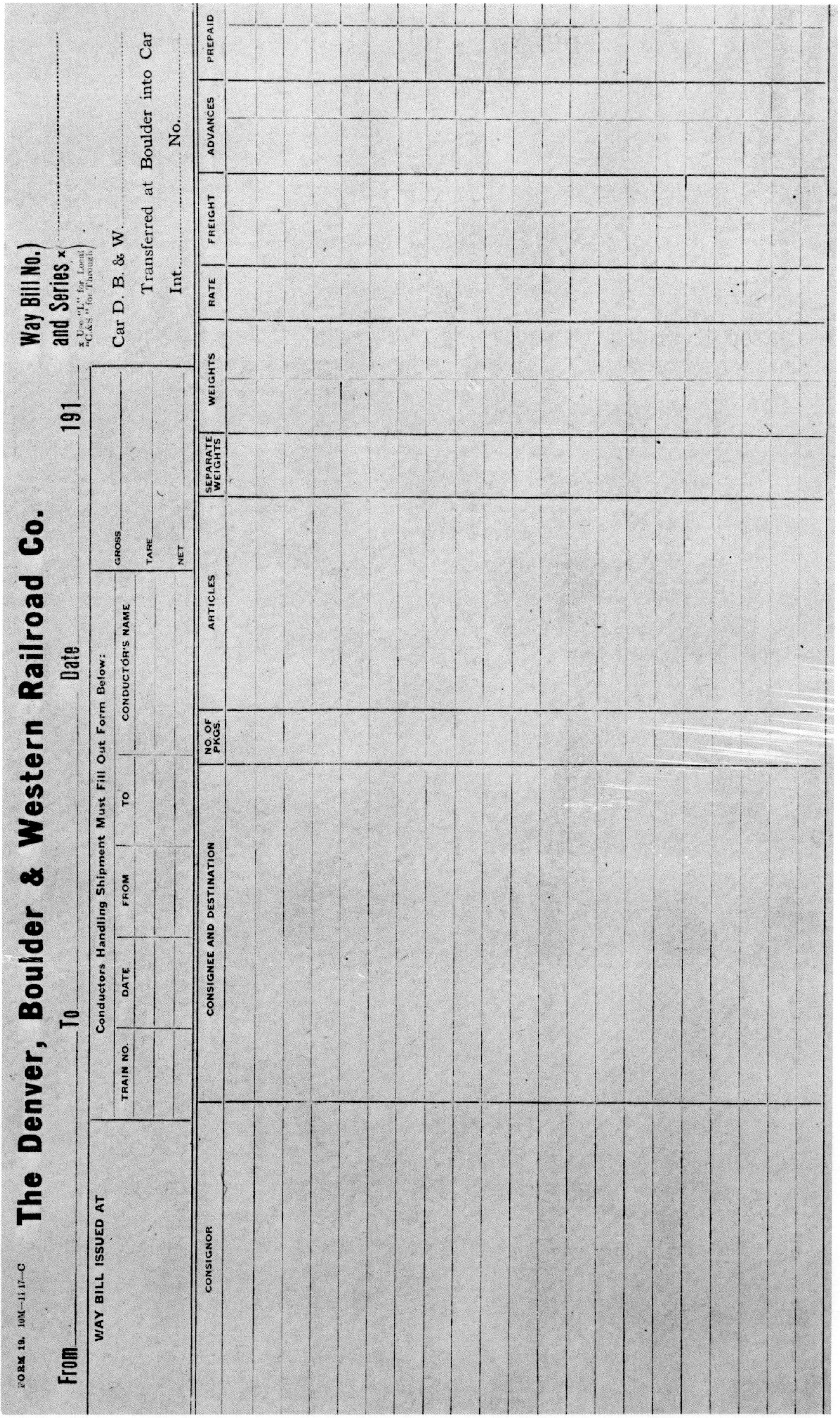

FORM 19. 10M—11-17—C

The Denver, Boulder & Western Railroad Co.

From .... **To** .... **Date** .... **191**....

Way Bill No.) and Series ×

× Use "L" for Local "C.&S." for Through

Car D. B. & W. ....

Transferred at Boulder into Car

Int.................... No....................

WAY BILL ISSUED AT

Conductors Handling Shipment Must Fill Out Form Below:

TRAIN NO.	DATE	FROM	TO	CONDUCTOR'S NAME

GROSS

TARE

NET

CONSIGNOR	CONSIGNEE AND DESTINATION	NO. OF PKGS.	ARTICLES	SEPARATE WEIGHTS	WEIGHTS	RATE	FREIGHT	ADVANCES	PREPAID

Courtesy Richard Lind

Way Bill form used by the Denver, Boulder & Western.

Engineer J. L. Frankeberger running the line for the Colorado & Northwestern. He saw the railroad finished to Ward, witnessing incidents that were unforgettable. Like the arrival of No. 25, the Shay locomotive.

"The crew limbered her up for several days, then they started up to Ward. But the engine was still so stiff that it took them all the first day to reach Salina. The next day they made it to Sunset, and the third day they pulled into Ward.

"The officials were pleased with the Shay, for it was commencing to run smoothly. They ordered her turned around and started down to Boulder. In the Ward yards were 105 cars which had been used in construction. All of these cars were coupled behind the Shay.

"All the engine crew had to do was to keep up enough steam to run the air pump and hold back a little on the engines. She was so stiff yet that the friction held her back strongly.

"The track was so rough that by the time the crew got to Boulder everything on the engine had been shaken loose. The bell was off, the headlight, the bolts in the cab were loose. The Shay was almost a wreck on her first trip!"

BILLY LOACH[14]

No one knew or appreciated the service of the Switzerland Trail better than William "Billy" Loach, the best known of all Boulder County pioneer tungsten producers and one of the railroad's heaviest shippers.

"We (the Firth-Sterling Steel Co. of Mc-Keesport, Pa.) started operations at Nederland in August, 1904," began Billy. "The very first mine we opened was the Oregon, near the Conger. The next was the Clyde. We bought the old Caribou Mill, which had been built to reduce silver ore freighted down from Caribou to bullion.

---

[14]*Boulder Daily Camera*, June 1, 1957.

"It was all steam power in those days. We burned wood in the mines and mill. It was good fuel but very expensive, we used so much of it. We paid $4 to $4.25 a cord. It was cut on the hills around Nederland.

"With the coming of the C&N we used coal. We bought coal from E. B. Hill in Boulder and had it shipped to Wolfram Junction. From there we hauled it by wagon.

"We shipped our concentrates down on the narrow gauge. At Boulder we had to transfer them to a standard gauge car. Our concentrates were all sacked and the sacks weighed about 125 pounds apiece.

"At Wolfram Junction there was a very short sidetrack. When we had coal set out there we had to haul it out in 24 hours.

"It was the same with other freight. Mining companies besides ours had shipments coming up.

"Another service that the narrow gauge improved on was the mail. When the railroad started in they had a mail compartment in the baggage car. A postal employee, Stanley Roberts, took care of the mail. When the standard gauge train came in from Denver in the morning, the mail sacks were transferred to the narrow gauge. Roberts sorted out the mail as the train came up.

"This was quite an improvement over the stages, which left after the train arrived from Denver. They could take only mail that had been sorted at the Boulder postoffice for the mining camps. Mail coming in on the morning train had to wait until the next day to go up by stage.

"The railroad rendered another big service. Suppose a mining operator broke a part on a Wilfley concentrating table or a pump. He'd call up one of the big supply houses in Denver and tell them to send it up on the next morning's train. He'd get it delivered at Wolfram Junction or Cardinal that day.

"We did a big business with the railroad. In 1907 I had about 200 men working for me.

Crossen photo

R. D. Ward standing beside the station at Ward where he served as agent for many years.

Crossen photo

R. D. Ward standing beside the station in Ward where he served as agent from 1905 until the close of the railroad in 1919. This building held a host of memories for him, most of them tender and pleasant.

OFFICE OF
GENERAL MANAGER.

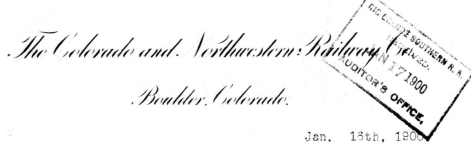

The Colorado and Northwestern Railway Co.

Boulder, Colorado.

Jan. 16th, 1900

Mr. Cooper Anderson,

      Auditor, The Rio Grande Southern Ry. Co.,

            D e n v e r,   C o l o.

Dear Sir:-

      Please accept thanks for Annual #561, and I hope I may find time to take a trip over your line.

                      Yours truly,

                      Gen'l. Frt. & Pass. Agt.

Courtesy of The Boulder Daily Camera

An example of courtesies exchanged between officials of two of Colorado's most romantic railroads back in the palmy days.

That included leasers. During World War I we had on about 400 men.

"The food that came up on the railroad was welcome. We had more fresh vegetables, fruit, and meat.

"When a person was hurt or taken ill and had to be rushed to the hospital, they could go quicker and easier on the train.

"People came to depend upon the little railroad. The crews would stop anywhere."

Billy's eyes were bright with the force of memories. "I rode the trains considerably between Boulder and Wolfram Junction or Cardinal. This saved time, for before I had to go by team and buggy.

"Jap Reed was the conductor I had most of my dealings with. Very accommodating, very fine man. He was very popular. All along the line he'd do things for people.

"That little railroad did a bigger service than it has ever been given credit for . . . I was sorry to see it abandoned."

RALPH PETERS[15]

We were watching the unloading of No. 30 in August, 1952, when she came home to Boulder permanently. Ralph, retired electrical engineer, began to chuckle.

"That engine once played a trick on me. She nearly scared the life out of me for a moment.

"During the summer of 1920 Morse Brothers of Denver had the contract to dismantle the Denver, Boulder & Western. I had a job with them during vacation at the University of Colorado. I ran a spike-straightening machine, but now and then I had to do general work around the yards.

"One Saturday afternoon they had me coaling up Number 30. The railroad had a conveyor run by a little steam engine to carry the coal off the ground and up into the locomotive tender. I connected the little conveyor engine to the steam line on the side of Num-

ber 30. I started the engine and then went up into the tender to spread the coal with a scoop shovel.

"Everything was running beautifully when, all of a sudden, old Number 30 jumped ahead about ten feet. The steam pipe to the conveyor engine broke. My, how she did roar!

"I got down out of that tender in a hurry —found the valve and shut off the steam.

"I went up to the roundhouse and told Bill Tipps, the engineer, about it. He began kidding me. 'Oh, you were playing with the throttle and she jumped on you.'

" 'No,' I said and stayed with my story.

"We repaired the broken steam line, and I went on with my work of coaling up Number 30. But Bill kept kidding me all that afternoon. I would fool with that throttle, would I?

"Finally he admitted that the throttle leaked a little. It had finally built up enough pressure in the cylinders to make the engine jump ahead."

WALLACE TANNER[16]

"The first time I went up to Nederland I went on the Switzerland Trail," said Wallace Tanner, pleasant, white-haired Boulder businessman. "Scared to death. I had never been in the mountains before. This was in September, 1905.

"When we got up above Sunset I got on the inside of the coach," he continued, his face wreathed in a smile. "I wasn't going to fall down the mountainside.

"Jap Reed was the conductor and Bill Tipps the engineer. I came to know them very well, for I did a lot of business with the railroad."

Nederland was then a busy place, with many nearby mines operating. It was reported that 75% of the tungsten produced in the United States came from a radius of five miles each side of Nederland. The big steel companies snapped up every pound of it.

[15]*Boulder Daily Camera*, August 30, 1952.

[16]*Boulder Daily Camera*, July 1, 1957.

357

"After a brief mining venture, I was taken into partnership in a new grocery store. This suited me fine.

"We shipped up most of our groceries on the narrow gauge. During summer they ran two daily trains. The freight came up on the afternoon train, arriving at Cardinal between five and six o'clock. I'd be there to meet it. Non-perishable groceries came up by freight, perishable stuff by express.

"The agent was John Conklin. He went from there to the Vasco (Mining Co.) people about 1916.

"I went up to Cardinal station once a day, rain or shine, sometimes three times a day. I've been out when my horses would stop; they couldn't face that wind. I'd have to turn my back to it. My horses' nostrils would be frozen over. The wind came right down from Caribou, where it was manufactured.

"As time went on I had other business with the railroad. I started leasing on the Colorado Tungsten (Company mines), and I shipped crude tungsten ore down to Boulder. For one year I had 8 to 10 men working on my leases.

"L. R. Ford, who was Traffic Manager and Auditor for the C&N, gave me a book of tickets to ride on the railroad. My freight and express at that time amounted to about $10 a day."

Mr. Tanner smiled. "In three years I never came down from Nederland, so I never used the tickets. The time limit ran out on them. I'm sorry I didn't keep them for a souvenir.

"I did business with the railroad until it quit. It always served me well, and I have many happy memories of men who worked for it. She was a great little railroad."

R. D. WARD[17]

"R. D." as he was affectionately known to thousands of people, went to Ward as sta-

tion agent July 10, 1905. He was a little above medium height, compactly built, friendly. After the Switzerland Trail ceased operation, he served as deputy assessor for Boulder County until his tragic death.

He came to Colorado from eastern Canada for his health. He liked Ward and after the brisk summer tourist season stayed on.

When howling winter blizzards closed the railroad, he began operating a stage line to and from Sunset. He operated this line for ten years.

Summer was the gay, busy time, with big picnics at Mont Alto Park, Glacier Lake, Ward, and Eldora. Snowball trips were organized in Boulder. Snowbanks lay within a half-mile of the track where Eastern and Southern visitors could pelt each other. When the wild flowers were at the greatest spread and beauty, the railroad ran wild flower specials, the train stopping at lovely fields so that people could pick them.

"When those flower trains pulled into Ward," explained R. D., eyes twinkling, "the children who had picked columbines and pond lilies gave each passenger a little bouquet."

The days carried excitement as well as tenderness. Now and again passengers arrived just as the train was pulling out. The agent arose to the occasion, took two saddles horses or a livery rig, and hurried down to the foot of Sawmill Hill, a distance of about one and one-fourth miles. Presently the train arrived, for it had to cover five miles to reach this point. The passengers were cheerfully taken aboard.

Once started talking, R. D. was full of stories of the Switzerland Trail.[18]

"The section crew, stationed over at Sunset, were all Old Country Italians. They were good men, and they kept the road in fine shape. Our little railroad kept everything up in first-class shape.

[17]*Boulder Daily Camera*, March 1, 1938.

[18]*Boulder Daily Camera*, August 15, 1957.

The Ox-Bow Curve today. In the distance rises Arapaho Peak and its glacier, source of Boulder's water supply. Mont Alto Park lies directly ahead to right of photo.

359

Sturtevant photo. M. R. Parsons Collection

Section crew on the C&N. Their push car lived up to its name. They could coast downgrade, but going back up called for steady effort.

"Phillip Gonneley was their foreman. He afterward became Roadmaster. He was a short stocky man, with a keen mind. He accumulated quite a bit of money. He was a great friend of mine. He liked our kids, so we used to have him over to the house for lunch when he'd have the crew up at Ward.

"One day I had a lot of ties on hand. I used to have men cutting and hauling them in on contract, also mine props and timbers. It was in the spring of the year, and the railroad was always hard up in the spring.

" 'Phillip, I've got to have some money,' I told him.

" 'All right,' he said. 'How much do you want?'

" '$500.'

"He pulled out a big roll and counted out five hundred. I wanted to give him a note.

" 'Don't want a note,' he said.

"But I gave him one anyway.

"One day he came in the office and left his coat there. Away he went. Before long I had a call from Chambers, the agent at Sunset.

" 'Did Phillip leave his coat up there?'

" 'Yes.'

" 'For God's sake hang onto it. He's got five hundred or a thousand dollars in it!' "

R. D. laughed. "Phillip didn't worry about money. He returned to Italy after the Switzerland Trail quit operating, a well-to-do man."

He paused, eyes keen behind his glasses.

"The first two or three years after I went to Ward they used to come in in the evenings with the train, go out in the mornings.

"Sometimes in stormy weather they wouldn't show up. I kept a saddle horse there, so I'd go out and find them.

"Sometimes the wind would blow snow in behind the train and block them. I'd take the mail, go back to Ward and send a message down to Boulder for the snowplow to come up and get them out.

"The train crew would have to stay there and keep the engine hot. Sometimes they had to shovel snow in the tender to melt down for water. They'd get along all right, for they carried food against such emergencies."

One evening I was visiting with Mr. and Mrs. Ward and their daughter, Mrs. Fanny Lewis. Before long the talk swung around to the Switzerland Trail.[19]

"Getting off the track was nothing unusual for that railroad," said Fanny lightly. "Once I was coming down to Boulder on the afternoon train to a circus. Mrs. Puddifoot, who was widely known as a good cook in the mountains, was taking me.

"There at Bloomerville the pony truck of the locomotive went off, right on the bridge. The train crew tried and tried but they couldn't get it back on. Finally somebody started up across the hills to Ward, to call down to Boulder for an engine.

"It was getting late, so Mrs. Puddifoot and I went over to Bob Duncan's cabin. He hadn't been there for years but the door was unlocked. She found some flour and made biscuits for everybody. We were eating when the engine from Boulder arrived."

A smile had gone over Mrs. Ward's face. "One time I was coming down. It was a beautiful morning, the clouds flying every which way. There were only a few passengers aboard and we all felt happy. . . .

"There on the curve this side of Camp Frances, going down hill, off went the locomotive. Everybody piled off but I sat right there in the coach, still enjoying the morning.

"Finally the train crew got the engine rerailed and we came on down without anything else happening."

Fanny was smiling at another memory. "We used to have fun with that railroad. We school kids used to be eating our lunches when we'd hear the engine whistling around the last big curve there below the station. We'd all hit out and try to get to the station before the train.

---

[19]*Boulder Daily Camera*, September 18, 1952.

361

Sturtevant photo. Courtesy Mrs. Erna Viele

Profile Rock in Boulder Canon on the Colorado & Northwestern, below mouth of Four Mile Creek.

362

"Pat Dinley was the engineer most of the time. He got so he'd delay blowing the whistle until he was nearly around the bend. This gave him the advantage and he'd beat us in."

It was easy to picture the laughing, shouting children around the locomotive. The Irish engineer had leaned out of the cab window, smiling broadly. The locomotive after its hard run was a living thing with fire in its belly, the rich smell of escaping steam, coal smoke, and hot valve oil enveloping it. Its air pump had throbbed hard, building up pressure for the brakes on the return trip. Over the train had hovered that mystical and wonderful aura of travel.

"The children loved the railroad," said Mrs. Ward. "One afternoon I missed Phil, who was just a little fellow. I hunted all around for him and was commencing to get scared.

"I went over to the store and inquired for him. A man in there said that his boy, who was older and quite a Smart Aleck, Phil, and another little boy had taken the railroad's handcar and started down the track.

"I was real worried but I hadn't more than gotten back to the house when Phil came in. The handcar had jumped the track and they'd all walked back to town."

Fanny nodded. "They left the handcar up there for Dad to use. We children used to push the car up to the wye. Then we'd get on and coast down, having a big time. We worked hard pushing it up there but the fun of coasting down was worth it."

R. D. spoke up. "I used to come all the way to Boulder on that little bicycle car. It was very light and you pedaled it just like a bicycle. Charley Williams used it a great deal. He used to go up to Salina on the train and come back on the car.

"One morning in the winter we started down from Ward. At Sunset some Italian section men started out on a handcar behind us. The rails were frosty, so they got to going too fast. Here they came, gaining on us, yelling and waving their arms.

"The engineer speeded up, trying to keep out of their way. The brakes on the handcar were no good on that slick rail, so they ran right into the rear of the train . . . The way they flew in all directions! They landed in the snow, so none of them was hurt."

We all laughed. "It's good to talk about those old days," said Fanny. "We had many a good time on the old DB&W or 'Drink Beer and Wine' as people laughingly called it."[20]

ELBERT HUBBARD[21]

"When I was a kid, I used to run a mile to see a train," said Elbert Hubbard of Wall Street. "We moved up here when I was three years old. They were building the Colorado & Northwestern. That's the first thing I can remember."

A happy smile wreathed Elbert's face. He is one of the most pleasant men around. He comes of old-time mountain mining people and the adventure zest of this colorful group has not been lost in him.

"That railroad was the most fascinating thing in my young life. I made friends with all the trainmen. At that time Jap Reed was conductor on the Eldora run. George Farnsworth was his brakeman.

"On days when I didn't have to go to school or in the summertime I'd be there to meet them. They'd take me to Eldora. They'd divide their lunches with me, which I thought was great stuff. It was always fun riding that mixed train.

"In 1912, when I was seventeen, I obtained the consent of my parents to go to work on the railroad. I made my first paying trip with Jap Reed as a brakeman."

He grinned at a sudden memory. "Braking used to be exciting up there. In November, 1915, we got stuck in the snow at the Big Five. We had the 31. Jap Reed told me to set

[20]*Boulder Daily Camera,* November 6, 1952.
[21]*Boulder Daily Camera,* August 25, 1954.

Crossen photo

Elbert Hubbard of Wall Street began working as a brakeman on the Denver, Boulder & Western in 1912. He was later advanced to fireman. Here he is standing on the old grade at Wall Street, nostalgia in his eyes for the Switzerland Trail that is no more.

A sweeping curve on the Switzerland Trail with the autumn gold of the aspens brightening the mountain land. This is a short distance south of Gold Hill station on the Ward branch.

the brakes, so I climbed up on top. Then Jap laughed and said, 'Heck, you don't have to set brakes in this snow. She won't move.'

"Pat Dinley was the engineer and Shorty Campbell his fireman. They uncoupled the engine and ran it ahead, trying to ram through that snowdrift. We had a string of freight cars, with one coach on the rear. There were fifteen passengers in it.

"Each time the engine came back, it bumped into the cars and moved them a foot or so. All of a sudden they broke loose and started down the line.

"Jap hollered out, 'Get on the coach.'

"I ran back—it was hard going through that snow—and managed to swing up on the steps. I looked in through the glass in the door. The passengers were all up on their feet, scared. I was scared too. There was a heavy grade there. If I couldn't get those cars stopped, we'd go off at the next curve and roll down the mountain.

"I didn't know whether I was going to get them stopped or not. The brake shoes were full of snow. But I commenced screwing down that brake wheel with all the strength I had, using the brake club.

"For what seemed like a long time nothing happened. The cars were picking up speed. Down below—not very far—was that sharp curve at the end of old Grassy Mountain.

"I threw myself against my brake club and managed to get the brake ratchet down another notch. Suddenly the brakes took hold. I felt our speed slacken, ever so little. I stood there, panting, hoping. We slowed down, down, gradually came to a stop. It wasn't any too soon. We were almost to the curve."

Elbert paused, his face brightening. "During the tungsten boom the railroad had lots of business. Harry Cluphf was a conductor and I was his brakeman. Harry was a great fellow, full of fun—and a good railroader.

"We had a bit of fun with Harry one time when I was firing for Pat Dinley. He'd taught me to fire an engine, so that gave me more work. We stopped up at Bloomerville, and right away Harry spotted a new gas handcar.

"Cluphf couldn't leave it alone. 'You go on to Frances,' he said. 'I'm going to run this gas buggy up there.'

"We started on. We didn't know it at the time but Cluphf couldn't get the gas engine started. At Frances we unloaded freight and waited. But no Cluphf.

"I looked up and saw him coming over the mountain on the short-cut trail. Pat Dinley was full of fun, so he started the train. Here came Cluphf, running hard. Pat kept on going.

"Finally he slowed down and let Cluphf get on the caboose.

"At Ward Cluphf came up to the engine. He was going to clean up on Pat. 'What would the "old man" (C. M. Williams, Superintendent) think if you came into Ward without any conductor?' he yelled out.

"Pat looked down at him; a grin on that Irish face. 'I'd say you went riding on the railroad's new gas buggy.'

"That ended the squabble. Harry had to laugh at himself."

Elbert laughed, then shook his head soberly. "Those old railroaders were characters. They were full of fun, weren't afraid of anything, and didn't give a rip what anybody thought. But they were railroaders. They could get the trains over the road under conditions that'd scare the average man half to death. They were big-hearted, real friends . . . as fine men as I've ever known."

One day a friend took Elbert and a few of us for a trip over the Eldora grade. We were rolling along east of Sunset when he asked to stop.[22]

"In 1913," he said, "when we had the big snow, they took the snowplow and two engines to Glacier Lake to try to open up the

---

[22]*Boulder Daily Camera*, January 5, 1955.

Crossen photo

Ward, Colorado, a few years ago. The Peak-to-Peak Highway, at left, was built on the former DB&W right-of-way. The big long building at left was the station, which was turned around and moved across road from its original location.

The railroad continued on up the highway to wye, around bend, then on to New Market, which can be seen in far background, near the skyline.

367

road. They got almost up there and ran out of water. So the only thing was back down to Sunset and hope they'd get to the tank all right.

"You see, when they were bucking snow the engines used a lot of water. You had to watch the glass (water gauge), for if you ran out of water. . . .

"The wind was blowing snow, so by the time they got down here there was about four feet on the track. Pat Dinley was on the head engine, Bill Tipps on the second. All of a sudden the tender of Tipps' engine began to raise up. The snow had lifted the truck wheels.

"Tipps whistled to Dinley to stop, but Pat couldn't hear him on account of the wind; I guess it was really blowing. Pat kept on coming. The tender kept raising higher and higher. It was about to go off the track.

"Finally Pat heard the whistle and shut off the steam. If he hadn't they might have gone down the mountain here." Elbert pointed to Four Mile Creek below. "That's a drop of 500 feet at least."

We reached the site of Sugar Loaf station and headed west, passing the site of Tungsten siding and Furlong station.

A little farther on Elbert began to chuckle, "Here's where they had a whistling post. The engineers would whistle here, and the agent down at Sunset would report where they were to the dispatcher. But that wasn't all.

"In the summertime there were lots of tourists to Eldora. Old George Farnsworth (brakeman) used to come through the cars and holler out, 'Sunset on the right.' You could actually see a little of the camp from here. Some of them wouldn't know what he was talking about. They thought he was pulling their legs; it was the wrong time of day for sunset."

These stories are only a small sampling of the stirring incidents that happened on the Switzerland Trail. I hope they have brought you a breath of the old wild days, when a breed of men now largely vanished rode out to new adventures on each train.

Crossen Collection

The summer lunch room at Glacier Lake stands cold and lonely as winter comes to the Eldora branch. To the left is the main line running west to Cardinal and Eldora.

Crossen Collection

DB&W freight charging up the Eldora grade out of Sunset, probably with freight for the Barker Dam, about 1909. The smoke from the second engine, which is pushing, can be seen at right.

Part II

Chapter XII

LOCOMOTIVES, ROLLING STOCK, AND EQUIPMENT

In this day of dull diesel units, it is refreshing and stimulating to turn to the equipment of a railroad like the Switzerland Trail of America and its predecessor.

The Greeley, Salt Lake & Pacific had no motive power or rolling stock of its own. It used Colorado Central and allied companies' equipment. Data on its locomotives comes from that excellent book, *Pictorial Supplement to Denver, South Park & Pacific*.

Colorado Central No. 6 came from Porter-Bell, date unknown. She was an 0-6-0, with 13 by 16-inch cylinders, 34-inch drivers, weighing 32,450 pounds on drivers. Rebuilt in September, 1882, she was scrapped in 1889.

Brooks built Colorado Central No. 10 and No. 153 in October, 1880. The same company turned out Colorado Central 154 and 155 in June, 1881. They were 2-6-0 engines, with 15 by 18-inch cylinders, 36-inch drivers, weighing 46,900 pounds on drivers. Old U. P. records lists their drivers as 38 inches. They were sold by the C&S by 1902.

Brooks built Denver, South Park & Pacific No. 160 in July, 1882. She was a 2-6-0, with 15 by 18-inch cylinders, 38-inch drivers, weighing 46,960 pounds on drivers.

Union Pacific, Denver & Gulf No. 108 was built by Cooke in February, 1884. She also was a 2-6-0, with 14½ by 18-inch cylinders, 40-inch drivers, weighing 58,300 pounds on drivers. She became C&S No. 13 in 1889 and operated until 1923, when she was scrapped.

The task confronting the C&N officials was enormous. To reach Ward, 14 airline miles from Boulder and 4,099 feet higher, the railroad had to twist and turn 26.1 miles. The average grade was 3½ percent, with curves as high as 30 degrees. Trainmen had to have powerful locomotives, sturdy rolling stock with the best braking equipment, and superb skill.

The two geared freight locomotives, the Climax and the Shay, had great power at slow speeds to haul big tonnages of coal and supplies up to the mines. They had the braking power to bring down long trains of ore. Had the mines fulfilled even part of their anticipated output, the Shay and the Climax might have had long and valuable service lives.

The Brooks Locomotive Works of Dunkirk, New York, sent out a sturdy 2-6-0 to conquer the grades. Someone erred in her design. Her 44-inch drivers were too high, her steam pressure of 150 pounds too low. She was soon retired to light duty.

The mistakes were corrected in Numbers 30, 31, and 32. They delighted all engineers. They had big boilers, plenty of grate surface, big cylinders, and low drivers. They were the heaviest and most powerful narrow gauge locomotives in Colorado. The Colorado & Southern in later years was very happy to buy them.

Number 33 was still more powerful.

Even today, in this age of super power, they are impressive. Howard Fogg, famous railroad artist, said of the Switzerland Trail's locomotives, "They are the most beautiful, most impressive narrow gauge engines I've ever seen."

The rolling stock was built or selected to stand the great strains of mountain railroading. It was the best that builders could supply.

Even the rail was far heavier than that ordinarily used on narrow gauge lines. It weighed 56 pounds to the yard and, with good ties and ballast under it, stood up very well.

From the start, the most careful maintenance was the rule of the road. Whenever a train came down from the mountains, expert mechanics went over it thoroughly.

The railroad was so small that people knew each locomotive by its whistle. They knew the trainmen by their first names. Toward the railroad they felt a warmth and a pride and a loyalty.

To tell the story of the Switzerland Trail's equipment, I was fortunate in securing a catalogue issued by the Morse Brothers Machinery & Supply Company after the road was abandoned. It was given to Dr. John B. Schoolland by the late John R. Wolff, who used it in his suits protesting the abandonment of the DB&W. It is reproduced later.

Additional information on the Denver, Boulder & Western's motive power, rolling stock, track, etc., comes to light in a lawyer's brief prepared by the late John R. Wolff of Boulder in 1920. Wolff represented mining companies and other protestants fighting the removal of the railroad.

Wolff's valuation of the road was as follows:

No. 1 locomotive was listed at $ 8,469.43
No. 25 locomotive was listed at   6,805.23
No. 30 locomotive was listed at   9,130.00
No. 31 locomotive was listed at   9,130.00
No. 32 locomotive was listed at   9,130.00
No. 33 locomotive was listed at   11,332.75

Total for six locomotives $53,997.41

Note: No. 32 was rebuilt in 1908 at the Colorado & Southern shops in Denver at a cost of $4,000.00. This included boring out her cylinders to 16½ inches.

The four Pullman Company coaches, Numbers 19 to 22 inclusive, were listed as having been purchased second-hand at $ 3,000.00
The five Barney & Smith coaches, new, at 15,310.22
Four Observation cars, second-hand, at 2,308.05
Combo No. 15 at 2,429.91
Combo No. 50 at 2,429.91

Total of 15 coaches $25,478.09

Twenty-three Barney and Smith boxcars $13,180.91
Thirty-five coal cars 16,963.68
Four flat cars 1,783.08
Two cabooses 1,670.56
One snow plow 445.76

Total of 65 units $34,043.99
49.91 miles of 56-pound rail, 4,392.08 tons, at $28 a ton, cost new $122,978.24
Angle bars, spikes, bolts, tie plates, rail braces, frogs, switches, etc., estimated 18,000.00

Total $140,978.24

49.91 miles, 150,000 ties, 6" x 8" x 7' @ 30¢ $45,000.00

Six water tanks, located one each at Boulder, Crisman, Sunset, Bloomerville, Glacier Lake, and Sulphide, estimated cost with attachments .... $ 5,000.00
1 pump house, gasoline engine, and pump at Glacier Lake 650.00

Total .... $ 5,650.00

All water tanks were gravity tanks, except the tank at Boulder, which was supplied with water from the Boulder City line at a cost of $120 a year. The water tank at Glacier Lake was supplied for six months of the year with water from a gravity pipe line; during the remainder of the year it could be supplied with water from a lake nearby by using the pumping plant installed for that purpose.

One pair of railroad track scales
    at Boulder .... $ 700.00
Three pair of wagon scales at
    Salina, Eldora, and Ward 300.00
Five platform scales at stations   200.00
                     ————
    Total .... $ 1,200.00

Twelve I-beam bridges, 6 members 7¼ X 24 inches, average length 54 feet, stone abutments, between Boulder and Salina.
Thirty-two wood trestles between
    Boulder and Ward. Seventeen
    wood trestles between Sunset
    and Eldora. Total 61 .... $73,059.00

Three passenger freight stations,
    one each at Salina, Sunset, and
    Ward @ $1,500 ....$ 4,500.00
One passenger and freight station
    at Sugar Loaf 250.00
One passenger and freight station
    at Cardinal 200.00
One passenger and freight station
    at Eldora 250.00
Two passenger waiting stations,
    one each at Orodell and Lake
    Eldora 400.00
Four freight warehouses, one
    each at Wall Street, Glacier
    Lake, Hill, and Wolfram 400.00
Four section houses, one each at
    Boulder, Salina, Glacier Lake,
    and Sunset 1,600.00
One restaurant building at Gla-
    cier Lake 250.00

One pavilion at Glacier Lake 1,500.00
One shop and warehouse at
    Boulder 500.00
                     ————
    Total .... $ 9,610.00

Land owned, exclusive of right-of-way, was:

Nine lots, Block 11 in the City of
    Boulder .... $ 1,600.00
Thirty-eight acres of land adjoin-
    ing the City of Boulder on the
    west purchased for Terminal
    facilities 5,000.00
Twenty acres of land on line from
    Sunset to Ward 500.00
One and one-half acres of land in
    the City of Boulder, near Boul-
    der Creek 150.00

Miscellaneous included hand and
    push cars, track tools, six plea-
    sure boats on Glacier Lake 350.00

The total, exclusive of right-of-way, grading, track laying, surfacing, engineering, etc., came to $396,816.93.

Attorney Wolff went on to say, "The above figures are actual cost or as near to actual cost as could be determined, with the exception of the value of $45,000.00 as shown for track ties. It is thought that this is a fair valuation based on actual cost, considering the kind, quality, and life of the ties.

"With the exception of the 4 observation cars, all of the Motive Power and Equipment is in good constitutional condition, barring, of course, usual running repairs. The mileage of the line being short, together with the fact that the cars are never interchanged with other lines, and being thoroughly inspected and repaired at Boulder after each trip, has added very materially to their physical condition, so that the usual charge to depreciation will not apply in this case."

Attorney Wolff then followed with another brief entitled "GENERAL INVENTORY OF D.B.&W.R.R. at AVERAGE SALE PRICES." It was a very detailed inventory, and its total came to $397,074.85. Thus the inventory showed that the railroad was worth $257.92 more than it cost.

There are two stories concerning the fate of No. 31 and 32. Both agree that in 1948, when still bearing Colorado & Southern numbers 75 and 76 respectively, they were sold by Morse Brothers Machinery & Supply Company of Denver to the Cerro de Pasco Copper Company of Lima, Peru. Their shipment to Peru followed shortly.

One account is that they were converted to standard gauge for use on the Central Railroad of Peru (Ferrocarrill Central del Peru), which is a standard gauge line.

The other is that the Cerro de Pasco Copper Company overhauled the engines in their shops at Lima. Then they turned them over to the government-owned Ferrocarrill Huancayo a Huancavelica—a narrow gauge line in a remote mountain district.

One of the locomotives is said to have fallen over a cliff and landed hundreds of feet below. The wrecking crew set her up on rails but the management delayed building the very extensive switchback line necessary to bring her back on the main track. She may still be there.

Efforts have been made to verify both stories. To date no concrete evidence has turned up to clinch the matter. Getting information about a steam locomotive in a Latin American country like Peru is entirely different from collecting it here. We hope full proof will be forthcoming.

Colorado & Northwestern No. 2, the Climax, rode out to new adventures when she left Boulder on a standard gauge flatcar in January, 1899. The story came from that very fine book, *Climax — An Unusual Steam Locomotive,* by Thomas T. Taber and Walter Casler, published by Railroadians of America, Inc.

The Pacific Contract Company of Skagway, Alaska, bought No. 2 from the C&N and operated it as No. 8. In 1901 they sold it to the White Pass & Yukon Railway, which retained its identity as No. 8. In 1903 this road sold it to the Maytown Lumber Company of Rochester and Maytown, Washington. The latter concern eventually scrapped this locomotive built at Corry, Pennsylvania, that traveled to and from Alaska by ship.

Photo by R. H. Kindig

Colorado & Southern No. 75, formerly C&N-DB&W No. 31 leaving Leadville with a train for Climax, Colorado, May 31, 1941. In the background of the Cloud City is Mount Massive.

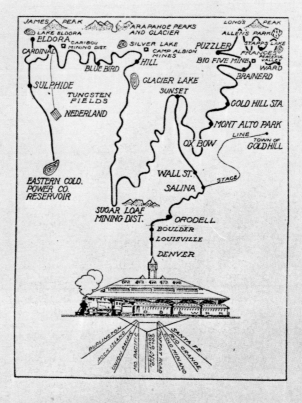

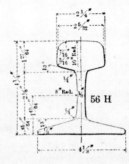

RAIL

The rail is all 56 pound per yard, 4¼" depth, 4⅛" base, 2¼" head.

The line from Boulder to Ward is Carnegie Steel Co. "E. T." Works.

The line from Sunset to Eldora is Lackawana Steel Works. There is 50.74 miles of track. The weight is 88 tons per mile, or 4465 gross tons. The rail being very heavy for 36" gauge road, it shows very little wear, even on curves. The rail has never been turned. It is in No. 1 condition.

SPLICE BARS

The Splice Bars are standard 56-pound bars. There is 600,000 lbs. of bars. These will only be sold with the rail.

SPIKES

The Spikes are ⁹⁄₁₆x5½". All spikes offered for sale are straight and serviceable. There is 450,000 lbs. of spikes.

TIE PLATES

270,000 lbs. of Tie Plates. Size of each tie plate 5 x 7 x ¼. Rail Joint Plates, 6½x7½x¼". Approximately 72,000 plates.

RAIL BRACES

44,000 lbs. 56-lb. Rail Braces. Approximately 16,000 braces.

SWITCHES

To Take The Angle of a Frog.

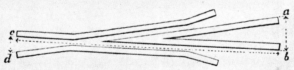

Measure A—B and C—D, then divide distance B—C by their sum. Example: A—B=8", C—D=4". Then 8+4=12. B—C 72". 72÷12=6, or No. 6 Frog. 64 Complete Switches, one in six split with No. 6 Frogs, as follows:

128 Split Points	64 Head Rods
64 Switch Stands	192 Tee Rods
64 Switch Locks	1024 Machine Bolts, ¾x1½"
266 Plain Side Plates	64 1-6 Frogs
266 Slide Plates and Rail Braces	3 1-6 Frogs Extra
64 Connecting Rods, 1¼" square	1 Extra Switch Stand

STEEL GIRDER BRIDGES

There is 4,164 feet of 24 I Beams from thirteen bridges. Dimension of I Beams: Height 24", width of flange 7¼", thickness of web ¾"; weight per foot, 100 lbs. The beams are in the following lengths:

12 beams 52' long.	12 beams 54' long.
24 beams 53' long.	6 beams 54' 8" long.
12 beams 53' 6" long.	6 beams 55' long.
6 beams 53' 11" long.	

WOOD BRIDGES AND TIMBER

There are 39 wood bridges and trestles of various lengths, 6 Howe Truss Bridges. All bridges will be dismantled and lumber sold. All bridge timber is Oregon Fir and of standard dimensions.

STRINGERS—

1736 pieces 7"x15"x15' 227,850

TIES—

1818 pieces 6"x8"x10' 72,720
480 pieces 8"x8"x8' 20,480
1575 pieces 8"x8"x8' 67,200

CAPS—

327 pieces 12"x12"x12' 47,088

SILLS—

261 pieces 12"x12"x18' 56,376
(Will run from 15' to 36' long.)

SWAY BRACES—

629 pieces 4"x12"x16' 40,256
(Some 3x12, 4x10 and 6x6.)

POSTS—

	Est. Ft. B. M.		Est. Ft. B. M.
8 pieces 12"x12"x 6'	576	20 pieces 12"x12"x16'	3,840
8 pieces 12"x12"x 5'	480	208 pieces 12"x12"x20'	49,920
16 pieces 12"x12"x 8'	1,536	52 pieces 12"x12"x24'	14,976
156 pieces 12"x12"x12'	22,444	24 pieces 12"x12"x26'	7,488
24 pieces 12"x12"x10'	2,880	80 pieces 12"x12"x30'	28,800
20 pieces 12"x12"x14'	3,360	48 pieces 12"x12"x40'	23,040
56 pieces 12"x12"x15'	10,080	40 pieces 12"x12"x45'	21,600
268 pieces 12"x12"x18'	57,888		

HOWE TRUSS BRIDGES—

84 pieces 5"x 8"x10'	2,800	12 pieces 7"x18"x56'	5,850
56 pieces 7"x15"x16'	7,840	8 pieces 5"x10"x44'	1,470
8 pieces 5"x12"x44'	1,760	4 pieces 10"x10"x44'	1,466
4 pieces 10"x12"x44'	1,760		

Boulder Terminal

LOCOMOTIVES

All locomotives are U. S. inspected and in A-1 condition; completely equipped with U. S. safety appliances.

LOCOMOTIVE No. 1
Gauge 36".

Make	Brooks Locomotive Works
Type—Mogul	2-6-0
Date built	November, 1897
Builder's No.	2851
Working weight on drivers	66,500
Weight on forward truck	4,000
Cylinders	15x22
Diameter drivers	44
Boiler pressure	150 lbs.
Tank capacity, coal tons	6
Tank capacity, water gallons	2,500
Extreme height from rail	13' 2"

Make	Lima Locomotive Works
Type	Shay
Date Built	January, 1898
Builder's No.	540
Working weight on drivers	107,500
Includes 28,000 lbs. coal and water in tender.	
Cylinders	12x12
Diameter, drivers	32
No. of drivers	8
Boiler pressure	150 lbs.
Tank capacity, coal, tons	5
Tank capacity, water, gallons	1,500
Extreme height from rail	13' 2"

LOCOMOTIVE NO. 25
Gauge 36".

LOCOMOTIVE NO 30
Gauge 36".

Make	Brooks Locomotive Works
Type, Cons.	2-8-0
Date built	July, 1898
Builder's No.	2951
Working weight on drivers	85,000
Weight on forward truck	8,000
Cylinders	16x20
Diameter, drivers	37
Boiler pressure	180 lbs.
Tank capacity, coal, tons	8
Tank capacity, water, gallons	3,000
Extreme height from rail	13' 2"

LOCOMOTIVES—Continued

LOCOMOTIVE NO. 31
Gauge 36".

Make	Brooks Locomotive Works
Type, Cons.	2-8-0
Date built	July, 1898
Builder's No.	2969
Working weight on drivers	85,000
Weight on forward truck	8,000
Cylinders	16x20
Diameter, drivers	37
Boiler pressure	180 lbs.
Tank capacity, coal, tons	8
Tank capacity, water, gallons	3,000
Extreme height from rail	13' 2"

Make	Brooks Locomotive Works
Date built	July, 1898
Builder's No.	2970
Working weight on drivers	85,000
Weight on forward truck	8,000
Cylinders	16x20
Diameter, drivers	37
Boiler pressure	180 lbs.
Tank capacity, coal, tons	8
Tank capacity, water, gallons	3,000
Extreme height from rail	13' 2"

LOCOMOTIVE NO. 32
Gauge 36".

LOCOMOTIVE NO. 33
Gauge 36".

Make	Brooks Locomotive Works
Type, Cons.	2-8-0
Date built	July, 1906
Builder's No.	41126
Working weight on drivers	87,500
Weight on forward truck	7,500
Cylinders	16x20
Diameter, drivers	37
Boiler pressure	200 lbs.
Tank capacity, coal, tons	9
Tank capacity, water, gallons	4,000
Extreme height from rail	12' 1"

PASSENGER CARS

All cars 36″ gauge.   Equipped with U. S. Safety Appliances and I. C. C. inspected.

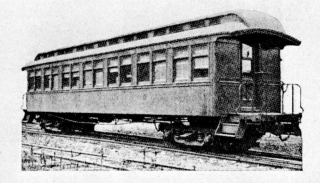

No's. 23 to 27 Inclusive

No. of coaches	5
Gauge	36″
Make	Barney and Smith
Seating capacity	46
Lighting	overhead chandeliers
Heater	Stove
Length	45′ 6″
Width	8′ 2″
Height from top of rail	12′ 2″

No's. 19 to 22 Inclusive

No. of coaches	4
Gauge	36″
Make	Pullman
Seating capacity	48
Lighting	overhead chandeliers
Heating	Baker Heater
Length	49′
Width	8′ 5″
Height from top of rail	12′ 2″

No's. 15 to 18 Inclusive

No. of coaches	4
Gauge	36″
Make	Denver
Seating capacity	68
Lighting	None
Heating	None
Length	42′ 6″
Width	8′ 3″
Height from top of rail	11′

COMBINATION CARS

No. 51

No. of coaches	1
Gauge	36″
Make	Barney & Smith
Seating capacity	28
Lighting	overhead chandeliers
Heating	Stove
Length	45′ 6″
Width	8′ 2″
Height from top of rail	12′ 2″

BAGGAGE CAR, No. 50

No. of coaches	1
Gauge	36″
Make	Barney & Smith
Lighting	Lamps
Heating	Stove
Length	32′ 2″
Width	8′ 2″
Height from top of rail	12′ 2″

COMPANY CARS

No's. 1 and 11 Caboose; length, 23′ 2″; width, 8′ 2″; height, 13′ 8″; gauge 36″.

SNOW PLOW

1 Snow Plow mounted on Flat Car; gauge 36″.

FREIGHT CARS

All Equipped with U. S. Safety Appliances.

BOX CARS

Total number 23
Gauge .... 36"
Capacity .... 40,000 lbs.
Doors .... Side

Inside Dimensions:

Length .... 31' 6"
Width .... 6' 11"
Height .... 6' 5"

Outside Dimensions:

Length .... 32' 3"
Width .... 7' 9"
Height from top of rail .... 10' 11"

GONDOLAS

Total number 35
Gauge .... 36"
Capacity 40,000

Inside Dimensions:

Length .... 30' 3"
Width .... 7' 2"
Height .... 3'

Outside Dimensions:

Length body .... 32' 4"
Width .... 8' 6"
Height from top of rail .... 6' 2"

FLAT CARS

Total number 4
Gauge .... 36"
Capacity 40,000

Outside Dimensions:

Length .... 32' 4"
Width .... 8' 6"
Height from top of rail .... 3' 2"

COAL LOADING ELEVATOR

1 Chain bucket elevator and hopper for loading coal on engines

OFFICE FURNITURE

3 Roll top desks
2 Flat top desks
2 Safes
6 Filing cases
Typewriter desk
Typewriter
Chairs

Station equipment, ticket racks, etc.

TRACK TOOLS

Large assortment of track tools of all kinds.

SCALES

3 Fairbanks-Morse 40-ton Track Scale, 36″ Gauge.
4 8-ton Fairbanks Wagon Scales   4 1500-lb. Fairbanks Platform Scales.

PUSH CARS

4 Heavy Type, 36″ Gauge   I Hand Car, 36″ Gauge

WATER TANKS

7 Wood water tanks with fixtures complete.

PIPE

10,000 feet 1, 2 and 3″ Water Pipe.

TIES

5,000 New Narrow Gauge Ties.   Used Ties that are serviceable, probably 50,000.

WHEELS AND AXLES

16 sets 28″ Wheels and Axles, 36″ gauge.   22 sets 26″ Wheels and Axles, 36″ gauge.
4 sets 24″ Wheels and Axles, 36″ gauge.

Boulder Terminal.

With cab boarded up and cold, C&S No. 76 awaits her fate in the Morse Brothers Machinery & Supply Company yards in Denver. Time: 1945.

Colorado & Southern No. 74, originally Colorado & Northwestern No. 30, on turntable at Leadville, Colorado, June 4, 1938.

Sturtevant photo. M. R. Parsons Collection

No. 30 with full steam up ready to leave Sunset for Ward in early days of the C&N. Her tonnage cannot be over 60, giving ample margin, for her allotted tonnage from Sunset to Gold Hill station was 90. Box car off track at left has Union Pacific on side, one of those left by the Greeley, Salt Lake & Pacific.

Photo by Otto C. Perry

No. 33, considered the largest and most powerful narrow gauge engine in the world, awaits her crew in the Boulder yards.

On this fine September morning in 1941, C&S No. 74 and her engineer are ready for a run out of Leadville, the Cloud City.

John W. Maxwell photo

The bright wonder of May has come again to Leadville, the Cloud City, as C&S No. 76 stands on the turntable, ready for duty. Note steam hose coiled around the sand dome and cinder catcher laid back.

Locomotives, Rolling Stock, and Equipment

Photo by M. C. Poor

Colorado & Southern No. 76, originally C&N No. 32, switching in the yard of the huge mill of the Climax Molybdenum Co. at Climax, Colorado, June, 1937.

389

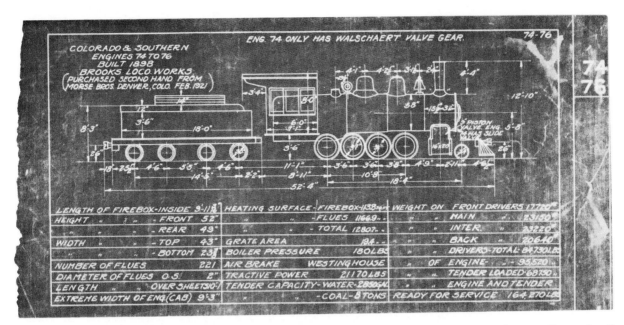

Colorado & Southern folio sheet with simplified drawing of former DB&W locomotives 30, 31 and 32.

The engine crew of C&N No. 1 are as well dressed as the train crew in this photo, which was evidently taken in the summer of 1898. Train is standing on track north of the recently finished station. Left to right, back row, unidentified brakeman, Conductor Jap Reed and Express Messenger George Farnsworth. The engineer at left is probably Jim Marsh, who was one of the first on the C&N. Bill Tipps, at right, was his fireman for a short time after coming to the new railroad. Location: Sunset.

Courtesy R. H. Kindig

C&N-DB&W No. 31 was C&S No. 75 when this photo was taken at Leadville, Colorado, July 3, 1941.

No. 30 has had another change of ownership by the time this photo was taken at Telluride, Colorado, September 1, 1951. She is now Rio Grande Southern No. 74.

392

Photo by W. D. Hollister

C&N No. 30 at Ward, Colorado, with a heavy train, February 22, 1902.

Handing up last train order for Colorado & Southern narrow gauge operations. It read: "Engine 76 run Extra Leadville to Climax and return to Leadville on Last trip of Narrow Gauge operations. Pick up at Climax and handle to Lead-ville all Narrow Gauge Cars."—from Denver, South Park & Pacific by M. C. Poor. Dated, Leadville, August 25, 1943.

Part II

Chapter XIII

THE RETURN OF NO. 30

When the Denver, Boulder & Western was dismantled, the adventures of its equipment were not ended. Railroads were our principal transportation, those of less advanced countries were still a-building. The DB&W's excellent locomotives, rolling stock, rails, and equipment were eagerly sought after. Some were destined for far strange places.

The freight and passenger equipment went to Mexico, most of the rails to Japan.

No. 25 is said to have been sold to a small railroad near Salt Lake City. No. 33 went to a lumber company in Louisiana. No. 1 was shipped to a railroad in Alaska.

Let us skip ahead three decades to the decision of a slender, likeable faculty member of the University of Colorado to take up a hobby for his retirement years. He was Dr. John B. Schoolland and his choice was narrow gauge railroading. This was strange for he had never had much interest in railroads.

His first research into Colorado's glorious narrow gauge past made him an avid fan. He rode on every existing line, camera in hand. He drove or walked over abandoned lines. Among the latter was Boulder's own railroad, the Switzerland Trail of America.

One day on the Rio Grande Southern he learned that its No. 74 was originally Colorado & Northwestern No. 30. He decided that she must be returned to Boulder for posterity. The days of the RGS were numbered. No. 30 must not be scrapped.

He lectured before Boulder clubs and groups—of which there are hundreds—showed slides taken from old photographs of Switzerland Trail operations. He featured No.

30 and his dream of bringing her back home.

The idea caught on. Boulder business and professional men and University of Colorado department heads formed a committee to help. It consisted of James Allen, Natt Burbank, Clarence Eckel, Dr. John Gillaspie, Frank Henderson, James Hickman, Bert Johnson, William "Billy" Loach, A. A. Paddock, Elmore Petersen, Francis E. Reich, and Dr. J. B. Schoolland.

In a meeting to discuss ways and means, Billy Loach, pioneer tungsten mining man and banker, said abruptly, "Let's make this a community enterprise. Let's raise the money by popular subscription, like people did in the Old West."

He wrote out a check for $100, handed it to Dr. Schoolland.

The campaign rapidly built up steam. The *Boulder Daily Camera,* radio station KBOL, and civic groups gave it full support. Contributions poured in, some as small as fifty cents. The total cost of exhibits and services, $8,000, was raised by voluntary contributions solely.

"In all the years I've lived in Boulder," said Loach, "I've never seen the community get behind a community project so enthusiastically."

One sunny morning in September, 1952, No. 30 as RGS No. 74 came home atop a standard gauge flatcar. A Colorado & Southern crew unloaded her, placed her in Central Park, her pilot pointed toward the mountains she had traversed so long.

A short time later Dr. Schoolland received a C&S bill for this work, $850. It was marked "Paid."

Photo by D. Ashton, CB&Q photographer
M. C. Poor Collection

Time is August 25, 1943. The next day a standard gauge train ran over this route. Note standard gauge rails already in place.

C&S No. 76 (C&N-DB&W No. 32) heads downhill toward Leadville from Climax on the last run of the Colorado & Southern narrow gauge system. In the background is the huge Climax Molybdenum Company's mill, atop Fremont Pass.

Photo by D. Ashton, who is standing at left
Courtesy of M. C. Poor

The end of narrow gauge operations on the Colorado & Southern. No. 76 bows out before her rival, No. 638, in Leadville, the Cloud City of Colorado, August 25, 1943.

The roundhouse crew at Ridgway were proud of their new No. 74. To left is D&RGW No. 455, one of the famous outside-frame "mud hens."

Against the backdrop of the towering Silvery San Juans, near Telluride, Colorado, RGS No. 74 stands proudly with the Rocky Mountain Railroad Club excursion, May 28, 1949.

John W. Maxwell photo

RGS No. 74 with the Rocky Mountain Railroad Club excursion crossing trestle No. 39A at Anderson, on the Telluride Branch. Time: September 1, 1951.

399

Photo courtesy of R. H. Kindig

Rio Grande Southern No. 74 (formerly C&N No. 30), heading a Rocky Mountain Railroad Club excursion special, drifts across a trestle near Brown, Colorado, on Sept. 1, 1951.

Courtesy R. H. Kindig

Former C&N No. 30, at this time carrying Number 74 of the Rio Grande Southern, crosses one of the spectacular trestles near Ophir, Colorado, with a Rocky Mountain Railroad Club excursion, on May 29, 1949.

400

The Denver & Rio Grande Western was not to be outdone. General Manager A. E. Perlman sent its freight bill for $776 marked "Paid."

Allen Hays, Boulder painting contractor, volunteered to paint No. 30. "If you can tell me how she looked originally, we'll do the work—free."

A short time later No. 30 was a shining black. On the sides of the tender was the original C&N insignia, red, white, and blue with black and white letters. Hays used as a model a painting done by Clint Dumm of Boulder in the yards prior to 1909.

The original brass 30 on the smokebox nameplate had been chiseled off. "She doesn't look right without it," said Cecil Case, Boulder machinist and metal worker. "I'll make new figures." He would take no pay.

Darrell Gibbs did some safety spot welding on the 30, locking one driver and the firebox door. It also was gratis.

No. 30 needed a coach to round out its short train. Dr. Schoolland and committee were able to secure one from the D&RGW, No. 280. On one side was stenciled "Colorado & Southern," for the close ties between that road and the C&N-DB&W. The C&S lent the stencils, Allen Hays doing the work without charge.

The Boulder Chapter of the D.A.R. under Regent Naomi Holloway furnished a handsome bronze marker plaque. It was mounted on a block of hard Eldora granite furnished and placed by Boulder County Commissioners Thurston, Austin, and Mc-Caslin. V. J. Emmett and L. O. Lewis of the Boulder Marble and Granite Works mounted the plaque. There was no charge.

On a soft August evening (6, 1953) the people of Boulder dedicated No. 30. High honors were paid to Dr. Schoolland and all who had contributed to bringing the proud old engine back to her home. Signaled out for recognition were former employees of the Switzerland Trail: R. D. Ward, station agent,

and Frank Tipps, fireman, the son of Engineer Bill Tipps.

No. 30 had completed her odyssey, as this article by Forest Crossen in the *Boulder Daily Camera* shows:

The narrow gauge locomotive which will remain with us as Colorado & Northwestern No. 30 has had a colorful, full life. She has served on four railroads. Her drivers have pounded the rails over most of Colorado's wonderland. She proves beyond doubt the reliability and durability of steam power; she is fifty-four years old.

Number 30 was built at Dunkirk, New York, by the Brooks Locomotive Works, afterward absorbed by the American Locomotive Company. She came out of the shops in April, 1898, and was shipped to Boulder, unloaded and started to work on the new Colorado & Northwestern Railway.

Number 30 was a Consolidation type, a 2-8-0 in wheel arrangement; she had two leading wheels, eight drivers and no trailing wheels under her firebox. She had flat valves, and her cylinders had a 16-inch bore by 20-inch stroke. Her drivers were 37 inches in diameter and her working steam pressure was 180 pounds. Her cab was built far up on her boiler, making her a 'deckless" engine. Her weight was listed as 85,000 pounds on drivers. Originally her valve gear was the inside time-honored Stephenson link; this was changed to the outside Walschaert by the Colorado & Southern in 1926.

She began operations on the C&N with high hopes. The mines at Ward were producing well and big tonnages of low-grade ores seemed assured. She and her sister locomotives would bring prosperity to all the mines along the railroad.

Shortly after the 30 steamed into Ward the mines there failed to produce the expected big tonnage, so the railroad began losing money. A branch from Sunset to Eldora was built to tap more territory. No. 30 went over this new line December 29, 1904.

She stood mutely by when the Colorado & Northwestern went into receivership and was reorganized as the Denver, Boulder & Western on March 29, 1909. She was to serve that road faithfully, pulling scores of excursion trains made up in Denver to Mont Alto Park and Glacier Lake.

When the sad abandonment came in 1919, she was shipped to Denver the next year with Numbers 31 and 32 to the Morse Brothers Machinery & Supply Company.

No. 30 comes home as Rio Grande Southern No. 74. Photo taken in the Boulder yards the morning of her arrival. Behind her is Rio Grande Southern caboose which was later blown up by criminals who have so far escaped punishment.

Floyd Walters photo. Courtesy J. B. Schoolland

Dedication of No. 30, August 6, 1953. People in foreground are registering for trip through train.

Floyd B. Walters photo

Dedication ceremony for No. 30. Forest Crossen, one of the reception committee, in engineer's seat.

Walters photo. Courtesy J. B. Schoolland

Dedication of No. 30, August 6, 1953. Left to right: Dr. J. B. Schoolland, Frank Tipps, J. B. "Skipper" Schoolland, R. D. Ward, Billy Loach, City Manager Bert Johnson.

In 1921 the three locomotives were acquired by the Colorado & Southern, which was operating a big narrow gauge system. Number 30 again felt the power of full steam pressure as she went out of Denver for Leadville on the historic Denver, South Park & Pacific line, by way of Como.

Through the years she worked up there in the high country, until August 25, 1943. On that day the C&S discontinued the last segment of its narrow gauge lines, the link from Leadville to the great mines of the Climax Molybdenum Company at Climax on Fremont Pass. She saw Number 32 (C&S No. 76) pull into Leadville with the last train before standard gauge operations began.

Number 30, 31, and the 32 were shipped to Denver and stored in the C&S yards until 1945, when they were again sold to Morse Brothers.

In 1948 the 30 was left alone and forlorn, her cab boarded up, her fires dead. The 31 and 32 were sold to the Cerro de Pasco Copper Company and shipped to Peru. Today the hard thud of their exhausts rings through the Andes Mountains.

March of 1949 was showing its gay green self when the 30 was again loaded on a flatcar and shipped away, this time to the Rio Grande Southern. She began pulling trains on this colorful little line from Ridgway to Durango by way of Dolores with side trips to Telluride.

One of Number 30's proudest moments came on Labor Day, 1951, when she stepped out ahead of a special passenger train filled with members of the Rocky Mountain Railroad Club of Denver and their guests. She left the Uncompahgre River at Ridgway, blasted her way up to Dallas Divide, eased down to the San Miguel River. Here she rolled along beneath the awesome and beautiful red, yellow, and chocolate cliffs to the junction with the Telluride line. A brakeman threw a switch and she drew the special up the winding rails to Telluride, where the thrilled excursionists stopped for the night. The next day she returned to the main line, climbed to Ophir, Trout Lake, and unforgettable Lizard Head Pass, in the heart of southwestern Colorado's majestic mountains.

Today and for untold years to come photos of old Number 30 as RGS No. 74 will be looked at proudly by people who rode this passenger train into Telluride and others who wish that they could have been there.

I for one would give much to hear old Number 30 working on a grade with full steam pressure in her boiler (which has never been replaced, to our best knowledge). I should like to sit down beside her on some mountain siding, hear the thumping exhaust of her air pump, smell the rich steam float out from her cylinder cocks, along with the heavy fragrance of hot valve oil.

If she could only talk, she could keep us entertained for many a night. Her stories would be of hard struggles upgrade in the face of tearing blizzard and driving rain, times when her drivers slipped on frosty and wet rails with showers of sparks. She would tell how she always answered to the knowing hand on her throttle, reverse lever and brake valve, of rounding many a sharp curve high on a mountainside near Boreas and Fremont Passes on her way to Leadville, the Cloud City. She would tell of the trips of her twilight years through the La Platta Mountains of lofty beauty and the Silvery San Juans to the busy narrow gauge hub of Durango. But most of all she would wax proud and a little sentimental as she talked of adventures, both wild and lovely, at Salina, Mont Alto, Frances, and Cardinal.

The Switzerland Trail lives on in the hearts of men. The Pioneer Museum of Boulder has an exhibit of Number 30: bell, a lantern, coach lamps, marker lamps, spikes and tie plates, and a clinker hook.

Each year thousand of motorists enjoy the great scenery and spectacular grades over a road built on the old roadbed.

The trip runs west from Boulder on Colorado Highway 119, passing over a bridge built on the stone piers laid up for the Greeley, Salt Lake & Pacific in 1882. Once inside the mouth of Boulder Canon, on the right is the shelf roadbed above dashing Boulder Creek. Here and there are trestle sites, the piers solid and enduring.

At the mouth of Four Mile Creek the route turns right, passing the site of Orodell and on to Crisman. From there to Salina, Wall Street, Copper Rock, and finally Sunset.

The road branches here. Take the abandoned grade to Mont Alto Park, pause to dream a little in this lovely spot and then on to the site of Gold Hill station. At the nearby intersecting road turn left and follow it across the hills and down Sawmill Hill, across Left Hand Creek and up to Ward. Here on the old Peak-to-Peak Highway is the former station.

South from Ward lie Frances, the site of

the tragic snowslide of 1901, and Bloomer-ville. On then to Glacier Lake.

The Eldora grade is open back to Sunset, through aspen and pine woods of peaceful beauty. To the west rise the cloud-sweeping peaks of the Continental Divide.

There are many dream places: cinder-marked abandoned sidings where firemen cleaned fires while waiting for meets, grades that engineers pulled with throttles wide and reverse levers in the corners. Here ran specials on moonlit nights when the whole world breathed romance.

The thirty-eight miles in this round trip are particularly lovely in the autumn, when the aspens turn to gold.

If I could have my grand wish, it would be that men with big money and big souls construct anew the lines from Sunset to Eldora and Ward, build duplicate locomotives, coaches, and cars, and gloriously operate again the Switzerland Trail of America.

A. A. Paddock Collection

Bronze plaque on a granite monument ahead of No. 30 in Central Park, Boulder, Colorado, reads: "Old Engine No. 30. Operated over the narrow gauge railroad (opened in 1883), affectionately known as "The Switzerland Trail of America" between Boulder, Eldora and Ward, 1898-1919, and over the Denver and South Park and the Rio Grande Southern until 1952. A memorial to Colorado railroad and mining pioneers."

No. 1 with the Combo passenger-mail-express coach on the Loop of the Ward line pauses for a photo.
J. B. Sturtevant photo. Courtesy Carl Tipps.

Part II

Chapter XIV

TRIBUTE TO AN ENGINEER

One day in the clubroom of the Elks Lodge at Boulder, Colorado I fell to talking with Carl Tipps, one of the senior members and an old-timer in this beautiful little city at the foot of the Rocky Mountains. Carl is a big man, tall, broad of shoulder, genial.

"I was born in Boulder," he said proudly, "at 406 Pearl (Street), July 30, 1903. My father was William Arthur Tipps, engineer on the narrow gauge, the Switzerland Trail—Denver, Boulder & Western."

This was at the west end of Boulder's principal downtown street, with the Foothills of the Rockies towering over it. The engine house and shops of the picturesque little railroad known as the Switzerland Trail of America were two blocks away. Bill had bought a house so that he could walk to work, as people did back in that less hurried day before the automobile.

"My father was born in Fairbury, Nebraska," Carl continued. "He worked first there on the Rock Island. When he was fifteen years old, he was working around the railroad. In those days the couplings (link and pin), they used their foot to shove the couplings up to get them to come together when they were backing into them. And at that time my dad put a foot up and slipped and got coupled himself. He was in a hospital for six months.

"He still continued his railroading. He came to Boulder around about 1895. He went to work on the Switzerland Trail as a fireman but shortly after that he was promoted to an engineer. He worked there as senior engineer until the railroad was dismantled."

Carl paused. "He was the last one there. The last engine he put on a standard gauge flatcar by havin' the steam up and knockin' the fire out of it and runnin' it up on rails onto the car. And that was the end of the Switzerland Trail. Morse Brothers had junked it and bought all the equipment."

The talk swung around to wrecks. "The wreck that happened to No. 30 at the Black Swan Curve. An engineer by the name of Flint had the engine," Carl explained. "My dad was out on (No.) 1, supposed to back on 2. (No. 35 and No. 36, according to the 1913 Employees' Time Table).

"When he didn't get back, my mother and I got worried, and we finally contacted Charlie Williams, the superintendent. And he says, 'Bills all right, but there's been a wreck.'

"When my dad got back to Glacier Lake, he had orders to turn his fireman and train over to Flint with Engine No. 30, which had a carbide headlight. My dad's engine had an electric headlight. The reason was they came down after night. They had a big excursion (July 4, 1915).

"After the wreck happened, they called my dad at the lake and asked him to split his train up with the rest of the engines there and come down light to the wreck. They only had one engine this side of the wreck, which was the One-Spot, which was a smaller engine. It had larger drivers but not as much power, and couldn't handle as many people. They only had three cars this side, a coach and two observation cars. The rest were all out. So they took gondolas and put burlap (bags) in them.

"My dad, being the senior engineer, they had him shuttle back and forth. They brought all the excursion people down there. They had to walk around the wreck and be taken into Boulder.

"This young Keith—his dad was the boiler-maker, Charley Keith. Young Keith was the

Sunset, Colorado 13 miles west of Boulder at the head of Pennsylvania Gulch. The railroad was new, with both trestles in. The one in the immediate foreground carried traffic to Ward, the one beyond after 1905 to carry trains to Eldora. The station lay between the two tracks.

J. B. Sturtevant photo. Courtesy Carl Tipps.

No. 1 headed for Ward has passed over one of the many trestles on this mountain scenic line.

J. B. Sturtevant photo. Courtesy Carl Tipps.

William Arthur Tipps, senior engineer on the Colorado & Northwestern Railway, the famous Switzerland Trail of America.

Courtesy Carl Tipps

No. 1 with a special, probably a photographic, train at the Salina station of the Colorado & Northwestern Railway in the early days of the railroad, 1898-99. Bill Tipps, second in the cab, serving his short period as a fireman, was soon promoted to engineer.

J. B. Sturtevant photo. Courtesy Carl Tipps.

fireman on this train. He had been out with my dad, but he had to clean coaches at night, and that's why they wanted him to come back earlier."

Carl shook his head slowly. "On that Black Swan Curve the tender turned over, to the right. The baggage car went through the cab of the engine and the first passenger car turned over on its side behind it.

"And this young Keith didn't have a chance. It broke the steam pipes and scalded him to death."

A few moments later Carl spoke up again. "There was a big grocers picnic at Glacier Lake. I can't recall the year. It was somewhere around '12 or '13.

"Anyway, my dad, of course, was out on 1, back on 2 (the regular passenger, mail and express trains). And some of these picknickers were still going up, for they had an evening up there. When my dad got back to Sunset, he got orders at Salina to meet certain trains. And then he got another order that changed it, changed the trains to Crisman. But in the second order they omitted one train.

"These orders came on tissue paper, yellow, hard to read. The engineer gets one, the conductor gets one. And after he got to Salina, heading for Crisman, all of a sudden, around a curve, here comes an engine at him.

"Well, he threw the Johnson Bar and got her reversed, spun his drivers, but they still touched cowcatchers (pilots), but there wasn't any damage.

"The next day he and his conductor were suspended to go into Denver to talk to the head people about this deal. After that they changed their orders so that every order had to include every engine."

Carl smiled at another memory. "There was another incident I could tell you about up at the Big Five Mine, up by Ward. On a snowslide. My dad was supposed to go out on that and there was an engineer here by the name of Cook. He

lived at our house and boarded there. Bob Cook.

"He went out in place of my dad. They kept my dad in to do some work on an engine that the Master Mechanic didn't know how to do. My dad knew everything about an engine, how to fix it. And he was madder than the dickens he didn't get to go out.

"That evening he got word. Somebody came to the house and they said, 'Cook's dead.'

"That was the first we knew about it. They had a snowslide and it killed Bob Cook (April 28, 1907). That was one of the times that my dad was lucky."

Carl's voice took on a lighter note. "There was a time during my dad's tenure there that the South Park (Denver, South & Pacific division of the Colorado & Southern) leased the old 25. They called it the 'Coffee Grinder.' A cog engine. A Shay. He had to go to Como.

"He spent three months up there with the Shay buckin' snow around Como one Winter."

Bill went up with the Shay, which was comparatively new then, in February, 1900. The South Park's locomotives could not get the railroad cleared.

I asked what wages Bill Tipps drew as an engineer.

"My dad drew $150 a month as pay, and they worked 365 days a year. They worked seven days a week and, until the 16-hour law came in—when they couldn't work over 16 hours without rest—there were times he was out all of that. After it came in, there were times he would go, instead of takin' the engine out, the Master Mechanic would take the engine, put a handcar on behind it. My dad's eight hours would be up about the time he got to Crisman or Salina. Then he'd take the engine and the Master Mechanic come back to Boulder on the handcar.

"But eventually he did get a raise, to $175 a month. That's as much as he ever drew as an engineer on that railroad."

INDEX

SUNSET AND WARD

Time Table No. 10
June 29, 1913

WEST BOUND SECOND CLASS 5 Mixed Leave D'ly AM	ALTITUDE	Length of Siding in Feet Between Head Blocks	Distance from Boulder	STATIONS	Distance from Ward	Station Number	Coal, Water and Turning Station	EAST BOUND SECOND CLASS 6 Mixed Arrive D'ly PM
10 50	7800	1065	13 3	DRT SUNSET SU	12 8	13	W Y	f 3 30
f11 11	8600		16 4	MONT ALTO PARK. No Siding	9 7	16		f 3 13
f11 21		330	17 8	*GOLD HILL	8 3	17		f 3 04
f11 35			20 0	BRAINERD. No Siding	6 1	19		f 2 51
f11 47		430	21 9	T PUZZLER	4 2	22		f 2 39
f11 53			23 0	BLOOMERVILLE. No Siding	3 1	23	W	f 2 33
11 57			23 6	†BIG FIVE JUNCTION	2 5	24		2 30
f12 03	9300	1230	24 6	FRANCES. No Siding	1 5	25		f 2 24
12 15	9450		26 1	DR WARD WA	0	26	Y	2 15
Arrive D'ly PM		430	26 6	†NEW MARKET	5	A 26		Leave D'ly PM

Station-to-station distances: SUNSET 3.1, GOLD HILL 1.4, BRAINERD 2.2, PUZZLER 1.9, BLOOMERVILLE 1.1, BIG FIVE JUNCTION .6, FRANCES 1.0, WARD 1.5, NEW MARKET .5

BIG FIVE BRANCH—Ward Line

Length of Siding	Distance from Boulder	STATIONS	Station No.
No Siding	23 6	†BIG FIVE JUNCTION 7	24
218	24 3	†BIG FIVE	A 25

Explanation of Characters

§—Telegraph Box.
‡—Local and Long Distance Telephone.
T—Composite Telephone.
D—Day Telegraph Office.
C—Coal.
W—Water.
Y—Turning Station.
S—Scales.
f—Stop on Signal.
g—Regular Stop.
*—Spur Connected at West End.
†—Spur Connected at East End.
R—Register.

SPECIAL INSTRUCTIONS

WEST BOUND TRAINS are superior to east bound trains of the same and inferior classes.

D. & I. trains will cross ahead of D. B. & W. trains at 12th street crossing, Boulder.

SPEED OF EXTRA TRAINS will not exceed the speed of scheduled trains of the same character.

EXTRA PASSENGER TRAINS may pass and run ahead of any train without orders.

EXTRA TRAINS may run ahead of second and third class trains without orders. Extras may pass extras.

ENGINES BACKING UP with or without cars will not exceed a speed of eight miles per hour. Shay Engine No. 25 will not exceed a speed of eight miles per hour on any train, except by special order.

OPERATORS will space all trains five minutes apart except in closing up at stations or at meeting and passing points. At register stations where no operators are provided, conductors will space their trains five minutes apart.

WHEN DOUBLE HEADERS ARE RUN air must be coupled to both engines but stop cock under engineer's valve in second engine must be closed and head engineer will handle air. Double headers ascending grades, rear engine will take water first then back up to spot head engine.

YARD LIMITS AT BOULDER extend from yard limit board one-half mile west of Boulder tank to Boulder Union Depot. Within these limits main track may be used, protecting against first and second class trains. Third class and extra trains must move within yard limits prepared to stop, unless the track is seen or known to be clear.

MAXIMUM SPEED over 12th Street Crossing, Boulder, must not exceed 6 miles per hour. Maximum speed at all other points within the city of Boulder 15 miles per hour.

CARS SET OUT ON SIDINGS ON GRADES must be kept coupled together, all hand brakes set, and derail set in derailing position. In addition at least two wheels of car next to derail must be securely blocked. Trainmen will take sufficient time to do this work properly.

ALL TRAINMEN are required to ride on the platforms of coaches or caboose on all descending grades, except when their duties require their presence inside, and make close observance for sliding wheels.

CARS MUST NOT BE CUT OFF on heavy grades until hand brakes are tested and known to be in good working condition. In switching cars on grades the air must be coupled and in working order.

DERAILING SWITCHES will be kept set in derailing position when not in use whether siding is occupied or not, except that derail at end of track at Eldora will not be set in derailing position except when track is occupied with cars. This rule, however, will not relieve trainmen from examining position of derail when cars are set out. When possible to avoid, coaches containing passengers must not